Rosemary Conley's
Low Fat
Cookbook
Two

Salmon with mango sauce, page 78

Rosemary Conley's
Low Fat
Cookbook
Two

Century Publishing

Published by Century in 2000

3 5 7 9 10 8 6 4

Copyright © Rosemary Conley Enterprises, 2000

Rosemary Conley has asserted her right under the Copyright, Designs and
Patents Act, 1988 to be identified as the author of this work

First published in the United Kingdom in 2000 by Century
Random House UK Limited
20 Vauxhall Bridge Road, London SW1V 2SA

Random House Australia (Pty) Limited
20 Alfred Street, Milsons Point, Sydney,
New South Wales 2061, Australia

Random House New Zealand Limited
18 Poland Road, Glenfield
Auckland 10, New Zealand

Random House (Pty) Limited
Endulini, 5a Jubilee Road, Parktown 2193, South Africa

The Random House Group Limited Reg. No. 954009
www.randomhouse.co.uk

A CIP catalogue record for this book is available
from the British Library

Papers used by Random House UK Limited are natural, recyclable products
made from wood grown in sustainable forests. The manufacturing processes
conform to the environmental regulations of the country of origin

ISBN 0 7126 6977 9

Photography by Peter Barry
Food styling by Dean Simpole-Clarke
Designed by Roger Walker

Printed and bound in Great Britain by
Butler & Tanner Ltd, Frome and London

Contents

Acknowledgements

This book has been another enjoyable challenge and I hope that everyone who uses it – and their family and dinner guests – enjoy the recipes. A book like this is a team effort and I want to thank all those who helped me.

Dean Simpole-Clarke is a chef and home economist with whom I have had the pleasure of working on my television programme, Rosemary Conley's Cookbook. Dean helped me with my last book and he not only happily agreed to help me with this one, but he has also brought with him his wonderful recipes plus his enthusiasm, skill, talent and attention to detail. Without Dean, this book would not be here! Thank you so much, Dean.

Thanks also to my assistant, Melody Patterson, who made this book her life work for ten months; to my PA, Louise Jones, for her valuable help and contribution; to Dr Susan Jebb, for her technical expertise. Another major player, as always, is my editor, Jan Bowmer, who has worked so hard to make this book work logically and easily for the reader. Her meticulous attention to detail never ceases to amaze me.

Thanks, too, to photographer Peter Barry; to art director Dennis Barker for designing the cover; to Roger Walker for designing the inside pages; and to Andy McKillop at Century Publishing for his support and encouragement throughout.

Thanks must also go to members of Rosemary Conley Diet and Fitness Clubs for supplying some of the recipes.

Useful Information

Weight conversions

All weights are given in imperial and metric. All conversions are approximate. Use only one set of measures and do not mix the two. The table below shows the conversions used.

Ounce (oz)	Pound (lb)	Gram (g)
1		25
2		50
3		75
4	$1/4$	115
5		150
6		175
7		200
8	$1/2$	225
16	1	450
	$1 1/2$	675
	2	900

Liquid measures

1 tablespoon = 3 teaspoons	= $1/2$fl oz	= 15ml	
2 tablespoons = 6 teaspoons	= 1fl oz	= 30ml	
4 tablespoons = $1/4$ cup	= 2fl oz	= 50ml	
5 tablespoons = $1/3$ cup	= $2 1/2$fl oz	= 75ml	
8 tablespoons = $1/2$ cup	= 4fl oz	= 120ml	
10 tablespoons = $2/3$ cup	= 5fl oz	= 150ml	
		($1/4$ pint)	
12 tablespoons = $3/4$ cup	= 6fl oz	= 175ml	
16 tablespoons = 1 cup	= 8fl oz	= 250ml ($1/2$ US pint)	

Note: A UK pint contains 20fl oz

American cup measures can be convenient to use, especially when making large quantities. However, although the volume remains the same, the weight may vary, as illustrated opposite.

Imperial	American
Flour	*Flour*
plain and self-raising	all purpose
1oz	$^1/_4$ cup
4oz	1 cup
Cornflour	*Cornstarch*
1oz	$^1/_4$ cup
generous 2oz	$^1/_2$ cup
4$^1/_2$ oz	1 cup
Sugar (granulated/caster)	*Sugar (granulated)*
4oz	$^1/_2$ cup
7$^1/_2$ oz	1 cup
Sugar (icing)	*Sugar (confectioner's)*
1oz	$^1/_4$ cup
4$^1/_2$ oz	1 cup
Sugar (soft brown)	*Sugar (light and dark brown)*
4oz	$^1/_2$ cup firmly packed
8oz	1 cup firmly packed

Useful measures

1 egg	56ml	2fl oz
1 egg white	28ml	1fl oz
2 rounded tablespoons breadcrumbs	30g	1oz
2 level teaspoons gelatine	8g	$^1/_4$oz

1oz (25g) granular aspic sets 600ml (1 pint).
$^1/_2$oz (15g) powdered gelatine or 4 leaves sets 600ml (1 pint).

All spoon measures are level unless otherwise stated.

Wine quantities

Average serving	ml	fl oz
1 glass wine	90ml	3fl oz
1 glass port or sherry	60ml	2fl oz
1 glass liqueur	30ml	1fl oz

Oven temperature conversions

Celsius (Centigrade)	Fahrenheit	Gas Mark	Definition
130	250	$\frac{1}{2}$	very cool
140	275	1	cool
150	300	2	warm
170	325	3	moderate
180	350	4	moderate
190	375	5	moderately hot
200	400	6	hot
220	425	7	hot
230	450	8	very hot
240	475	9	very hot

Abbreviations

oz	ounce
lb	pound
kg	kilogram
fl oz	fluid ounce
ml	millilitre
C	Celsius (Centigrade)
F	Fahrenheit
kcal	kilocalorie (calorie)

Equipment and terms

British	American
baking tin	baking pan
base	bottom
cocktail stick	toothpick
dough or mixture	batter
frying pan	skillet
greaseproof paper	waxed paper
grill/grilled	broil/broiled
knock back dough	punch back dough
liquidiser	blender
muslin	cheesecloth
pudding basin	ovenproof bowl
stoned	pitted
top and tail (gooseberries)	clean (gooseberries)
whip/whisk	beat/whip

Ingredients

British	American
aubergine	egg plant
bacon rashers	bacon slices
bicarbonate of soda	baking soda
black cherries	bing cherries
boiling chicken	stewing chicken
broad beans	fava or lima beans
capsicum pepper	sweet pepper
cauliflower florets	cauliflowerets
celery stick	celery stalk
stock cube	bouillon cube
chicory	belgium endive
chilli	chile pepper

British	American
cooking apple	baking apple
coriander	cilantro
cornflour	cornstarch
courgette	zucchini
crystallised ginger	candied ginger
curly endive	chicory
demerara sugar	light brown sugar
essence	extracts
fresh beetroot	raw beets
gelatine	gelatin
head celery	bunch celery
icing	frosting
icing sugar	confectioner's sugar
plain flour	all purpose flour
root ginger	ginger root
self-raising flour	all purpose flour sifted with baking powder
soft brown sugar	light brown sugar
spring onion	scallion
stem ginger	preserved ginger
sultanas	seedless white raisins
wholemeal	wholewheat

Introduction

Low-fat cooking is easier than you think and the results taste delicious too. With a little know-how and imagination there is no excuse why you shouldn't eat scrumptious food that is healthy, nutritious and which, at the same time, will help you to lose weight if that is your aim. After the success of my first Low Fat Cookbook, I decided to extend the selection of recipes in this new book. I have included some of the food facts that appeared in my last cookbook as an easy source of reference, but all the recipes are new.

There are some tasty ideas for meals for one, microwave menus, vegetarian recipes, dinner party ideas, buffet and party food, plus lots of recipes for all the family to enjoy.

My expert chef Dean Simpole-Clarke and I have worked together to arrive at a selection of recipes that we hope will leave your tastebuds dancing. And, just think, eating this food is actually good for your health.

I want you to enjoy using this book. You don't need to be an expert cook – the recipes will work for everyone. Each recipe lists the calorie and fat content per serving, and if you are trying to lose weight it is important for you to be aware of your daily calorie intake. However, there is no need to start counting fat grams. Almost all the ingredients used in the recipes in this book contain 4 per cent or less fat and so the total fat content of your diet will look after itself. The only exceptions are foods such as oily fish, which contain valuable nutrients, or items such as seasonings – curry powder, mustard, and so on – which are used in such small quantities that the fat content is immaterial.

Please note that the calorie calculation is based on the recipe only and does not include the calories from any accompaniments.

Whether your motivation to cook low fat is for your waistline or your health, this book will help you to get it right and enable you to enjoy your food at the same time as helping your body to stay healthy and trim. If you like the taste of oil in your food, it may take a little time to acclimatise to the taste of non-oily food, but once you get used to it there will be no looking back.

Happy cooking!

Do you want to lose weight?

Imagine your body is like a bank account. Every day your body spends energy rather like money. In this body bank account there are only two kinds of payments – cheques and standing orders. Cheques pay for the energy you spend in going about your daily work and activities, and the standing orders pay for the energy you spend in keeping your body functioning, including just staying alive – breathing, heart circulating blood around the body, digestion, body repairs, and so on.

The energy spent in maintaining these bodily functions is beyond your direct control, and the term used to describe this basic energy requirement is the basal metabolic rate (BMR). Even if you stayed in bed all day, this energy would still be spent.

However, *you* decide how physically active you are, so *you* decide how much energy you spend. If you have an inactive day, you don't write many energy cheques, but if you are active you spend more.

What about income into this special energy account? Income comes from the food and drink you consume and, in this metaphorical bank account, the currency is calories. The energy content of all food is measured in calories (kcal). The calorie content of different foods varies considerably. Butter, for instance, contains 185 calories per 25g (1oz), whereas tomatoes contain just 5 calories. Obviously, you must eat in order to stay alive, and every time you eat you pay income into your energy bank account.

This energy bank account is rather different from your normal current account into which you pay your monthly salary cheque. In this energy bank account there has to be a nil balance at the end of each day, which means that there has to be a 'savings' account into which any unused balance can be transferred.

This special savings account doesn't store cash; instead it stores body fat. The balance of fat goes up or down according to the number of calories you eat and the amount of energy you spend. If you eat more than you spend, you increase your savings of fat. If you spend more calories than you pay in (eat), you have to make up the balance by taking extra calories from your savings account of fat to make up the difference.

So, to lose weight, you need to eat fewer calories than you spend each day and, to lose weight even faster, you can spend more calories by increasing your level of physical activity so that you draw even more fat from your savings account. Every time you go upstairs, or play energetic games with your children or grandchildren, or go for a walk, you are writing more cheques and drawing more fat from your savings account!

Quite simply, losing weight is a matter of physics. Your body needs a certain number of calories to keep you alive and give you the energy to live your daily life. If you eat more calories than you use, you will gain weight. If you eat an equal number of calories to those you use, your body weight will remain constant. If you eat fewer calories than your body uses, you will lose weight.

It is important to remember that, weight for weight, the fat we eat contains more than twice as many calories as carbohydrate and protein. Fat does not add bulk to food, but it adds lots of extra calories – in the form of fried foods, oily dressings, butter on bread or toast, the 'invisible' fat in cakes and biscuits, and so on. Since the body stores fat much more readily than it stores protein or carbohydrate, if you are trying to lose weight it is important to cut down your intake of fat.

To prove my point, let me tell you about an experiment I witnessed in 1996, when I made a series of films for ITV's highly popular *This Morning* programme. I went along with the film crew to the Dunn Nutrition Centre in Cambridge, where Dr Andrew Prentice, who at that time was Head of the Energy Metabolism Research Group, showed us an experiment.

A volunteer was given a high-carbohydrate meal – a plate of pasta. After eating it, a plastic hood with a breathing tube connected to a computer (called a metabolic hood) was placed over the volunteer's head. As he continued to breathe quite normally the computerised machine registered an increase in energy expenditure, signifying metabolic activity by the volunteer's body in digesting the calories supplied by the carbohydrate in the pasta. It was as though someone had turned the gas up on this volunteer's body!

A similar test was run on another volunteer. This time the volunteer was given a bar of chocolate that was high in fat but which contained the same number of calories as the plate of pasta. Again, the metabolic hood was placed over the volunteer's head to check the energy expenditure created by the eating of the chocolate. There was, however, almost no recognition by the computer that the volunteer had eaten anything! In other words, the body had digested and absorbed the high-fat chocolate without burning any extra calories.

Working out the calories

Most people who decide to shed a few pounds want to do it fast! There is an understandable temptation to eat fewer and fewer calories in the belief that the less you eat, the more weight you lose. There are three main problems with this theory. Firstly, eating too little stretches your willpower to its limits, leaves you feeling very hungry and deprived and always – yes, always – ends in disaster when the inevitable eating binge takes over. A sense of failure, desperation and disappointment follow and your good intentions are replaced by a feeling of resignation that you are meant to be fat!

The second problem is that the body doesn't like being starved and automatically changes down a gear towards self-preservation. The body becomes as efficient as possible and tries not to waste a single calorie. In fact, on the most severe diets, your metabolic rate can actually decrease by up to 20 per cent.

There is yet another problem. Since there isn't enough energy in your food, your body takes the energy it needs from its reserves. Normally, this would come from its fat stores, but during rapid weight loss brought about by crash dieting, the energy comes from the muscles. Yes, you lose weight on the scales – possibly lots of it – but it is weight from the wrong places. The worst news of all is that the less muscle you have, the lower your metabolic rate. Crash dieting – eating fewer than 800 calories a day for a woman and 1,200 calories for a man – is bad news on all sides. It is counterproductive, it doesn't re-educate your eating habits, so it doesn't work in the long term, and because you don't actually lose much body fat, you can end up with a flabby body. Anyway, why crash diet when you can lose weight much more efficiently by eating more?

So how many calories should we take in to lose weight? Your BMR varies according to your age, sex and weight. The heavier you are, the more calories your body needs to keep you alive and to carry out your daily activities.

On pages 19–24 you will find tables giving approximate calculations of your basic daily calorie requirements. Use these tables to work out your personal BMR figure and base your daily calorie allowance on this. If you stick to this calorie intake you will lose weight at the optimum rate.

Once you reach your goal weight, aim to gradually increase your daily calorie allowance by working out your most accurate activity level on the tables on pages 19–24. Providing you don't exceed this calorie intake, your weight should remain constant.

You will notice that as you get older your basal metabolic rate falls. While this seems unfair, it is a fact that body composition changes as we get older. When we are young our bodies have a greater proportion of muscle to fat, but as we get older, we automatically find it easier to store body fat and more difficult to retain muscle. This is a good reason for continuing to exercise regularly right into old age. Exercise increases your muscle mass, which in turn increases your metabolic rate, helps keep you healthy and certainly makes you look leaner.

Daily energy (kilocalorie) requirements of women aged 18–29 years

Body Weight (Stones)	Basal Metabolic Rate	Total energy requirement (kcal per day)		
		Sedentary	Active	Very Active
7	1146	1720	1950	2180
7.5	1193	1790	2030	2270
8	1240	1860	2110	2360
8.5	1288	1930	2190	2450
9	1335	2000	2270	2540
9.5	1382	2070	2350	2630
10	1428	2140	2430	2710
10.5	1476	2210	2510	2800
11	1523	2280	2590	2890
11.5	1570	2360	2670	2980
12	1618	2430	2750	3070
12.5	1664	2500	2830	3160
13	1711	2570	2910	3250
13.5	1758	2640	2990	3340
14	1806	2710	3070	3430
14.5	1853	2780	3150	3520
15	1900	2850	3230	3610
15.5	1945	2918	3306	3696
16	1992	2988	3386	3785
16.5	2040	3060	3468	3876
17	2087	3130	3548	3965
17.5	2133	3200	3628	4053
18	2180	3270	3706	4142
18.5	2228	3342	3788	4233
19	2274	3411	3866	4321
19.5	2320	3480	3944	4408
20	2370	3555	4029	4503

For every additional stone increase daily calorie intake by 100

Body Weight (Stones)	Basal Metabolic Rate	Total energy requirement (kcal per day)		
		Sedentary	Active	Very Active
7	1215	1820	2070	2310
7.5	1242	1860	2110	2360
8	1268	1900	2160	2410
8.5	1295	1940	2200	2460
9	1323	1980	2250	2510
9.5	1348	2020	2290	2560
10	1374	2060	2340	2610
10.5	1400	2100	2380	2660
11	1427	2140	2430	2710
11.5	1454	2180	2470	2760
12	1480	2220	2520	2810
12.5	1505	2260	2560	2860
13	1532	2300	2600	2910
13.5	1559	2340	2650	2960
14	1586	2380	2700	3010
14.5	1612	2420	2740	3060
15	1639	2460	2790	3110
15.5	1645	2468	2796	3126
16	1671	2506	2841	3175
16.5	1700	2550	2890	3230
17	1723	2584	2929	3274
17.5	1750	2625	2975	3325
18	1774	2661	3016	3371
18.5	1800	2700	3060	3420
19	1825	2738	3102	3468
19.5	1852	2778	3148	3519
20	1880	2820	3196	3572

Daily energy (kilocalorie) requirements of women aged 30–59 years

For every additional stone increase daily calorie intake by 50

Daily energy (kilocalorie) requirements of women aged 60 years and over

Body Weight (Stones)	Basal Metabolic Rate	Total energy requirement (kcal per day)		
		Sedentary	Active	Very Active
7	998	1500	1700	1900
7.5	1028	1542	1750	1950
8	1057	1590	1800	2010
8.5	1087	1630	1850	2070
9	1116	1670	1900	2120
9.5	1146	1720	1950	2180
10	1174	1760	2000	2230
10.5	1204	1810	2050	2290
11	1233	1850	2100	2340
11.5	1263	1890	2150	2400
12	1292	1940	2200	2450
12.5	1320	1980	2250	2510
13	1350	2030	2300	2570
13.5	1380	2070	2350	2620
14	1409	2110	2400	2680
14.5	1439	2160	2450	2730
15	1469	2200	2500	2790
15.5	1552	2298	2590	2907
16	1581	2372	2688	3004
16.5	1610	2415	2737	3059
17	1639	2458	2786	3114
17.5	1667	2500	2834	3167
18	1697	2546	2885	3224
18.5	1726	2589	2934	3279
19	1754	2631	2982	3333
19.5	1783	2674	3031	3388
20	1810	2715	3077	3439

For every additional stone increase daily calorie intake by 50

Body Weight (Stones)	Basal Metabolic Rate	Total energy requirement (kcal per day)		
		Sedentary	Active	Very Active
8	1456	2180	2480	2770
8.5	1509	2260	2570	2870
9	1557	2340	2650	2960
9.5	1606	2410	2730	3050
10	1652	2480	2810	3140
10.5	1701	2550	2890	3230
11	1749	2620	2970	3320
11.5	1797	2700	3060	3410
12	1846	2770	3140	3510
12.5	1892	2840	3220	3600
13	1940	2910	3300	3690
13.5	1990	2980	3380	3780
14	2037	3060	3460	3870
14.5	2086	3130	3550	3960
15	2134	3200	3630	4050
15.5	2180	3270	3710	4140
16	2220	3330	3770	4220
16.5	2278	3420	3870	4330
17	2330	3490	3950	4420
17.5	2365	3548	4020	4494
18	2410	3615	4097	4579
18.5	2460	3690	4182	4674
19	2510	3765	4267	4769
19.5	2555	3832	4344	4854
20	2605	3908	4428	4950

Daily energy (kilocalorie) requirements of men aged 18–29 years

For every additional stone increase daily calorie intake by 100

Daily energy (kilocalorie) requirements of men aged 30–59 years

Body Weight (Stones)	Basal Metabolic Rate	Total energy requirement (kcal per day)		
		Sedentary	Active	Very Active
8	1458	2190	2480	2770
8.5	1495	2240	2540	2840
9	1532	2300	2600	2910
9.5	1569	2350	2670	2980
10	1604	2410	2730	3050
10.5	1641	2460	2790	3120
11	1678	2520	2850	3190
11.5	1715	2570	2920	3260
12	1752	2630	2980	3330
12.5	1787	2680	3040	3400
13	1824	2740	3100	3470
13.5	1861	2790	3160	3540
14	1898	2850	3230	3610
14.5	1934	2900	3290	3680
15	1970	2960	3350	3750
15.5	2007	3010	3410	3810
16	2037	3060	3460	3870
16.5	2080	3120	3540	3950
17	2117	3180	3600	4020
17.5	2150	3225	3655	4085
18	2184	3276	3713	4150
18.5	2220	3330	3774	4218
19	2260	3390	3842	4294
19.5	2295	3442	3902	4360
20	2330	3495	3961	4427

For every additional stone increase daily calorie intake by 50

Body Weight (Stones)	Basal Metabolic Rate	Total energy requirement (kcal per day)		
		Sedentary	Active	Very Active
8	1182	1773	2009	2246
8.5	1220	1830	2074	2318
9	1256	1884	2135	2386
9.5	1294	1941	2200	2459
10	1331	1996	2263	2529
10.5	1368	2052	2326	2599
11	1406	2109	2390	2671
11.5	1443	2164	2453	2742
12	1480	2220	2516	2812
12.5	1517	2276	2579	2882
13	1555	2332	2644	2954
13.5	1591	2386	2705	3023
14	1629	2444	2769	3095
14.5	1666	2499	2832	3165
15	1704	2556	2897	3238
15.5	1740	2610	2958	3306
16	1777	2666	3021	3376
16.5	1815	2722	3086	3448
17	1852	2778	3148	3519
17.5	1888	2832	3210	3587
18	1926	2889	3274	3659
18.5	1964	2946	3339	3732
19	2000	3000	3400	3800
19.5	2038	3057	3465	3872
20	2075	3112	3528	3942

Daily energy (kilocalorie) requirements of men aged 60 years and over

For every additional stone increase daily calorie intake by 50

Creating a healthy diet

We only need to walk into the doctor's surgery to see an abundance of leaflets and posters recommending that we eat a healthy diet. But so often we associate foods that are healthy with foods that are boring. Well, it needn't be that way.

We need to eat a variety of foods to obtain the nutrients we need for good health. I find it easier to think of nutrients as falling into two categories – tangible and intangible. Tangible nutrients are carbohydrates, proteins and fats. Minerals and vitamins fall into the intangible category because they are found *within* carbohydrates, proteins and fats. The key to good nutrition is getting the balance right. Eating too much of one thing can be as bad as eating too little of another. Here are some basic nutritional guidelines.

Carbohydrates

Carbohydrates include foods such as bread, rice, potatoes, pasta, cereals, as well as fruit and vegetables. These foods provide bulk in the diet and will only be stored as fat on the body if eaten in great excess. One gram of carbohydrate yields 4 calories. Carbohydrate should feature as the largest component in every meal, as out of all the food groups, it is the most important supplier of energy, and 60 per cent of the calories we consume each day should come from this food group.

Proteins

Proteins include foods such as meat, fish, poultry, eggs, cheese and milk. Their primary use is to help the body grow and to renew and repair existing tissues. Protein contains 4 calories per gram. It should be eaten in moderation, forming about a seventh of our daily calorie intake. Too much protein can be harmful because it has to be metabolised by the kidneys, so high-protein diets are not healthy or recommended. If we eat more protein than we need, the excess cannot be stored by the body. Instead, part of the protein will be excreted from the body and the remainder will be used to provide energy, therefore delaying the burning of fat.

Fats

Fats include foods such as oil, butter, margarine, cream and lard. Fat is also found in varying amounts in other foods such as meat and fish. It is a concentrated form of energy that is efficiently stored by the body for emergencies and also supplies some valuable nutrients for health. Fat contains 9 calories per gram, which is more than twice the number of calories contained in one gram of carbohydrate or protein.

On a weight-reducing diet, women should allow between 23 and 40 fat grams per day, while men should allow between 35 and 50 grams. When seeking to maintain weight, rather than trying to lose it, the maximum fat intake should not exceed 70 grams a day for women and 100 grams for men.

A small amount of fat is necessary for good health, and oily fish such as salmon, mackerel and herrings contain essential fatty acids that are particularly beneficial. For this reason I allow moderate amounts of oily fish on my diets.

Minerals

There are many minerals, all of which play an important role in helping us achieve good health. In most cases, a varied and healthy diet will ensure we are not missing out. However, there are two important minerals – calcium and iron – which require special mention. Since dairy products are the richest source of calcium, and red meat is the richest source of iron, on a low-fat diet it is particularly important to make sure you are taking in sufficient amounts. If you consume 450ml (3/4 pint) of skimmed or semi-skimmed milk plus a small pot of yogurt (150g/5oz) each day and eat red meat four times a week, you will probably meet your needs.

We need calcium to help maintain our bones and teeth and we need iron to make haemoglobin which carries oxygen around the body in the red blood cells. Too little iron, and we become anaemic; too little calcium, and we get osteoporosis. The tables on pages 29 and 30 will help you check if you are getting enough of each nutrient. If you're not, you need to amend your diet accordingly.

Please note, these tables are intended as a rough guide only, since the iron and calcium content of foods may differ slightly for different cuts of meat and different brands of cereals, especially if they have been fortified.

Vitamins

Vitamins fall into two categories: fat soluble and water soluble. Vitamins A, D, E and K are fat soluble and do not need to be consumed daily, since the body is able to store them. However, the B complex vitamins and vitamin C are water soluble. Since these cannot be stored by the body, they need to be consumed daily. Each vitamin has its own special function and all are essential for good health.

Even though my diets are designed to be healthy and nutritionally balanced, I do recommend you take a multivitamin tablet daily, just to make doubly sure you have all the vitamins you need. This will ensure that you always get all the micronutrients your body needs. The time-released type of vitamin tablet is best and they are widely available from healthfood stores and chemists. Always follow the recommended dose.

These days much attention has been focused on the antioxidant vitamins (vitamins A, C, and E). These vitamins help to zap the free radicals that occur naturally in the body. For thousands of years, the balance between antioxidants and free radicals in the body has been just fine, naturally. But now, with increased pollution, radiation from microwaves, mobile phones, TVs and computers and even electric light bulbs, as well as increased exposure to stress, the body is producing more free radicals. These are the bad guys. To neutralise them, we need to increase the number of antioxidants (the good guys) by eating more of the foods that contain the ACE vitamins. They're easy to spot because many of these vitamins are found in brightly coloured vegetables and fruit. Many other chemical compounds, such as flavonoids, which occur naturally in some fruit and vegetables (particularly onions and apples), also act as antioxidants. Flavonoids are also found in green tea, red wine (from the grape skins) and lycopene (the substance which makes tomatoes and some other fruits turn red). Some minerals, such as zinc and selenium, can also act as antioxidants.

So, make sure you eat a wide range of foods to get all the vitamins and minerals you need. If in doubt, consider taking a micronutrient supplement.

Alcohol

Alcohol is a mixture of good and bad. It is a relaxant and has been acknowledged by the medical profession as having a real benefit in relieving stress. Alcohol also helps to reduce the risk of heart disease. It is, nevertheless, a mild form of poison and the body works hard to get rid of it. On my diets, I allow a single unit of alcohol each day for women and two for men, plus three bonus drinks that can be taken at any time during the week. Remember, too, that, alcohol can be addictive, and we need to be mindful of the dangers. As with all things, moderation is the key.

There have been many trials to determine the benefits and disadvantages of consuming alcohol, ranging from whether it helps your heart to whether it makes you fat. It was even suggested at one point that the calories from alcohol didn't count because the body processed calories from alcohol in a different way from other calories. But alcohol calories *do* count.

In its neat form, alcohol yields 7 calories per gram, but of course we never consume alcohol in its pure state. It is always diluted by water, even in the strongest spirits. The calories in your favourite tipple may not always be directly related to the alcohol content, since many drinks contain sugar, carbohydrate and sometimes even fat.

Alcohol is easily absorbed by the stomach, but the only way the body can rid itself of alcohol is by burning it in the liver and other tissues. Since alcohol is essentially a toxin and the body has no useful purpose for storing it, the body prioritises the elimination of it at the cost of processing other foods you have eaten. Consequently, other foods may be converted to fat more readily than usual, thereby increasing your fat stores.

In the many trials I have carried out for my diets I have always found that slimmers who do drink a little alcohol while following a weight-loss diet do at least as well as those who don't and, in some cases, lose more weight. But rather than suggesting that alcohol has any miracle effect, I believe it's down to the fact that if you are allowed a drink you feel less restricted, can still socialise and feel as if you are leading a 'normal' life.

The key is to have a little each day, rather than drinking a lot on the occasional drinking binge. Perhaps the greatest danger from drinking alcohol when you are dieting is that it is extremely effective at diluting your willpower. Because it is a relaxant, it's so easy to think, 'oh, what the heck, I'll diet tomorrow', and then really overindulge on the food front!

Reading nutrition labels

Nowadays we are fortunate that most food products we buy contain lots of useful information on the nutrition label. This provides us with a breakdown of their nutritional content

Iron content of foods

Food	Serving size	MG	
Liver	100g cooked weight	8	
Kidney	100g cooked weight	7	
Venison	100g cooked weight	8	
Lean beef	100g cooked weight	3	
Lean lamb	100g cooked weight	2	
Pork	100g cooked weight	1	
Ham	100g cooked weight	1	
Duck	100g cooked weight	3	
Chicken/turkey	100g cooked weight	1	
Egg	1	1	
Chickpeas	100g cooked weight	3	
Lentils	100g cooked weight	2.5	
Baked beans	1 small can	2	
Potatoes	100g	0.5	
Spinach	50g cooked weight	2	
Watercress	50g	1	
Cabbage	50g cooked weight	0.5	
Broccoli	50g cooked weight	0.5	
Dried fruit	50g	1	
White bread	1 slice	0.5	
Wholemeal bread	1 slice	0.8	
Branflakes	25g	7	(fortified)
Weetabix	25g	4	(fortified)

The reference nutrient intake (RNI) for the female population is 14.8mg per day and 8.7 mg for the male population.

Calcium content of foods

Food	Weight	MG
Milk	600ml	680
Cheddar cheese	25g	225
Cottage cheese	1 small pot	60
Yogurt	1 small pot	360
Egg	1	25
Sardines	50g cooked weight	250
Pilchards (canned)	50g	150
Prawns	50g cooked weight	75
Tofu	100g	500
Ice cream	50g	70
White bread	1 slice	30 (fortified)
Wholemeal bread	1 slice	7
Weetabix	25g	10
Shredded wheat	25g	12
Spinach	50g cooked weight	300
Watercress	50g	110
Dried fruit	50g	30

The reference nutrient intake (RNI) for both the female and male population is 700mg per day (800mg per day for 15- to18-year-olds).

as well as the number of calories and amount of fat. To simplify matters, as far as weight control is concerned, the two key things to look at are 'energy' and 'fat'.

The figure relating to 'energy' tells you the number of calories in 100g of the product (you can ignore the kJ figure – just look at the kcal one). You then need to calculate how much of the product you will actually be eating to work out the number of calories per portion.

The fat content may be broken down into polyunsaturates and saturates but, for anyone on a weight-reducing diet, this is not significant. It is the total fat content per 100g that is relevant in our calculations. I make the general and simple rule that my dieters should only select foods where the label shows the fat content as 4g or less fat per 100g of product, i.e. 4 per cent or less fat. I believe the actual amount of fat per portion is of lesser importance. If you follow the simple 4 per cent fat rule and restrict your calorie intake to a figure equal to your BMR (see tables

NUTRITIONAL INFORMATION	
	Per 100g
ENERGY	172 kJ/40 kcal
PROTEIN	1.8g
CARBOHYDRATE	8.0g
(of which sugars)	(2.0g)
FAT	0.2g
(of which saturates)	(Trace)
FIBRE	1.5g
SODIUM	0.3g

on pages 19–24), the fat content of your food will look after itself. The only exceptions to this rule are lean cuts of meat such as beef, lamb and pork, which may be just over the 4 per cent yardstick, and oily fish such as salmon and mackerel, which may yield as much as 17 per cent fat. I make these exceptions because these foods contain important nutrients. Vegetarians may use the occasional drop of oil in the preparation of their food.

Food facts <small>Meat</small>

Meat is a valuable source of protein and also contains a variety of vitamins and minerals. Fortunately, in recent years, meat producers have managed to reduce the fat content of much of the meat we buy. According to the Meat and Livestock Commission in the United Kingdom, cattle are now about 25 per cent leaner than they were 30 years ago, and pork has an even more impressive track record with a 50 per cent reduction in fat. Meat is one category of food where I am not too strict on my 4 per cent rule, and any meat with a fat content of up to 6 per cent is acceptable on my diets.

You can buy meat where much of the fat has already been trimmed off, but, before cooking, you should remove any remaining white strands of fat that are still visible. Meat can be cooked by using either dry heat methods such as roasting, baking, grilling or dry-frying or by using moist heat methods such as poaching, braising and steaming. While it is safe to serve beef and lamb undercooked or 'rare', pork on the other hand must be cooked thoroughly.

When grilling or roasting meat, make sure the grill or oven is preheated so that once the meat is placed under the heat the juices can be sealed quickly. Likewise, when dry-frying, make sure the pan is hot before adding the meat.

When roasting, I always use foil to cover the joint, placing it so that it completely covers the edges of the roasting tin. This allows a certain amount of steam to be retained, which results in a moist joint at the end. Twenty minutes before the end of cooking I remove the foil to allow the joint to crispen. It is important not to overcook beef, otherwise it will go dry. To check that pork is thoroughly cooked, insert a skewer into the thickest part. The juices that run out should be clear and not pink.

The fat content of meat can vary according to the cut. For instance, belly pork and neck of lamb are much fattier than fillet. With beef, topside, rump, sirloin and fillet are among the leanest cuts. Extra lean minced beef is now widely available in food stores and supermarkets. It can be much more expensive than ordinary lean mince, but there is less waste. However, I find that if I dry-fry lean mince and drain off all the fat that emerges during cooking, I am left with very lean mince. As always, it is the removal of the fat that is important. For a change, try minced turkey or chicken. These make good alternatives to minced beef, since they are very lean and do add a different flavour to some standard dishes.

Whether you are barbecuing, grilling, dry-frying, roasting, braising, pot roasting or even just stewing, never add any oil, fat or butter. If you are able to make a casserole in advance, allow it to cool and then skim off the fat. Reheat thoroughly before serving. There are many kinds of marinades, glazes and stocks that will enable your meat to be full of flavour and moisture.

Glazes

You can glaze chops, steaks and joints to add extra flavour and create an attractive appearance. Spread the glaze over joints 20 minutes before the end of cooking, or brush over the surface of chops or steaks prior to grilling. Try the following.

Beef
Honey, ginger and orange juice
Mustard and honey
Garlic, root ginger and honey

Pork
Honey, soy sauce, garlic and pineapple juice
Plum jam, tomato ketchup and Worcestershire
    sauce
Maple syrup, orange juice and cinnamon

Lamb
Wholegrain mustard and brown sugar
Redcurrant jelly, garlic and fresh mint
Lemon juice, honey and fresh ginger

Gammon
Honey or brown sugar and ginger or cinnamon
Orange marmalade and orange liqueur
Plum jam and apple juice

Marinades

Marinating adds flavour and helps to tenderise meats. To ensure the flavours are absorbed successfully, you should leave meat to marinate overnight, or for at least four hours, covered and in the refrigerator. Try combining some of the following flavours or make up your own.

Beef

Fresh herbs and lots of garlic

Soy sauce, lemon juice, garlic, sherry and sesame seeds

Horseradish, mustard and red wine

Soy sauce, sherry, garlic and ginger

Pork

White wine, orange rind and juice and fresh coriander

Honey, orange juice and cinnamon

Pineapple juice, soy sauce and fresh ginger

Cider vinegar, apple juice and fresh sage

Lamb

Lemon juice, garlic and dried mixed herbs

Rosemary and garlic

Redcurrant jelly, red wine and fresh herbs

Yogurt, fresh mint and garlic

Yogurt, coriander and cumin

More flavour enhancers

Joints can be studded, spiked or covered with a crust to add extra flavour and/or texture. Try the following ways to add flavour:

- Stud or spike with fresh rosemary sprigs and garlic slivers.
- Stud or spike with finely chopped garlic and crushed black peppercorns.
- Sprinkle with a Creole mixture of black peppercorns, paprika and dried mixed herbs.
- Twenty minutes before the end of cooking, spread the joint with a mixture of parsley and mustard and then sprinkle with breadcrumbs.

Offal

Offal includes heart, liver and kidneys, although nowadays heart is rarely used in cooking.

Liver is a particularly good source of iron and, like meat, the iron in liver is more easily absorbed by the body than iron from sources such as bread, fortified breakfast cereals, dried fruits and eggs. Liver is not recommended for pregnant women because of its high vitamin A content. Too much vitamin A during pregnancy could cause problems for the foetus.

Liver provides 137 calories and 6.2g fat per 100g. Since it is higher in fat than kidneys, you are advised not to eat more than two portions a week. You can choose from ox's, pig's, or lamb's liver, although lamb's liver is considered to be the most tender. To tenderise liver, leave it to soak in skimmed milk for a minimum of 30 minutes. The most satisfactory low-fat way of cooking liver is to dry-fry it quickly in a non-stick pan.

Kidneys provide 91 calories and 2.6g fat per 100g and are used primarily in casseroles, but they can also be dry-fried or grilled. You should remove all the fat prior to cooking, then slice the kidneys lengthways and remove any membrane and the tough centre core. Quickly dry-fry the kidneys, or, alternatively, lay each one flat and skewer with two cocktail sticks at right angles to each other (this will help hold the kidneys flat), then place under a grill until cooked.

Poultry

Chicken is probably more popular than ever before. It is plentiful, cheap, low in fat and versatile and ideal for inclusion in a low-fat diet. If you are on a weight-reducing diet, the main thing to be aware of with chicken is that most of the fat is in the skin. A chicken breast weighing 100g grilled with the skin on will provide 173 calories and 6.4 per cent fat, compared with 148 calories and only 2.2 per cent fat if grilled without the skin. So, next time you consider eating the skin off your roast chicken, remember that 100g of chicken with skin will give you 218 calories and 12.5g fat, compared to 164 calories and 7.2g fat if you eat just the flesh.

The key is to buy skinless chicken breasts to keep in your freezer for stir-fries, casseroles, and so on, and when roasting whole chickens make sure you remove the fat found around the neck before cooking and then remove the skin before serving. Roasting a chicken on a wire rack will enable all the fat from it to drip below the bird and keep it as low fat as possible. This has the same effect as spit roasting or grilling. When I'm roasting chicken I always cover it with foil for the first three-quarters of the cooking time and then remove it at the end to crispen the chicken for an attractive end result.

If you are using a frozen chicken, it is important to allow it to thaw out slowly and completely, ideally in a refrigerator, before cooking. Always make sure chicken is thoroughly cooked before you eat it. To test this, pierce it with a skewer in the fleshiest part of the leg, and if the liquid that pours out is clear, the chicken is cooked, but if the liquid is pink, it is not cooked.

CALORIE AND FAT CONTENT OF CHICKEN, DUCK AND TURKEY		
	kcal per 100g	fat grams per 100g
Roast chicken with skin	218	12.5
Roast chicken without skin	164	7.2
Roast duck with skin	423	38.1
Roast duck without skin	195	10.4
Turkey mince, stewed	176	6.8

Interestingly, skinless chicken or turkey breast has more protein than fatty steak but only about one-tenth the fat and half the calories. Even the flesh of fattier poultry such as goose or duck still contains substantially less fat than fatty red meat. It is always a good idea to buy smaller, younger birds as these are less fatty than older ones. Minced chicken or turkey is a useful alternative in certain dishes where beef mince would normally be used.

Fish

Rich in protein, minerals and vitamins A and D, fish is one of the most nutritious foods we can eat. Fish falls into various categories but is simply classed as white fish or oily fish. White fish includes fish such as cod, halibut, skate, sole, and so on, and oily fish includes herrings, salmon, kippers, anchovies, mackerel and sardines. The reason I recommend oily fish in my low-fat diets is because it contains a unique group of polyunsaturated fatty acids called omega-3. Not only do these omega-3 fatty acids decrease the levels of the artery-choking LDL (low density lipoprotein) cholesterol, but it is believed that they also raise the levels of artery-clearing HDL (high density lipoprotein) cholesterol. Try to eat oily fish at least once a week, but no more than three times a week and avoid ones canned in oil.

Many studies have shown that in communities where increased amounts of fish were eaten, the incidence of heart disease has decreased. Fish oil is also known to help prevent hardening of the arteries by thinning the blood and is also effective in reducing the likelihood of blood clots. Furthermore, salmon and sardines are particularly rich sources of calcium. Try to eat the soft bones they contain to bolster your calcium intake.

Tuna contains less fat than oily fish such as salmon but more fat than white fish. Although it is not a particularly rich source of fish oils, it forms a good alternative to meat.

Shellfish is reasonably low in fat, although the fat it contains is high in cholesterol. However, it is now recognised that high blood cholesterol is made worse by a high-fat diet rather than by cholesterol itself. This is good news for low-fat dieters, since prawns, crab and lobster can add a delightful variation to a salad or sandwich. However, as with oily fish, limit your intake to three servings a week.

Fish can be cooked in many ways, and we have included some interesting and varied recipes in this book. Remember, white fish is so low in fat and calories that you can have a large portion yet still keep within your calorie allowance.

Grilling

Fish does not take long to cook. Placing it on some foil on the grill pan will make it easier to handle and also prevent other foods from picking up the fish odour. Moisten the flesh with lemon or lime juice or a light marinade, according to the recipe you are using. To prevent the fish from drying out, baste regularly during cooking. Serve with a low-fat sauce.

Microwaving

Microwaving is an ideal cooking method for fish. Covering the fish with food wrap helps to retain the moisture, as the fish cooks in its own liquid.

Poaching

Poaching is a satisfactory way of cooking large whole fish. It keeps the fish moist and encourages it to take on the flavourings of the liquor in which you are poaching it. You can use fish stock, milk, water or wine and add whatever flavours you choose, such as lemon or herbs. Always add plenty of freshly ground black pepper. Just keep it on a gentle heat to simmer and avoid any furious boiling.

A fish kettle is one of those utensils you might use only two or three times a year, but on those occasions when you do use it, it is worth its weight in gold. Cooking a whole salmon is almost impossible without one, so next time you wonder what to put on your Christmas list, I suggest you ask for one.

CALORIE AND FAT CONTENT OF WHITE FISH

	kcal per 100g	fat grams per 100g
White fish, grilled	95	1.3
White fish, coated in breadcrumbs and fried	235	14.3
White fish, coated in batter and fried	247	15.4

CALORIE AND FAT CONTENT OF SHELLFISH

	kcal per 100g	fat grams per 100g
Prawns, boiled	99	0.9
Crab, boiled	126	5.5
Lobster, boiled	103	1.6

CALORIE AND FAT CONTENT OF OILY FISH

	kcal per 100g	fat grams per 100g
Salmon, grilled	215	13.1
Mackerel, grilled	239	17.3
Herrings, grilled	181	11.2
Sardines, grilled	195	10.4

Baking

When baking fish in the oven, it's best to wrap it in aluminium foil or to place in a covered ovenproof dish. Make sure there is some liquid surrounding the fish to encourage it to stay moist. You can use any liquid left after cooking to add to a sauce.

Fish in curries and casseroles

Depending on the recipe you are using, it may be appropriate to add the fish towards the end of the cooking time. For instance, when cooking a curry or casserole, if you add the fish too early, you may find it has disintegrated into almost invisible strands by the time you come to serve it.

Pulses

Kidney beans, lentils, chickpeas, blackeye beans, haricot beans, baked beans are all different types of pulses. Nowadays, pulses are available dried or, much more conveniently, ready to use in a can.

Pulses provide more protein than any other plant food. They are low in fat and are a valuable source of soluble fibre which can help to reduce blood cholesterol. Also rich in B vitamins and the minerals iron, zinc, and copper, pulses are an extremely nutritious food for vegetarians and non-vegetarians alike and make a great low-calorie but satisfying option for dieters.

Great care must be taken during the preparation and cooking of dried pulses. So, follow the three steps below.

Cleaning

Pick over the beans, peas or lentils carefully, removing any sediment or unwanted extras.

Soaking

Most pulses need rehydrating after the ripening and drying process. Immerse in water, then remove and discard any that float to the top. Rinse and top up with fresh boiling water and leave to soak for 8 hours.

Cooking

Place in a saucepan of cold water, using three parts water to one part beans, peas or lentils. Bring the water slowly to the boil and skim off the starchy scum that rises to the surface. Boil until tender (this may take an hour or more). During the initial stages of cooking, it is very important that pulses are boiled vigorously to destroy their lectins (these are toxins that can cause gastrointestinal distress). Most dried pulses should be boiled vigorously for at least ten minutes, but two to three minutes is sufficient for lentils and split peas.

Eggs

Basically a protein food, eggs offer many and varied nutrients. They are extremely versatile, forming a delicious meal on their own or as a vital ingredient to a recipe. As far as fat is concerned, the white is the good guy and the yolk is the bad guy. The white is high in protein yet very low in fat. For this reason, I use it widely in sorbets, meringues, mousses, and so on. The white of an egg contains 11 calories and zero fat. The yolk, on the other hand, is high in calories (61 calories per yolk), relatively high in fat (5.5g), and high in cholesterol. For this reason I recommend that non-vegetarians consume around two egg yolks per week, while vegetarians may have more because of the absence of meat in their diet.

Egg yolk is a rich source of iron, which will be absorbed more efficiently if the egg is eaten at the same meal as a food containing vitamin C. This is why, throughout my diets, I always include either a glass of orange juice or half a grapefruit when I suggest an egg for breakfast.

Eggs used in recipes do not need to be counted into your weekly allowance, since the proportion of egg per serving is minimal. It's important to remember that young children, the elderly, and pregnant women should not eat slightly cooked or soft boiled eggs because of the risk of salmonella.

Butter, margarine and low-fat spreads

Butter contains 80 per cent fat, margarines approximately 70 per cent fat, and even spreads that are labelled 'low fat' can contain as much as 60 per cent fat! Of all the spreads I know, Tesco's low-fat spread has the lowest fat content, at 5 per cent fat, and so is acceptable in small quantities if you find you really cannot live without having something to spread on your bread.

There is much confusion among the general public about whether polyunsaturated fats are beneficial for health. The confusion arises between those who have high blood cholesterol or a heart problem and those who need to reduce their weight. For someone who is slim but needs to eat a low-cholesterol diet because of a heart problem, then polyunsaturated margarine is a better choice than saturated fat such as butter. If, however, a heart patient is overweight, then it is better to eat a low-fat diet and avoid polyunsaturated margarines in order to lose weight. At 9 calories per gram, fat offers more than twice as many calories as protein or carbohydrate, weight for weight. If you need to lose weight, then you need to reduce your fat intake dramatically. The amount of fat necessary for good health is very small and will be provided by other foods, without the need to eat butter or mayonnaise.

New cholesterol-lowering foods containing plant stanol esters have appeared on the supermarket shelves. Stanol esters are natural substances which are extracted from certain plants and added to foods during their manufacture. These new cholesterol-lowering foods contain much higher levels of stanol esters than occur in the original plants. They have been sold in Scandinavia for many years but have only recently been introduced in Britain, firstly as a margarine and also as a cream cheese spread. These foods help to reduce cholesterol by blocking its absorption from the gut into the bloodstream. It is important to realise, though, that these foods specifically reduce the absorption of cholesterol – not total fat. They may help decrease blood cholesterol levels, but they won't help you to lose weight. Moreover, it is not yet clear exactly what effect this reduction in blood cholesterol may have on the chances of suffering from heart disease.

Even if you have lost weight successfully and are just seeking to maintain your new weight, I do not recommend you start reintroducing low-fat spreads into your diet. There is no question that butter tastes better than low-fat spreads and, once you get the taste for fat again, you may find yourself on a very slippery slope and slide back into your old eating habits. But if you never start reintroducing it, then your new lifestyle habit will stay a lifetime habit – and so will your figure!

Cheese

Most hard cheeses contain 30 per cent fat and eating them is one of the surest ways to trap you into consuming more fat and calories than you realise. I know regular hard cheese tastes terrific, but it is high in fat, high in sodium, high in cholesterol and high in fattening power, so if you want to have a great body, this is one sacrifice you have to make.

If you are trying to lose weight in the fastest possible time, hard cheese is off the menu, except for small amounts used in recipes. Once you reach your goal weight, you may treat yourself occasionally, ideally with the reduced-fat variety, which we have used in some dishes in this book.

Cottage cheese, on the other hand, is high in nutrients and low in fat. I used to detest it. Strangely, though, as soon as I stopped eating high-fat Cheddar, I grew to like cottage cheese, and now I adore it. I eat it with fruit, I make delicious sandwiches by spreading Marmite onto the bread and filling it with cottage cheese – try it, it's delicious – and I'm very happy to have it on a jacket potato or in a salad.

You can substitute Quark, (skimmed soft cheese) for full-fat cream cheese in many recipes and you won't even notice the difference when you come to eat the finished dish.

CALORIE AND FAT CONTENT OF CHEESE		
	kcal per 25g	fat grams per 25g
Cheddar	103	8.6
Cheddar (reduced fat)	65	3.7
Cottage cheese (full fat)	25	0.9
Cottage cheese (reduced fat)	20	0.3

If you do need to keep cheese in your fridge for the rest of the family, then keep it wrapped in foil and out of sight. It is probably the single most dangerous food to have in your fridge to tempt you. If it's in a see-through plastic container, begging you to slice off a chunk each time you go to the fridge, then it's not surprising that the weight loss on the scales is disappointing.

Milk

Milk is an extremely valuable source of nutrients. It provides high-quality protein as well as many minerals and vitamins. While the fat-soluble vitamins A and D, which are found in whole milk, are removed when the fat is removed from whole milk, they are often added to skimmed milk, so no loss is suffered. Milk also contains the B vitamins and a small amount of vitamin C. By far the most important mineral found in milk is calcium, but other minerals include phosphorous, potassium and a very small but easily absorbed amount of iron, as well as magnesium and copper.

Semi-skimmed milk has about half the fat content (2 per cent fat) of whole milk (4 per cent fat). Skimmed milk has almost no fat and yields only half the number of calories of whole milk. The drawback with skimmed milk, in my view, is that it is so unpalatable – it looks and tastes watery. Whether you choose skimmed or semi-skimmed milk, though, is entirely up to you. Both supply as much calcium as whole milk, because the calcium contained in milk is not in the fatty

bit. We are likely to get most of our calcium requirements through the milk we drink.

Not everyone can tolerate milk because of its lactose content. Such problems arise when the digestive enzyme lactase, which helps to break down lactose into its component sugars, is produced in insufficient amounts by the body. If you have a lactose intolerance, try consuming cultured milk products such as live cultured yogurt. You can also buy milk products that have been treated with lactase, or you can buy lactase and add it to dairy products at home. If you do not consume any milk or dairy products it is important that you take a calcium supplement or eat significant quantities of calcium rich non-dairy products such as green leafy vegetables. A good intake of calcium is essential to build and maintain strong bones and to reduce the risk of osteoporosis in later life.

Yogurt, fromage frais and cream

Yogurt is simply milk that has been fermented by several strains of bacteria such as Lactobacillus acidophilus and Bifidobacteria bifidum. The bacteria curdle the milk by converting the milk sugar to lactic acid. Yogurt is made from a skimmed milk base with added skimmed milk powder. The milk is pasteurised, cooled and special bacteria are added to cause fermentation. The milk is then incubated in large tanks at a constant temperature until it thickens, after which it is cooled.

One of the main nutritional benefits of yogurt is to reinforce additional 'friendly' bacteria in the intestines, promoting the growth of beneficial intestinal flora. The bacteria of the intestinal flora aid digestion and absorption of food, produce B vitamins and prevent the growth of pathogenic bacteria (such as candida) which cause disease. These bacteria also promote a healthy intestinal acidity. In this respect, yogurt is especially beneficial for people who are taking antibiotics, and for those who eat a lot of sugary products or who drink chlorinated water, all of which deplete friendly bacteria. Yogurt also helps to synthesise vitamin K, preventing internal

CALORIE AND FAT CONTENT OF CREAM, YOGURT AND FROMAGE FRAIS

CREAM	kcal per 100g	fat grams per 100g	kcal per 15ml tablespoon	fat grams per 15ml tablespoon
Double	449	48	134	14
Single	198	19.1	29	2.8
Soured	205	19.9	62	5.9
Clotted	586	63.5	263	28.5
Whipping	373	39.3	167	17.6

YOGURT	kcal per 100g	fat grams per 100g	kcal per average portion (150g)	fat grams per average portion (150g)
Low-calorie	41	0.2	61	0.25
Low-fat flavoured	90	0.9	135	1.4
Low-fat fruit	90	0.7	135	1.05
Low-fat plain	56	0.8	84	1.2
Soya	72	4.2	108	6.3

FROMAGE FRAIS	kcal per 100g	fat grams per 100g	kcal per 15ml tablespoon	fat grams per 15ml tablespoon
Fruit	131	5.8	59	2.6
Plain	113	7.1	51	3.2
Very low fat	58	0.2	29	0.1

haemorrhages, and it lowers cholesterol levels and reduces the risk of colon cancer.

Yogurt is a good source of high-quality protein, vitamins and minerals. It contains vitamins A, B complex, D and E, and is an excellent source of easily absorbed calcium, potassium and phosphorus, with just a modest sodium content. Yogurt is easily digestible – in fact most of its protein is digested within an hour. It also has a valuable role in the treatment of gastroenteritis, colitis, constipation, bilious disorders, flatulence, bad breath, high cholesterol, migraine and nervous fatigue. Moreover, yogurt can often be tolerated by people who are unable to consume other forms of milk due to lactose intolerance.

Yogurt is more widely available now than ever before, with many varieties to choose from. Most yogurt produced in the UK is low in fat. If you find natural yogurt too acidic for your taste, you can add fruit, fruit juice, muesli, honey or any other flavourings you like.

Unless yogurt is pasteurised after preparation (it will say on the label), it will contain 'live' bacteria which remain dormant while kept cool. If the yogurt is not kept in the refrigerator or a similarly cool place, the bacteria will become active again and produce more acid until the yogurt eventually separates.

You can buy commercially frozen yogurt or freeze your own, using homemade or shop-bought flavoured yogurt, providing it contains sugar.

Low-fat yogurt is just as valuable a source of protein, calcium and other nutrients as the full-fat brands, and forms an invaluable part of a low-fat diet. The use of artificial sweeteners or artificial sweetening agents in certain brands means there is a wide variety of low-calorie ones to choose from. Find a brand you enjoy, but do check the fat content and the total number of calories per pot before purchasing. Many yogurts which are virtually fat free offer 180 calories per pot. Why use up so many calories on one pot of yogurt when you can buy another of the same size that yields only 60 calories? For the same number of calories, you could have a sandwich as well as the pot of yogurt!

Yogurt is extremely versatile and a useful substitution for cream. Eat it with fruit, or use it to dress a dessert. A pot of yogurt is also ideal to include in the children's packed lunch for school.

Alternatives to cream

All cream, whether single, whipping, double, soured, or crème fraîche, is extremely high in fat and therefore high in calories. It has no place on a low-fat diet, but fortunately, there are some great alternatives. Yogurt (plain or flavoured) is a good alternative to single cream, while low-fat fromage frais, (try the Normandy kind), 0% fat Greek yogurt and set bio yogurts are excellent alternatives to the thicker varieties of cream.

Cream is high in cholesterol and very high in fattening power, but if we're used to eating it, then we like the taste. It takes time for our tastebuds to adjust to eating the low-fat alternatives, but, given time, you will be amazed how you find you come to dislike the taste of cream and grow to love the taste of these healthier options.

The golden rule to remember when using yogurt or fromage frais in cooking is never to boil them. If they become too hot, they will curdle, so add them at the end of cooking when the dish has been removed from the heat.

Ice cream and sorbets

The fat content of ice cream varies enormously, from being quite modest for an almost synthetic product to being high fat when made with real cream and egg yolks. It is, however, a versatile and often quite nutritious dessert and certainly one of my favourites! When buying branded ice creams, remember to look at the nutrition label. As well as checking the fat content, look at the number of calories too and make sure they fit into your daily allowance. Wall's 'Too-Good-To-Be-True' and other brands offer some excellent low-fat iced desserts which taste every bit as good as the real thing. You could also try yogurt-based ice cream as an alternative.

Sorbets are naturally low in fat and make a delicious dessert to follow any meal. Check out the ones in your local supermarket – Marks & Spencer has a particularly good range.

Potatoes

Potatoes play an invaluable role in a low-fat diet. They are cheap, versatile, low in calories and virtually fat free. You can create a whole meal around this humble vegetable. Baked or 'jacket' potatoes are a firm favourite, and baby new potatoes can honour the most lavish dinner party menu.

Potatoes provide around 20 calories per 25g and are a good carbohydrate food, which means the calories are not easily stored as fat on the body but are easily burned as energy. It was once thought that potatoes were fattening, but this was only because most people used to eat them with lots of added fat. Now that we've learned ways of cooking and eating them without fat, potatoes are a real friend of the dieter because they are so filling. They contain valuable nutrients such as folic acid and thiamine as well as vitamin C. In fact, until relatively recently when fruit and vegetables became more popular, Britain's population used to acquire most of its vitamin C intake through potatoes, simply because we ate them so much.

Potatoes can be boiled with or without their skins, dry-roasted, or mashed with yogurt or fromage frais instead of butter. You can even buy readymade oven chips with a fat content of less than 4 per cent. It's interesting to note that a serving of regular chips has three times the number of calories and 12 times the amount of fat of boiled potatoes. If you want to have chips occasionally, make sure you go for thick-cut ones and not the small crinkle-cut varieties which have a greater surface area to absorb the fat.

Bread

I could devote half this book to the different kinds of breads and the differences between them. For simplicity's sake, I recommend you always check the fat content on the packaging before purchasing. Almost all bread requires some form of fat to make it into a finished loaf. The fat can be anything from olive oil to butter, margarine, and so on. Some of the newer exotic breads in the supermarkets today contain surprisingly large amounts of fat. Watch out, too, for those with added high-fat ingredients such as olives, cheese or sun-dried tomatoes.

Wholemeal bread contains flour which is less processed than that used for white bread and thereby retains more natural ingredients. With white bread, most of the fibre and the wholegrain has been removed, although in the UK it is fortified with many nutrients and, fibre content aside, is just as healthy as wholemeal. In fact, white bread contains more calcium than brown bread. Brown bread doesn't necessarily mean that it's wholemeal, so do check the label to ensure that it meets your particular requirements. If you want a high-fibre loaf, then choose a wholegrain one or one with added fibre – this will be stated on the packaging.

On average, bread provides 70 calories per 25g and its fat content can vary enormously. Warm, freshly baked bread tastes superb without any fat spread on it and can become a firm favourite on a low-fat diet. If you have eaten butter or margarine on bread for many years, it

CALORIE AND FAT CONTENT OF POTATOES		
Type	kcal per 100g	fat grams per 100g
New potatoes, boiled	75	0.3
Old potatoes, boiled	72	0.1
Potatoes, dry-roasted	72	0.2
Potatoes, roasted with fat	149	4.5
Instant potato powder made up with water	57	0.1
Chips, fried	189	6.7
Chips, crinkle-cut, fried in corn oil	290	16.7
Frozen oven chips, baked	162	4.2
Frozen oven chips, microwaved	221	9.6

CALORIE AND FAT CONTENT OF BREAD

Type	Portion	kcal	fat grams
Brown	average slice	78	0.7
Granary	average slice	84	0.9
Wheatgerm	average slice	83	0.9
White	average slice	84	0.9
Wholemeal	average slice	77	0.9
Garlic	1/3 baguette	290	15.8
Naan	1 naan	469	13
Pitta	1 pitta	163	0.5
Ciabatta	1/6 ciabatta	108	1.6
Soda	40g	92	0.8

will probably come as a shock to start eating bread without a greasy layer. Give yourself 30 days to get used to having marmalade spread directly onto dry toast and mustard, or low-fat dressing spread directly onto bread for sandwiches. As long as there's some moisture there, you won't miss the butter or margarine. If you're eating bread prior to a meal in a restaurant, a good restaurant will bring you hot rolls, and these taste delicious on their own.

Bread is a carbohydrate and is easily burned by the body. However, some people are intolerant to wheat and may need to follow a gluten-free diet. You can purchase gluten-free bread in cans from many high street chemists or fresh loaves from health food shops. Rice cakes are a good alternative for anyone who has an allergy to wheat flour.

Pasta

Pasta is a carbohydrate and, as such, is burned easily as energy by the body. Pasta is made from wheat flour and can be home-made or purchased fresh or dried. There are many varieties and shapes and sizes available, some made with just flour and water and some with added egg. On a low-fat diet, obviously, it is preferable to choose the egg-free varieties. Dried pasta is convenient to have in the store cupboard. Cooked properly, it tastes excellent, and it can be used in lunch and dinner menus.

Pasta adds variety to a low-fat diet, forming a delicious high-carbohydrate, low-fat accompaniment to many dishes. Dry pasta yields 85 calories per 25g (1oz). Twenty-five grams (1oz) of dry pasta when boiled will weigh almost 75g (3oz) and, providing you add no butter or oil

CALORIE AND FAT CONTENT OF PASTA

Type	kcal per 100g	fat grams per 100g
Dried egg pasta	358	3.5
Dried pasta without egg	345	2.0
Fresh egg pasta	279	3.6

to the finished pasta, you can make your calorie calculations based on 85 calories per 25g (1oz) dry weight or 85 calories per 75g (3oz) cooked weight. When cooking pasta, I always add a vegetable stock cube to the water for extra flavour. Make sure there is plenty of water in the pan so that the pasta does not need to be rinsed after cooking. This will help retain the delicate flavour that has been absorbed from the stock cube. Cooked pasta can be saved in a covered dish and served on a later occasion.

Pasta can be served hot or cold with a variety of different sauces. Many children love it, and the small spirals and shell-shaped pasta are ideal to pack for school lunches.

One word of warning: it is easy to underestimate how much pasta you are eating. This is one of the first things I ask my dieters to check when they tell me their weight-loss progress is proving too slow. So, if this applies to you, do check your serving sizes.

Rice

Long grain, short grain, basmati, patna, wild – there are so many different types of rice to choose from. In each of the recipes in this book I have stated what type of rice should be used if a special one is needed. Otherwise, use long-grain rice for a savoury dish and short-grain rice for a sweet dish.

Twenty-five grams (1oz) of dry weight rice yields 96 calories, and 25g (1oz) of dry weight rice weighs 65g (2½oz) when cooked. On a low-fat eating plan, the simple message is to boil rice and never fry it. You can save many grams of fat and loads of calories simply by never frying rice. Rice is a carbohydrate and is easily burned by the body but the quantities are deceptive and a typical portion is surprisingly high in calories. Mixing boiled rice with boiled or steamed beansprouts is an excellent way of making the rice go further and help fill you up.

Rice can be eaten hot or cold in savoury and sweet dishes and is a highly absorbent substance. I always boil my rice in plenty of water with a vegetable stock cube and, providing I am using easy cook rice, I find no need to rinse the rice before serving. However, If you wish to cook rice for a cold dish or in advance for a dinner party, then rinse it and cool it right off with cold water. You can reheat rice easily by just pouring boiling

NUTRIENT VALUES OF RICE			
Type	energy per 100g	protein per 100g	fat per 100g
Brown rice, raw	357 kcal	6.7g	2.8g
White rice, easy cook, raw	383 kcal	7.3g	3.6g

water over it or reheating in a microwave. The key is not to overcook rice, as this makes it go soft and soggy. Rice is cooked when it doesn't taste grainy. It should be firm but soft in texture. If you add a vegetable stock cube to the cooking water there is no need to add butter or oil, as the tiny amount of fat contained in the stock cube will ensure that the particles of rice stay separated. Cooked rice can be kept in a cool cupboard or refrigerator for up to two days and used hot or cold on a later occasion.

I always buy the easy cook variety of rice for everyday use, as it's so quick and easy to prepare. However, for dinner parties and special occasions I use basmati rice. Wild rice is very attractive and is also excellent for dinner parties.

Brown rice has the husk still attached, which gives extra fibre, although it requires almost four times more cooking time than the easy cook or white varieties.

Fruit and vegetables

Fruit and vegetables are a real friend of the low-fat dieter, but one of the greatest myths of low-fat eating is the belief that, because fruit is virtually fat free, you can eat it quite freely between meals, as if the calories disappeared into obscurity! Fruit contains more sugar and therefore more calories than vegetables. On average, fruit contains around 10 calories per 25g (1oz) compared with vegetables, which have just 5 calories per 25g (1oz), with some

exceptions such as potatoes, peas and sweetcorn.

Fruit and vegetables have a valuable role to play in the daily diet and should be consumed in generous quantities within your calorie allowance. Try to vary your choices so that you eat a wide range of different types and colours to gain maximum benefits from the vitamins and minerals they contain. Rather than stocking up on large amounts in one go, aim to buy smaller amounts regularly so that they don't become stale and lose some of their vitamin content. Fruit and vegetables eaten raw will yield a greater vitamin content than when cooked. In most of my diets I recommend you eat three portions of fruit and three portions of vegetables each day. One portion of fruit can be in the form of 150ml ($\frac{1}{4}$ pint) fruit juice, or a piece of fruit, or 115g (4oz) of fruit such as strawberries, cherries, raspberries, blackberries, etc.

When cooking vegetables, never add any fat, although you can add a vegetable stock cube to the cooking water for extra flavour. If you do this, there is no need to add salt. Vegetables act as a great filler and are the only foods that I suggest can be eaten between meals on my diets. Cucumber, cherry tomatoes, celery and carrot sticks all offer few calories yet have lots of munching and filling power. It's a good idea to create a nibble tray each morning and keep it in the refrigerator or take it to work so that if you feel peckish between meals you have an instant low-fat alternative to a chocolate bar.

Three vegetables which deserve a special mention here are mushrooms, onions and tomatoes. I use these a lot in my cooking, because they are cheap and also great for adding flavour and bulk to low-fat recipes, making a more satisfying meal without adding too many calories.

Mushrooms

Mushrooms come in many shapes, sizes and varieties, and the flavours between the different types vary enormously. Since they contain very few calories (2 calories per 25g/1oz), they are a real friend of the low-fat dieter. They act as a useful filler as well as adding a special flavour to any low-fat recipe. However, when fried in any type of fat, mushrooms are like little sponges and their calorific value increases from 13 calories per 115g (4oz) in their natural state to 157 calories per 115g (4oz) when fried in oil or butter. The golden rule when using mushrooms in low-fat recipes is to avoid the use of fat and allow them to absorb moisture from flavoured sauces.

Mushrooms contain quite a lot of their own liquid, so if you slice and cook them in a non-stick frying pan with no added liquid, you will be surprised how much liquid they make. They also taste great when sliced and served raw in salads. You can buy dried mushrooms from the supermarket, which means you can have a supply of exotic ones to hand in the store cupboard ready for that special occasion when you require a different flavour.

Onions

Onions, like mushrooms, are low in calories in their natural state, but as soon as you put them near fat, they soak it up like a sponge. Onions yield only 36 calories and 0.2g fat per 115g (4oz), but, when fried, that figure bumps up to a massive 164 calories and 11.2g fat. The calorie and fat content is roughly the same for any type of onion, whether it be Spanish, cooking, red, spring, pickling or shallots.

Cooking onions offer the strongest flavour, followed by Spanish onions and then red onions, which makes the latter particularly suitable for salads. Onions are a great way to bulk up a low-fat recipe, add lots of flavour and bring moisture to the dish. Again, try cooking in stock for added flavour. They also dry-fry magnificently. All round, they are a useful ally for the low-fat dieter.

Tomatoes

Tomatoes are another vegetable full of flavour but with very few calories and virtually no fat, and they are a rich source of vitamin C. Available all year round and generally inexpensive, they are extremely versatile and can be used in many dishes, hot or cold. Tomato purée adds a richness to any sauce and a tin of chopped tomatoes takes all the hard work out of preparing tomatoes in a spaghetti bolognese sauce. There is no need to add butter or cream or oil to any tomato-based recipe, as the flavour of cooked tomato will be enhanced by allowing it to reduce and thicken. The end result is a sweeter, stronger-tasting tomato flavour.

Another useful tomato-based item is in the unlikely form of tomato ketchup. Although this contains some sugar, it is a useful low-fat addition to any store cupboard and can be mixed with reduced-oil salad dressing to make a low-fat Marie Rose dressing, or with cottage cheese to make a tasty topping for potatoes.

Sun-dried tomatoes have come into their own in recent years, but do avoid those canned or bottled in oil.

Sugar

Sugar is a simple carbohydrate offering what some nutritionists term empty calories. In other words, apart from energy-giving carbohydrate, there are no other nutrients in sugar, yet it has a very positive role to play in a low-fat diet. In the absence of high amounts of fat, the body will naturally yearn energy-giving foods, and by including a moderate amount of sugar in a low-fat diet, I firmly believe it is easier to hold our willpower intact. I do in fact advocate having a small teaspoon of sugar in tea or coffee, since I find this is one of the best ways to resist the temptation to eat biscuits or cakes between meals. Sugar taken in moderation is easily burned by the body as energy and is not easily stored, but you still need to count the calories.

This does not mean I am giving licence for everyone to eat a high-sugar diet. Certainly not. All I am suggesting is that sugar, in moderation, can still be included in a weight-reducing diet. Remember, though, that calories do count, but within a daily calorie allowance of 1,400 calories, I believe there is room for small amounts. Like fat, sugar is an acquired taste and if we decrease our liking for it, then it will be easier to moderate our intake. One of the easiest ways of cutting our sugar intake is to avoid high-sugar fizzy drinks, since these not only contain a high proportion of sugar offering unnecessarily high amounts of calories but can also be harmful to teeth. Substitute diet brands instead or, even better, try fizzy water. There are now many flavoured varieties available.

I am not a great advocate of sugary confectionery, as I believe it is habit forming and

CALORIE AND FAT CONTENT OF SUGAR		
Type	kcal	fat grams
White sugar, per 25g	99	Nil
White sugar, per 5ml teaspoon	24	Nil
Demerara sugar, per 25g	91	Nil
Demerara sugar, per 5ml teaspoon	24	Nil

has no part in a healthy eating plan. I would prefer you to have a spoonful of sugar in your tea than have a packet of mints every other day. To make my point further, I suggest you look at your friends – who takes sugar in their tea and who doesn't? Often it's the overweight ones that don't and the slim ones that do. I believe that those who have a little sugar in their tea have no need to yearn for sweets and biscuits. Be aware, also, that a lot of confectionery, such as chocolate or toffee, is high in fat as well as sugar.

I'm also not a great advocate of reduced-sugar brands of foods such as baked beans, as the difference in calories and fat between these and the ordinary varieties is minimal. Far better to go for the real thing and feel that you are eating normal food.

Jams, marmalades, preserves and honey

In the absence of butter or margarine on your toast, marmalade, honey, jams and preserves come into their own. Offering easily released energy-giving carbohydrate as well as moisture, they add a delightful taste to freshly toasted wholemeal bread. Again, be aware of the calories, so don't spread them onto your toast an inch thick! There is no need to buy reduced-sugar varieties of jams and preserves unless you find one that you prefer to the full-sugar version. Otherwise, the number of calories you save are at the expense of the flavour, and this will only leave you with a feeling of deprivation which, in turn, could lead to cheating. Better to have a teaspoon of the real thing than to go off the rails because you didn't enjoy a low-calorie alternative.

Sauces and dressings

When cooking and preparing everyday food without fat, sauces and dressings are important for adding flavour, moisture and taste. Today, we are spoilt for choice with the numerous varieties available on supermarket shelves, but do check the fat content before you buy. These are a convenient and helpful aid to anyone following a low-fat eating plan, but it can be quick and easy to make your own.

Experiment with different dressings when preparing salads or sandwiches. Soy sauce on a salad made of rice, beansprouts and mixed vegetables, or with grated raw beetroot or carrot tastes superb. Try mixing some ready-made mustard with balsamic vinegar, a little sugar and plenty of freshly ground black pepper for an instant dressing. Soon they will become part of your everyday menu planning.

Cooking the low fat way

To cook the low fat way you will need some basic non-stick kitchen utensils such as a non-stick frying pan or wok, some non-stick baking tins and the appropriate utensils to go with them. The first time you cook a stir-fry in a non-stick wok without a drop of oil is quite a revelation. The moisture that comes from the meat and vegetables prevents the food from sticking or tasting dry.

Once you have got used to low-fat cooking there will be no turning back. It really is easier than you think. In the following pages I have included advice on the kinds of utensils you need and how to care for them, as well as outlining the various low-fat cooking techniques and suggestions for flavour enhancers to help your food taste delicious.

Equipment you will need

Utensils

At one time, non-stick surfaces used to have a very short lifespan before becoming scratched and worn. Fortunately, in recent years great progress been made with non-stick pans, although the old adage 'you get what you pay for' still holds firm. Buy a cheap non-stick pan, and the first time you slightly burn the pan, the surface begins to peel.

It is worth investing in a top-quality non-stick wok and a non-stick frying pan, both with lids. I use these two pans more than anything else in my kitchen. The lid is crucial, since this allows the contents of the pan to steam which adds moisture to the dish.

Non-stick saucepans are useful, too, for cooking sauces, porridge, scrambled eggs and other foods that tend to stick easily. Lids are essential for these too. Also, treat yourself to a set of non-stick baking tins and trays. Cakes, Yorkshire puddings, scones, and lots more can all be cooked the low fat way.

To clean a non-stick pan, always soak the pan first to loosen any food that is still inside, then wash with a non-abrasive sponge or cloth. Any brush or gentle scourer used carefully will do the trick of cleaning away every particle without effort and without damage to the surface. Overheating and allowing pans to boil dry is the biggest danger for non-stick pans, so, when cooking vegetables, keep on eye on the water levels!

Non-scratch implements

Wooden spoons and spatulas, Teflon (or similar) coated tools and others marked as suitable for use with non-stick surfaces are a must. If you continue to use metal forks, spoons and spatulas, you will scratch and spoil the non-stick surface of pans. Treat the surfaces kindly, and good non-stick pans will last for years.

Other equipment

You will no doubt already have some of the items listed below, but I have made the list as comprehensive as possible, including the things I use most often.

Aluminium foil
Baking parchment
Chopping boards (1 small, 1 medium, 1 large)
Clingfilm
Colander (1 small and 1 large)
Fish kettle (stainless steel)
Flour shaker
Food processor
Garlic press
Good quality can opener
Juicer
Kitchen paper
Kitchen scales (ones that weigh small amounts
   accurately)
Lemon squeezer
Measuring jugs (1 × ½ litre/1 pint, 1 × 1 litre/
   2 pints)
Melon baller
Mixing bowls (1 × 1 litre/2 pints /1.2 litre,
   1 × 2 litres/4 pints, 1 × 4 litres/8 pints)
Multi-surface grater
Ovenproof dishes

Palette knife
Pasta spoon (non-scratch)
Pastry brush
Pepper mill
Pizza cutter
Plastic containers with lids
Potato masher (non-scratch)
Ramekin dishes
Rolling pin
Scissors
Set of sharp knives (all sizes)
Sieve (1 small and 1 large)
Slotted spoon (non-scratch)
Steamer
Vegetable peeler
Whisk (balloon type)
Wire rack
Zester

Store cupboard

There are many items that are very useful to have in stock. Build up your store cupboard over a period of time to avoid a marathon shopping trip!

Arrowroot
Cornflour
Plain flour
Self-raising flour
Gelatine
Marmite
Bovril
Dried herbs

Tomato ketchup
HP sauce
Fruity sauce
Barbecue sauce
Reduced oil salad dressing
Balsamic vinegar
White wine vinegar
Black peppercorns
Salt
White pepper
Vegetable stock cubes
Chicken stock cubes
Beef stock cubes
Lamb stock cubes
Pork stock cubes
Long-grain easy cook rice
Basmati rice
Pasta
Oats
Tabasco sauce
Soy sauce
Worcestershire sauce
Caster sugar
Brown sugar
Artificial sweetener

Fresh items
Eggs
Fresh herbs
Garlic
Lemons
Oranges
Tomatoes

Low-fat cooking techniques

Dry-frying meat and poultry

The secret of dry-frying is to have your non-stick pan over the correct heat. If it's too hot, the pan will dry out too soon and the contents will burn. If the heat is too low, you lose the crispness recommended for a stir-fry. Practice makes perfect and a simple rule is to preheat the pan until it is quite hot (but not too hot!) before adding any of the ingredients. Test if the pan is hot enough by adding a piece of meat or poultry. The pan is at the right temperature if the meat sizzles on contact. Add the rest of the meat or poultry and toss it around. Once it is sealed on all sides (when it changes colour) you can reduce the heat a little as you add your seasonings, followed by vegetables and any other ingredients.

Cooking meat and poultry is simple, as the natural fat and juices run out almost immediately, providing plenty of moisture to prevent burning.

When cooking mince, I dry-fry it first and place it in a colander to drain away any fat that has emerged. I wipe out the pan with kitchen paper to remove any fatty residue and then return the meat to the pan to continue cooking my shepherd's pie or bolognese sauce.

Dry-frying vegetables

Vegetables contain their own juices and soon release them when they become hot, so dry-frying works just as well for vegetables as it does for meat and poultry. When dry-frying vegetables, it's important not to overcook them. They should be crisp and colourful so that they retain their flavour and most of their nutrients. Perhaps the most impressive results are with onions. When they are dry-fried, after a few minutes they go from being raw to translucent and soft and then on to become brown and caramelised. They taste superb and look all the world like fried onions but taste so much better without all that fat.

Good results are also obtained when dry-frying large quantities of mushrooms, as they 'sweat' and make lots of liquid. Using just a few mushrooms produces a less satisfactory result unless you are stir-frying them with lots of other vegetables. If you are using a small quantity, therefore, you may find it preferable to cook them in vegetable stock.

Alternatives to frying with fat

Wine, water, soy sauce, wine vinegar, balsamic vinegar, and even fresh lemon juice all provide liquid in which food can be cooked. Some thicker types of sauces can dry out too fast if added early on in cooking, but these can be added later when there is more moisture in the pan.

When using wine or water, make sure the pan is hot before adding the other ingredients so that they sizzle in the hot pan.

Flavour enhancers

Low-fat cooking can be bland and dry, so it's important to add moisture and/or extra flavour to compensate for the lack of fat.

I have found that adding freshly ground black pepper to just about any savoury dish is a real flavour enhancer. You need a good pepper mill and you should buy your peppercorns whole and in large quantities. Ready-ground black pepper is nowhere near as good. Sometimes it has other things mixed with the ground pepper, so give this one a miss.

When cooking rice, pasta and vegetables, I always add a vegetable stock cube to the cooking water. Although the stock cube does contain a little fat, the amount that is absorbed by the food is negligible and the benefit in flavour is very noticeable. I always save the water I've used to cook vegetables to make soups, gravy and sauces. Again, the fat from the stock cube that will be contained in a single serving is very small.

When making sandwiches, spread sauces and pickles such as Branston, mustard, horseradish and low-fat or fat-free dressings straight onto the bread. This helps the inside of the sandwich to stay 'put' and, because these sauces or dressings are quite highly flavoured, you won't miss the butter. Make sure you use fresh bread for maximum taste.

Here is a quick reference list of ingredients or cooking methods that can be substituted for traditional high-fat ones.

Cheese sauces Use small amounts of low-fat Cheddar, a little made-up mustard and skimmed milk with cornflour.

Custard Use custard powder and follow the instructions on the packet, using skimmed milk and artificial sweetener in place of sugar to save calories.

Cream Instead of double cream or whipping cream, use 0% fat Greek yogurt or fromage frais. Do not boil. For single cream, substitute natural or vanilla-flavoured yogurt or fromage frais.

Cream cheese Use Quark (skimmed soft cheese).

Creamed potatoes Mash the potatoes in the normal way and add fromage frais in place of butter or cream. Season well.

French dressing Use two parts apple juice to one part wine vinegar, and add a teaspoon of Dijon mustard.

Mayonnaise Use fromage frais mixed with two parts cider vinegar to one part lemon juice, plus a little turmeric and sugar.

Marie Rose dressing Use reduced oil salad dressing mixed with yogurt, tomato ketchup and a dash of Tabasco sauce and black pepper.

Porridge Cook with water or skimmed milk and make to a sloppy consistency. Cover and leave overnight. Reheat before serving and serve with cold milk and sugar or honey.

Roux Make a low-fat roux by adding dry plain flour to a pan containing the other ingredients and 'cooking off' the flour. Then add liquid to thicken. Alternatively, use cornflour mixed with cold water or milk. Bring to the boil and cook for 2–3 minutes.

Thickening for sweet sauces Arrowroot, slaked in cold water or juice, is good because it becomes translucent when cooked.

Herbs

Herbs are fine fragrant plants that have been used to enhance and flavour food since the development of the art of cookery. As well as adding the finishing touches to a dish, many are attributed with hidden medicinal strengths that contribute to our wellbeing. Never before has there been such a wide variety of herbs introduced to our palate, from Mediterranean influences and worldwide cultures. You can buy them fresh, freeze-dried or dried, or grow your own. They all have an important role to play. Since dried herbs have a stronger flavour, they should be used more sparingly than fresh ones.

Fresh herbs fall into two categories: hard wood and soft leaf. Generally, hard wood herbs, such as rosemary, thyme and bay, are added at the beginning of a recipe in order to allow the herbs to soften and release their flavours. Soft leaf herbs, such as parsley, chervil, and basil, have more delicate flavours and are added near the end of cooking time so that they retain their flavour.

Fines herbes

This is a French blend of sweet, aromatic herbs that complement each other and is used as a complete flavour enhancer. The most common blend consists of parsley, chervil, chives, and tarragon, which is ideal for fish and salads, egg dishes (especially omelettes), poached chicken, and sauces.

Bouquet garni

A fresh bouquet garni is a small bundle of selected herbs such as parsley stalks and thyme, wrapped in bay leaves. Sometimes a celery stalk or the green part of the leek is also included.

A bouquet garni can also contain dried herbs. Commercially produced ones come in sachets that look rather like tea bags and usually contain equal quantities of dried thyme, bay and parsley. You can make your own by placing a selection of dried herbs in a small square of muslin and tying with a piece of string.

A bouquet garni is used to flavour soups, stews and casseroles and other dishes that need considerable cooking. It should be removed from the dish before serving.

Lemongrass

This sharp woody grass herb, commonly used in East Asian cooking, is unlike any other herb and has the appearance of a dried iris stem. The outer leaves are removed before using so that the softer core can be finely chopped. As its name implies, it has a strong lemon fragrance, and it can also be bought dried and chopped.

Fennel

This strong robust plant with sturdy dark green foliage has an anise flavour. Both the leaf and seeds are commonly used in cooking. The seeds are crushed or used whole in curries and casseroles or as a topping for breads.

Bay leaves

These green waxy leaves of the bay tree or Mediterranean laurel have a strong, spicy flavour. They are commonly used in soups and stews, and to flavour infusions of milk in sauces such as bread sauce.

Mint

There are many varieties of mint, from spearmint to applemint and fruit mint. The most aromatic of all herbs, mint is particularly known for its affinity with lamb. Spearmint or garden mint is the one most commonly used in cooking. You can use it to make mint sauce, serve with roast lamb, and add to the cooking water for vegetables such as new potatoes and peas. Mint is also ideal for decorating desserts and puddings. Freshly chopped mint has a strong aroma with which dried mint cannot compare.

Basil

This Mediterranean leaf with its pungent taste and aromatic scent can be used in salads and is perfect with tomatoes. Its main use is in pesto – a paste made with basil, garlic, olive oil and pine nuts. You can make low-fat pesto by omitting the pine nuts and substituting lemon juice for the olive oil.

Marjoram and oregano

These two plants are very similar (oregano is a member of the marjoram family), with small round leaves on woody stems. Marjoram has a more gentle flavour than oregano and is good in stuffings, egg dishes and on roasts. Oregano is commonly used in Italian dishes such as pizza. Both marjoram and oregano are available fresh or dried.

Chives

A member of the onion family, these long green strands have a light onion flavour. When in flower they hold a purple ball of tiny flowers at the pinnacle of the stem. The flowers as well as the strands can be finely snipped and used in salads and dressings and to garnish soups. Choose ones that have dark green and dry firm stems. Avoid yellow tinged ones, as these may be old.

Dill

This is a wispy dark green, feather-like plant. Both the leaves and seeds are cultivated. Fresh leaves are traditionally used with cured salmon such as gravadlax. The seeds are crushed or left whole to impart an anise flavour. Dried dill has a particularly concentrated flavour – use sparingly.

Chervil

This green leafy herb is very similar in appearance to parsley but is a much finer, delicate plant with a light flavour of aniseed. It is used a great deal in French cuisine. Freeze-dried chervil is excellent.

Tarragon

There are two types of tarragon: French and Russian. Russian has a more pungent taste. This large ganglion plant has long, thin greyish green leaves and is used to flavour vinegar and sauces.

Coriander

A member of the carrot family, this pretty plant is probably the most used herb throughout the world. The plant yields both leaf and seed for culinary use. The seeds are crushed or used whole and have a sweet, almost orange zest flavour. Coriander is used as a component in pickling spice and also sold in ground form. The leaf is very delicate with a distinctive flavour that is considered an acquired taste. Both the seeds and leaf are used for flavouring Indian curries and many Moroccan and Mexican dishes.

Parsley

There are two types – curly and flat leaf – and both are full of vitamins and minerals. Flat leaf parsley is better for cooking, as it has a stronger flavour than the curly leaf. Curly parsley, with its strong keeping qualities, is used as a garnish. The leaves can be chopped and sprinkled on many savoury dishes and vegetables, whereas the stalks are ideal for use in soups and stocks.

Rosemary

This hard wood herb has silver grey needle-like leaves and is widely used in Mediterranean cookery. It is used for marinades and spiking lamb or roasting with fish. This versatile herb can also be used with strongly flavoured vegetables, jams and jellies.

Sage

A strong and powerful herb which is used in stuffings and to add flavour to sausages. It can also be used to flavour casseroles and meat dishes (especially pork), but use sparingly.

Thyme

It is believed that there are about 100 different varieties of thyme. This special herb flavours a dish without overpowering it. It is used in soups and casseroles to add depth and a light flavour.

Herbes de Provence

This mixture of southern French herbs, which usually includes oregano, rosemary, marjoram, savory, basil, bay and thyme, is used in stews and is good with pizza, tomatoes and sauces.

Spices

Spices were originally used to disguise ill-flavoured meat and sour foods as a result of insufficient means of chilled storage. Mainly derived from distant shores such as Sri Lanka and the East Indies, spices have over the years developed into flavour-enhancing additions. Today, they are appreciated for their aroma, colour and ability to blend together to give unique flavours.

Since spices are made from seeds, they are quite high in fat. However, because of the relatively small quantities used in recipes, their fat content is insignificant.

Spices can be kept longer than herbs, although once opened they will deteriorate. Keep out of direct sun and seal well after use.

The strongest flavours are achieved by grinding fresh seeds or whole spices as opposed to buying them already ground.

Always add spices at the beginning of a recipe, as they need to be allowed to 'cook out' to allow the flavour to develop fully. Berries such as juniper need to be crushed before cooking to release their flavours, whereas some spices such as fennel or cumin seeds benefit from being toasted in a non-stick pan.

The best way is to experiment with different spices, adding them in tiny quantities, to give a unique flavour to your cookery.

Garlic

Garlic is a fundamental ingredient in many savoury dishes. Once native to the Mediterranean, China and Central Asia it is now grown all over the world, varying in size, colour and flavour.

A bulb or head of garlic contains several cloves, each covered with a thin film of skin and are held together by an outer thicker skin. The most common garlic is the white-skinned type, followed by pink-skinned, which is much stronger in flavour. Then there is Elephant garlic with its giant cloves that are much milder in strength and flavour.

A member of the onion family, garlic, like most vegetables, is seasonal. Fresh pungent bulbs are harvested in late spring and then hung and stored in cool, well-ventilated dark rooms.

In its raw state, garlic is strong and fiery. Cooking with garlic is very much a matter of personal taste. The longer it is cooked, the sweeter and more mellow the flavour. Crushed or chopped garlic can be dry-fried at the beginning of a recipe to release its flavour. However, do not allow it to burn or it will add a bitter flavour to the finished dish.

If you only like a little garlic, try rubbing the inside of a cooking pan or casserole dish with a peeled clove. This will impart a hint of garlic flavour.

Stocks

Any chef will tell you that the secret of a good sauce relies on a very good stock. Home-made stock is very time-consuming to make but well worth the effort, as the final flavours are quite different from any convenient stock cube alternatives. If you do decide to make your own stock, be sure to chill it completely. This allows the fat to set, making it easy to remove and discard before adding the stock to your cooking.

There are four basic stocks which are used as a base for many dishes. White stock is pale and light and made from meat and poultry. Unbrowned beef and chicken are excellent for this purpose, while lamb, pork and duck contain much higher levels of fat. Brown stock is made by browning the meat or bones first – you can either dry-fry the meat in a non-stick pan or roast in a hot oven (the latter method gives a darker colour). Both white and brown stock are then flavoured with root vegetables such as carrot, celery, onion and leek and left to simmer in plenty of water for $1\frac{1}{2}$–2 hours. A brown stock may be coloured with tomato purée or gravy browning for a deep finish.

Fish stock is quite different and needs careful cooking. The stock should not be allowed to simmer for more than 20 minutes, as the bones will make the stock bitter. You can use the bones, heads, skin and tails of any white fish such as sole, brill, plaice. Avoid fatty fish such as mackerel, which will make the stock oily.

Vegetable stock can be made easily by simmering a wide selection of fresh vegetables, taking care not to overpower the flavour with one particular ingredient. You can add tomato purée for additional colour.

The majority of recipes in this book use stock cubes for convenience and it is well worth spending a little extra on the better quality ones. Generally, one stock cube will make up with 600ml (1 pint) water.

Meals in minutes

Modern day lifestyles have changed our eating habits, forcing many of us to choose convenience foods or ready prepared meals. Although these meals can act as good alternatives, nothing beats a freshly prepared meal using good cuts of meat and fresh young vegetables bursting with nutrition.

This section contains easy-to-follow recipes designed to produce a tasty meal for 2 or 4 people in 35 minutes or less. Choose from dishes ranging from grilled sardine baguettes to smoked paprika vegetable pasta, and tuna and onion hash to Mediterranean couscous.

As with many recipes in this book, most of these meals can be prepared in advance and then stored in the refrigerator to save time later.

Quick chicken korma

SERVES 4
PER SERVING:
285 KCAL / 3.7G FAT
PREPARATION TIME:
15 MINUTES
COOKING TIME:
20 MINUTES

4 skinless chicken breasts, cut
into chunks
2 medium onions, finely
chopped
2 garlic cloves, crushed
1–2 tablespoons korma curry
powder
1 vegetable stock cube,
dissolved in 150ml (¹⁄₄) pint
boiling water
1 tablespoon plain flour
300ml (¹⁄₂ pint) skimmed milk
1 tablespoon chopped fresh flat
leaf parsley
2 tablespoons virtually fat free
Normandy fromage frais
salt and freshly ground black
pepper

1 Season the chicken pieces with salt and black pepper and dry-fry in a preheated non-stick pan for 6–7 minutes until they start to colour. Remove from the pan and set aside.
2 Add the onions and garlic to the pan and cook gently until soft. Sprinkle the curry powder over, add 2 tablespoons of stock and mix well. Add the flour and cook for 1 minute, stirring continuously.
3 Gradually add the remaining stock and the milk, stirring continuously to prevent any lumps from forming.
4 Return the chicken to the pan, add the parsley and simmer gently for 8–10 minutes to ensure the chicken is fully cooked. Remove from the heat and stir in the fromage frais.
5 Serve with boiled rice.

Baked leek and ham mornay

For a vegetarian alternative, omit the ham and cover the leeks with sliced beef tomatoes or finely sliced mushrooms.

1 Simmer the leeks in a saucepan of boiling salted water for 5 minutes, then drain well.
2 Heat the milk, stock cube and bay leaves in a separate non-stick saucepan and bring to the boil.
3 Slake the cornflour with a little cold water and stir into the milk mixture. Add the mustard and chives, reduce the heat and simmer gently, stirring continuously as the sauce thickens. Season with salt and black pepper.
4 Wrap the ham slices around the leeks and arrange in the bottom of an ovenproof dish.
5 Pour the sauce over and cover with the grated cheese. Place under a preheated grill for 2–3 minutes until golden brown.
6 Serve with crusty bread and a mixed salad.

SERVES 4
PER SERVING:
155 KCAL/3.8G FAT
PREPARATION TIME:
10 MINUTES
COOKING TIME:
20 MINUTES

8 baby leeks, washed and cut in half
600ml (1 pint) skimmed milk
1 vegetable stock cube
2 bay leaves
1 tablespoon cornflour
1 teaspoon English mustard
1 tablespoon finely chopped fresh chives
8 thin slices smoked ham
50g (2oz) low-fat Cheddar cheese, grated
salt and freshly ground black pepper

Grilled sardine baguettes

SERVES 2
PER SERVING:
238 KCAL / 6.2G FAT
PREPARATION TIME:
5 MINUTES
COOKING TIME:
15 MINUTES

1 small French baguette, split in
    half lengthways
1 garlic clove, peeled and cut in
    half
115g (4oz) canned sardines in
    brine
2 tablespoons virtually fat free
    Normandy fromage frais
1 teaspoon lemon or lime juice
2 tomatoes, sliced
salt and freshly ground black
    pepper

An express lunch – perfect for when you have little time to spare.
Make sure you spread the mixture right up to the edges of the
bread, as these may burn slightly when the baguette is returned to
the grill.

1 Preheat the grill to high.
2 Lightly toast the bread on both sides, then, using the cut side of
    the garlic, rub the cut side of the toasted bread.
3 Drain the sardines and place in a small bowl. Mix in the
    fromage frais, lemon or lime juice and season with plenty of salt
    and black pepper.
4 Spread the mixture onto both pieces of bread, making sure it
    goes right up to the outside edges, and top with the sliced
    tomatoes. Place under the grill until brown and bubbling.
5 Serve immediately with salad and pickles.

Turkey and ginger stir-fry

This recipe is ideal for using up any oddments of vegetables you have in the store cupboard. You can substitute leeks or root vegetables such as thinly sliced carrots or parsnips for the red pepper, courgettes and mushrooms, but they may need slightly longer cooking times.

1 Heat a non-stick wok or frying pan, add the turkey strips and dry-fry for 5–6 minutes or until just cooked. Remove from the pan and set aside.
2 Return the pan to the heat and add the onion, red pepper and courgettes and dry-fry for 2–3 minutes. Add the mushrooms and ginger, mixing well.
3 Return the turkey to the pan and continue cooking.
4 Mix together the soy sauce, honey and chilli and add to the pan, coating the meat and vegetables. Stir-fry, combining all the ingredients, until the meat is fully cooked.
5 Serve immediately on a bed of noodles or instant rice.

SERVES 4
PER SERVING:
229 KCAL / 2.4G FAT
PREPARATION TIME:
10 MINUTES
COOKING TIME:
15–20 MINUTES

450g (1lb) turkey fillets, cut into strips
1 medium red onion, finely sliced
1 red pepper, seeded and sliced
2 small courgettes, sliced
115g (4oz) chestnut mushrooms, sliced
2 teaspoons fresh ginger, peeled and finely chopped
1 tablespoon light soy sauce
1 tablespoon runny honey or mango chutney
2 teaspoons chilli sauce

Tuna and onion hash

Canned tuna is nothing like the real thing, but it comes into its own as a convenience food, as it is high in nutrients and low in fat. We tend only to use it cold in salads or as a sandwich filler, but it can be served hot, as in this recipe, or in a clear vegetable soup.

1 Preheat a non-stick wok or frying pan.
2 Dry-fry the potatoes over a high heat, moving them around with a spatula, for 4–5 minutes until they start to colour.
3 Add the onions, garlic and chilli and continue to move the ingredients around the pan to prevent sticking.
4 When the potato is cooked, add the remaining ingredients and mix well, seasoning with lots of black pepper. Cook until the greens are wilted yet crisp in texture.
5 Pile onto serving dishes and garnish with the lemon slices and coriander.

SERVES 2
PER SERVING:
246 KCAL/1.04G FAT
PREPARATION TIME:
10 MINUTES
COOKING TIME:
15–20 MINUTES

2 large baking potatoes, diced
2 medium onions, finely sliced
1 garlic clove, crushed
1 small red chilli, seeded and
    finely chopped
50g (2oz) pak choi or dark
    cabbage leaves, shredded
115g (4oz) canned tuna steak in
    brine
1 tablespoon light soy sauce
juice from half a lemon
freshly ground black pepper
4 slices fresh lemon
1 tablespoon chopped fresh
    coriander

Sweet potato and pepper casserole

SERVES 4
PER SERVING:
221 KCAL/2.4G FAT
PREPARATION TIME:
10 MINUTES
COOKING TIME:
20 MINUTES

4 large sweet potatoes, peeled
and cut into small dice

2 × 400g (2 × 14oz) can
chopped tomatoes

2 bay leaves

4 baby leeks, washed and finely
chopped

2 large red peppers, seeded and
diced

1 vegetable stock cube,
dissolved in 300ml ($\frac{1}{2}$ pint)
boiling water

1 tablespoon plain flour

1 tablespoon finely chopped
fresh herbs

$\frac{1}{2}$ teaspoon cayenne pepper

$\frac{1}{2}$ teaspoon fennel seeds

50g (2oz) low-fat Cheddar
cheese, grated

This cheesy casserole is perfect for home freezing. It forms a complete meal in itself, or you can serve with crusty bread and salad for a more substantial meal.

1 Place the potatoes in a saucepan. Add the tomatoes and bay leaves and bring to the boil. Reduce the heat and simmer gently for 10 minutes until just cooked.

2 In a separate non-stick pan dry-fry the leeks and peppers for 2–3 minutes. Add 2 tablespoons of stock and sprinkle the flour over, mixing it in with a wooden spoon. Cook out the flour for 1 minute, then gradually add the remaining stock, along with the herbs and spices and then the potato and tomato mixture.

3 Pour into a large shallow dish or into individual gratin dishes and cover with the cheese. Brown under a medium hot grill.

4 Serve with crusty bread and a mixed salad.

Pork in tomato cream sauce

The creamy tomato sauce in this recipe also goes well with chicken, grilled fish and roasted peppers. Simply add different herbs or spices to change the flavour to suit the dish.

1 Preheat the grill to its highest setting.
2 Season the steaks on both sides with salt and black pepper and place on a wire rack under a hot grill for 5–6 minutes each side or until cooked.
3 In a non-stick pan, dry-fry the onion and garlic until soft. Add the stock powder and passata and stir well. Bring the sauce to a gentle simmer.
4 When the steaks are ready to serve, transfer them to plates. Remove the sauce from the heat, stir in the basil and fromage frais and pour over the pork.
5 Serve with boiled new potatoes and a selection of fresh vegetables or salad leaves.

SERVES 2
PER SERVING:
383 KCAL/11.3G FAT
PREPARATION TIME:
10 MINUTES
COOKING TIME:
15 MINUTES

2 lean pork steaks
1 medium red onion, finely chopped
1 garlic clove, crushed
1 teaspoon vegetable bouillon stock powder
300ml ($\frac{1}{2}$ pint) tomato passata
a few basil leaves, shredded
2 tablespoons virtually fat free Normandy fromage frais
salt and freshly ground black pepper

Mediterranean couscous

SERVES 4
PER SERVING:
180 KCAL/3.4G FAT
PREPARATION TIME:
15 MINUTES
COOKING TIME:
20 MINUTES

1 vegetable stock cube,
    dissolved in 400ml (14fl oz)
    boiling water
4 sun-dried tomatoes (non-oil
    variety), finely chopped
1 red onion, finely chopped
1 small aubergine, diced
1 red pepper, seeded and diced
1 yellow pepper, seeded and
    diced
2 small courgettes, sliced
115g (4oz) chestnut mushrooms,
    sliced
1 tablespoon chopped fresh
    mixed herbs (oregano, thyme,
    basil, marjoram)
175g (6oz) couscous
25g (1oz) Parmesan shavings

Couscous is an ideal alternative to pasta or rice. It can be made up in advance and reheated either in a microwave or steamed over boiling water.

1 In a saucepan, bring the vegetable stock to the boil, add the sun-dried tomatoes to allow them to soften.
2 In a non-stick frying pan, dry-fry the onion and aubergine for 4–5 minutes until they start to colour. Add the peppers and courgettes and continue cooking for a further 4–5 minutes.
3 Add the mushrooms, herbs, stock and tomatoes to the frying pan and bring to the boil. Sprinkle the couscous over and cover with a lid for 1 minute to allow the couscous to steam.
4 Remove the lid and, using 2 forks, fluff up the couscous grains. Transfer to a warm serving bowl and cover with the Parmesan shavings.

Smoked paprika vegetable pasta

Smoked paprika gives this popular spice a different dimension and adds a delicate smoked flavour when used to season foods.

1 Cook the pasta in a pan of boiling salted water with the vegetable stock cube.
2 Preheat a non-stick pan and dry-fry the vegetables very quickly until they start to colour. Sprinkle the stock powder, paprika and rosemary over the vegetables, stir in the passata and bring to the boil to create a rich sauce.
3 Drain the pasta and transfer to serving plates. Top with the tomato sauce.
4 Serve with a mixed green salad.

SERVES 2
PER SERVING:
273 KCAL/4G FAT
PREPARATION TIME:
10 MINUTES
COOKING TIME:
25 MINUTES

115g (4oz) pasta shapes
1 vegetable stock cube
1 small red onion, finely chopped
1 carrot, coarsely grated
1 courgette, coarsely grated
50g (2oz) mange tout
8 cherry tomatoes
1 teaspoon vegetable stock bouillon powder
1–2 teaspoons smoked paprika powder
$\frac{1}{2}$ teaspoon finely chopped fresh rosemary
300ml ($\frac{1}{2}$ pint) tomato passata
sea salt

Potato biarritz

SERVES 2
PER SERVING:
403 KCAL/5.5G FAT
PREPARATION TIME:
10 MINUTES
COOKING TIME:
15 MINUTES

4 large baking potatoes, peeled
and diced

1 vegetable stock cube

1 garlic clove, chopped

2 tablespoons virtually fat free
fromage frais

1 large red pepper, seeded and
finely diced

1 yellow pepper, seeded and
finely diced

4 spring onions, finely chopped

2 thin slices ox tongue, diced

1 tablespoon chopped fresh
parsley

salt and freshly ground black
pepper

*A tasty quick and easy lunch with lots of colour and flavour. The
hot potato semi-cooks the peppers, leaving them with a crunchy
texture.*

1 Cook the potatoes in a saucepan of boiling water with the stock
cube and garlic. Drain well and mash with a potato masher,
adding the fromage frais to soften the mix.

2 Add the remaining ingredients to the mashed potato and
season well with salt and black pepper. Pile into individual
gratin dishes and brown under a hot grill.

3 Serve hot with grilled tomatoes and a few steamed mange tout
or green beans.

Meals for one

If you are cooking for yourself and want something quick to rustle up, then these simple, no-fuss recipes are ideal. They use practical ingredients so that you don't have to open endless jars and tins and any wastage is kept to a minimum. You will find something to your taste, from easy toast toppers to a delicious aubergine and chickpea rogan josh as well as toasted sandwiches that make the perfect hot snack.

Smoked bacon and mushroom fritters

SERVES 1

PER SERVING (2 FRITTERS):
130 KCAL/2.2G FAT

PREPARATION TIME:
25 MINUTES

COOKING TIME:
25 MINUTES

115g (4oz) firm waxy potatoes
½ medium onion, finely
    chopped
1 rasher lean smoked bacon,
    finely chopped
25g (1oz) chestnut or button
    mushrooms, finely sliced
½ tablespoon light soy sauce
½ tablespoon chopped fresh
    chives
salt and freshly ground black
    pepper

1 Peel the potatoes, then coarsely grate into a mixing bowl.
2 Place the grated potaotes in the centre of a clean tea towel.
   Draw together the corners of the towel and squeeze tightly to
   remove as much of the liquid as possible.
3 Shake the grated potato into a clean bowl and season well with
   salt and black pepper. Add the onion, bacon, mushrooms, soy
   sauce and chives and mix well.
4 Using your hands, shape the mixture into 2 equal-sized balls.
5 Preheat a non-stick frying pan, add a little vegetable oil, then
   wipe out the pan with kitchen paper (wear an oven glove if
   necessary).
6 Lightly flatten the fritters with the palm of your hand and place
   in the hot pan.
7 Cook over a moderate heat for 4–5 minutes, then turn the
   fritters over and cook for a further 4–5 minutes until golden
   brown.
8 Serve with salad or vegetables.

Peppered steak with chive and tarragon sauce

1 Preheat the grill to the highest setting.
2 Prepare the steak by removing any fat, then, using the palms of your hands, gently flatten the steak to help it cook more quickly. Place on one side.
3 Crush the peppercorns in a pestle and mortar or place on a chopping board and crush with the broad edge of a heavy chopping knife. Place the crushed peppercorns on a flat plate.
4 Season both sides of the steak generously with sea salt, then dip both sides of the steak into the peppercorns, pressing them well into the meat.
5 Place the steak on a non-stick baking tray and cook under a hot grill to your requirements (2–3 minutes each side for rare, 3–4 minutes each side for medium, and 5–6 minutes each side for well done).
6 When the steak is almost cooked, strain off the meat juices collected on the baking tray into a saucepan. Add the flour and cook over a low heat for 1 minute to cook out the flour.
7 Gradually add the milk and the stock powder or cube, stirring continuously to prevent lumps from forming. Add the mustard and herbs and simmer gently.
8 Place the steak onto a serving plate and pour the sauce over.
9 Serve with boiled potatoes and fresh vegetables or salad.

SERVES 1
PER SERVING:
374 KCAL/14.1G FAT
PREPARATION TIME:
20 MINUTES
COOKING TIME:
20 MINUTES

1 × 225g (8oz) lean fillet steak
2 tablespoons mixed peppercorns (green, black, red and white)
1 teaspoon plain flour
150ml (1/4 pint) skimmed milk
1/2 tablespoon stock powder or 1 vegetable stock cube
1/2 teaspoon Dijon mustard
1/2 tablespoon finely chopped fresh chives
1/2 tablespoon finely chopped fresh tarragon
sea salt

Grilled sausages with balsamic shallot sauce

SERVES 1
PER SERVING:
331 KCAL/9G FAT
PREPARATION TIME:
5 MINUTES
COOKING TIME:
25 MINUTES

2 large low-fat pork or beef
   sausages (4% or less fat)
2 long shallots or 2 small red
   onions, finely sliced
1 small Bramley apple, grated
1 tablespoon balsamic vinegar
2 tablespoons apple juice
1 teaspoon cornflour
2 teaspoons finely chopped
   fresh chives
salt and freshly ground black
   pepper

Apples and onions transform plain grilled sausages into glazed fruity delights. If you like mustard, try mixing a teaspoon of wholegrain mustard into the sauce.

1 Grill the sausages until brown and cooked.
2 Preheat a non-stick frying pan. Add the shallots or onions and dry-fry over a high heat until they start to change colour. Add the grated apple and continue cooking for 2–3 minutes, mixing all the ingredients together and seasoning with salt and black pepper.
3 Add the vinegar and apple juice. Slake the cornflour with a little cold water and stir into the mixture to form a smooth sauce, adding more water if required. At this stage the sausages can be added to keep warm.
4 Serve the sausages with the sauce, accompanied by mashed potatoes and vegetables.

Salmon with mango sauce

1 Preheat the oven to 200C, 400F, Gas Mark 6.
2 Place the salmon fillet in an ovenproof dish and season on both sides with salt and black pepper.
3 Combine the remaining ingredients and spread over the salmon.
4 Bake in the oven for 6–8 minutes until just cooked.
5 Serve with boiled rice and vegetables or salad.

SERVES 1
PER SERVING:
242 KCAL/11.8G FAT
PREPARATION TIME:
5 MINUTES
COOKING TIME:
10 MINUTES

1 × 115g (4oz) salmon fillet
150ml ($\frac{1}{4}$ pint) low-fat yogurt
$\frac{1}{2}$ tablespoon mango chutney
1 level teaspoon mild curry powder
$\frac{1}{2}$ small red chilli, seeded and finely chopped
$\frac{1}{2}$ tablespoon chopped fresh coriander
salt and freshly ground black pepper

Baked basil haddock

SERVES 1

PER SERVING:

273 KCAL/5.6G FAT

PREPARATION TIME:

5 MINUTES

COOKING TIME:

20 MINUTES

1 fresh haddock steak
   (approximately 120g/4¼oz)

300ml (½ pint) skimmed milk

2 spring onions, finely sliced

1 teaspoon vegetable bouillon
   stock powder

6–8 fresh basil leaves, shredded

2 teaspoons cornflour

salt and freshly ground black
   pepper

You can use either plain or smoked haddock in this recipe. Baking fish in the oven is a good method of cooking as it tends to stay in one piece. Sometimes poaching loose textured fish can result in the fish breaking up and becoming watery, thus losing valuable flavour.

1 Preheat the oven to 180C, 350F, Gas Mark 4.

2 Season the steak on both sides with salt and black pepper and place in an ovenproof dish.

3 In a saucepan heat the milk with the spring onions, stock powder and basil. Slake the cornflour with a little cold water and whisk into the milk. Continue whisking as the sauce thickens to prevent any lumps from forming, then pour over the fish.

4 Bake in the oven for 12–15 minutes until cooked.

5 Serve with mashed potatoes and a selection of freshly cooked vegetables.

Smoked ham macaroni cheese

1 Preheat the oven to 190C, 375F, Gas Mark 5.
2 Cook the pasta in boiling salted water until tender. Drain through a colander and rinse under cold water to prevent further cooking.
3 In a saucepan, heat the milk and the stock powder. Slake the cornflour with a little cold water and stir into the sauce. Stir continuously as the sauce thickens, then reduce the heat and simmer for 2–3 minutes.
4 Stir in the remaining ingredients and season well with salt and black pepper. Add the cooked pasta, mix well, and pour into an ovenproof dish.
5 Bake in the oven for 20 minutes until golden brown.

SERVES 1
PER SERVING:
324 KCAL / 4.8G FAT
PREPARATION TIME:
5 MINUTES
COOKING TIME:
45 MINUTES

50g (2oz) macaroni pasta
75ml (2$\frac{1}{2}$fl oz) skimmed milk
1 teaspoon vegetable stock powder
1 teaspoon cornflour
$\frac{3}{4}$ teaspoon Dijon mustard
1 rounded tablespoon grated low-fat Cheddar cheese
1 slice smoked ham, cut into strips
1 teaspoon chopped fresh chives
salt and freshly ground black pepper

Chilli bean mince

SERVES 1
PER SERVING:
491 KCAL/17.2G FAT
PREPARATION TIME:
5 MINUTES
COOKING TIME:
40 MINUTES

115g (4oz) extra lean mince
   beef
3 spring onions, chopped
1 teaspoon plain flour
1 teaspoon freeze dried herbes
   de Provence
1 teaspoon vegetable bouillon
   stock powder
1 tablespoon chilli sauce
1 small can baked beans
150ml ($\frac{1}{4}$ pint) tomato passata
salt and freshly ground black
   pepper

This recipe can be prepared in advance and refrigerated for up to 2 days, or frozen for a longer period. When reheating, make sure the mixture remains at boiling point for at least 10 minutes before serving.

1 In a non-stick pan, dry-fry the mince until it changes colour.
2 Drain the mince through a metal sieve to remove the fat, then wipe out the pan with kitchen paper.
3 Return the drained mince to the pan and add the spring onions. Sprinkle the flour over and mix well. Cook over a low heat for 1 minute to cook out the flour.
4 Add the remaining ingredients and mix well. Simmer over a low heat for 15–20 minutes until the meat is tender, adding a little water if required. Season with salt and black pepper.
5 Serve hot with a jacket potato or boiled rice and vegetables.

Aubergine and lentil rogan josh

Rogan josh is a spicy curry usually associated with beef or lamb. The spice flavour contrasts well with the aubergine, especially when the aubergine has been well browned, which adds a lightly toasted flavour.

1 Preheat the oven to 200C, 400F, Gas Mark 6.
2 Using a dessertspoon, carefully scoop out the centre of one aubergine half and place on a chopping board. Place the shell face down on a non-stick baking tray and bake in the oven for 10–15 minutes until soft.
3 Meanwhile, chop the scooped out aubergine flesh and the other half of the aubergine into small dice and place in a non-stick frying pan. Add the onion and garlic and cook over a moderate heat, turning regularly, until the aubergine is browned all over.
4 Place the lentils, vegetable stock, tomato purée and curry powder in a saucepan and bring to the boil. Cook until the lentils are soft.
5 Add the aubergine mixture to the lentils and stir in the tomato and coriander. Season with salt and black pepper.
6 Place the baked shell on a serving plate and pile the aubergine mixture into the centre.
7 Serve hot with salad or vegetables.

SERVES 1
PER SERVING:
255 KCAL / 3.3G FAT
PREPARATION TIME:
20 MINUTES
COOKING TIME:
40 MINUTES

1 small aubergine, cut in half lengthways
$\frac{1}{2}$ red onion, finely chopped
1 garlic clove, crushed
2 tablespoons red lentils
300ml ($\frac{1}{2}$ pint) vegetable stock
1 tablespoon tomato purée
1 tablespoon rogan josh curry powder
1 tomato, skinned, seeded and diced
1 tablespoon chopped fresh coriander
salt and freshly ground black pepper

Turkey schnitzel

An escalope is a thin slice of meat that can be cooked quickly, usually by grilling or coating in egg and breadcrumbs and frying. Make sure the pan is hot before you add the floured escalope, to ensure a cripsy coating.

1 Place the turkey escalope on a chopping board and beat with a rolling pin until thin. Season well with salt and black pepper.
2 Pour the milk into a shallow container. Combine the flour, cheese and paprika and place in another shallow container.
3 Preheat a non-stick frying pan.
4 Wrap the slice of ham around the turkey and dip the covered escalope into the milk, coating both sides. Immediately place it in the flour, turning it over to coat both sides.
5 Transfer to the frying pan and cook over a moderate heat for 8–10 minutes on each side.
6 Garnish with the lemon slices and parsley and serve with vegetables of your choice.

SERVES 1
PER SERVING:
408 KCAL/4.5G FAT
PREPARATION TIME:
15 MINUTES
COOKING TIME:
25 MINUTES

1 × 175g (6oz) turkey escalope
2 tablespoons skimmed milk
1 tablespoon plain flour
1 teaspoon grated Parmesan cheese
$1/4$ teaspoon hot or sweet paprika
1 slice lean ham
salt and freshly ground black pepper
2 slices fresh lemon
chopped fresh parsley

Broccoli and mushroom mornay

SERVES 1
PER SERVING:
396 KCAL/8.2G FAT
PREPARATION TIME:
5 MINUTES
COOKING TIME:
35 MINUTES

1 small head broccoli, trimmed

300ml (½) pint skimmed milk

1 teaspoon Dijon mustard

2 teaspoons cornflour

4 mushrooms, sliced

25g (1oz) low-fat Cheddar
   cheese, grated

1 tablespoon sage and onion
   stuffing mix

If you find you do not require the full quantity of sauce in this recipe, save some for the following day and spread onto toasted bread as a light lunch.

1 Cook the broccoli in boiling salted water, drain and place in an ovenproof dish.
2 Place the milk and mustard in a saucepan and bring to the boil. Slake the cornflour with a little cold water and add to the milk, stirring well to prevent any lumps from forming.
3 Add the mushrooms and cheese and mix well. Simmer gently until the sauce is of a coating consistency, adding a little extra milk or diluted cornflour if necessary. Pour over the broccoli and sprinkle with the stuffing mix.
4 Place under a medium grill until golden brown.
5 Serve hot as a light lunch with grilled tomatoes and crusty bread.

Italian toast toppers

1 Very lightly toast the bread on both sides and set aside.
2 Preheat a non-stick frying pan, add the onion and dry-fry for 2–3 minutes until soft.
3 Add the red pepper, garlic, courgette and mushrooms and cook briskly over a high heat, turning the vegetables over regularly.
4 Stir in the tomatoes and herbs and simmer gently for 5–6 minutes until the liquid has reduced to leave a thick chunky paste.
5 Spread the mixture onto the toasted bread and place under a hot grill for 2–3 minutes to brown. Serve hot.

SERVES 1
PER SERVING:
248 KCAL / 2.6G FAT
PREPARATION TIME:
10 MINUTES
COOKING TIME:
15 MINUTES

2 slices medium-cut white or
   brown bread
$1/2$ medium onion, thinly sliced
$1/2$ red pepper, seeded and finely
   sliced
1 garlic clove, crushed
$1/2$ courgette, finely sliced
50g (2oz) chestnut mushrooms,
   sliced
115g (4oz) canned chopped
   tomatoes
$1/2$ tablespoon chopped fresh
   oregano
salt and freshly ground black
   pepper

The ultimate BLT

SERVES 1
PER SERVING:
312 KCAL/8.5G FAT
PREPARATION TIME:
5 MINUTES
COOKING TIME:
10 MINUTES

2 rashers lean bacon
2–3 leaves of romaine or crisp
  lettuce
2–3 sweet cherry tomatoes
2–3 cornichon or pickled baby
  gherkins
1 tablespoon low-fat salad
  dressing
1 tablespoon tomato ketchup
$\frac{1}{4}$ teaspoon cayenne pepper
2 slices medium-cut white or
  brown bread

1 Preheat the grill on the highest setting.
2 Place the bacon on a wire rack over a grill tray and grill on each
   side until cooked.
3 Remove the bacon from the rack and place on a piece of
   kitchen paper to absorb any remaining fat.
4 Shred the lettuce, slice the tomatoes and the cornichon or baby
   gherkins.
5 In a small bowl, mix together the salad dressing, ketchup and
   cayenne pepper and spread on both slices of bread.
6 Place the lettuce on one slice of bread, followed by the bacon
   and then the tomatoes and cornichon or baby gherkins. Place
   the remaining slice of bread on top and press down lightly. Slice
   in half and serve.

Mushroom frittata

1. Preheat a non-stick frying pan, add the mushrooms and spring onions and dry-fry for 2–3 minutes until lightly coloured, seasoning well with black pepper.
2. In a mixing bowl, whisk the eggs, gradually adding the milk and the soy sauce.
3. Pour the mixture into a frying pan, reduce the heat and cook gently until the frittata is just set. If you wish, you can then place it under a hot grill for 30 seconds to brown.
4. Fold the frittata in half and slide onto a warmed plate.
5. Serve with salad.

SERVES 1
PER SERVING:
219 KCAL/13G FAT
PREPARATION TIME:
10 MINUTES
COOKING TIME:
10 MINUTES

115g (4oz) chestnut mushrooms, sliced
2 spring onions, finely chopped
2 eggs
1 tablespoon skimmed milk
$1/2$ tablespoon light soy sauce
freshly ground black pepper

Spanish omelette

As the vegetables will release liquid during cooking, there is no need to add any milk to the egg mixture, although a teaspoon or two won't hurt.

1. Preheat a non-stick frying pan. Add the onion, pepper and garlic and dry-fry for 3–4 minutes until soft.
2. Add the beaten egg and cook gently, using a wooden spatula to bring the set mixture from around the outside of the pan into the centre.
3. When the omelette is almost completely set, add the diced tomatoes and turn the omelette over, either whole or split down the centre to make this easier.
4. Serve immediately with salad.

SERVES 1
PER SERVING:
240 KCAL/13.6G FAT
PREPARATION TIME:
10 MINUTES
COOKING TIME:
10 MINUTES

$1/2$ red onion, finely sliced
$1/2$ red pepper, seeded and diced
1 garlic clove, crushed
2 eggs, beaten and seasoned with salt and freshly ground black pepper
1 tomato, skinned, seeded and finely diced

Hot field mushroom sandwich

SERVES 1
PER SERVING:
143 KCAL/2.7G FAT
PREPARATION TIME:
5 MINUTES
COOKING TIME:
10 MINUTES

1 × 10cm (4in) piece of French bread or a small baguette
1 large Portabello or field mushroom
2 teaspoons light soy sauce
2 teaspoons low-fat salad dressing
$\frac{1}{2}$ teaspoon Dijon or grain mustard
2–3 crisp lettuce leaves
a little fresh lemon juice

A great simple hot sandwich. Add other ingredients if you wish, such as sliced raw onion or sweet peppers. The big mushroom gives the sandwich a really meaty juicy bite.

1 Cut the bread in half lengthways and lightly toast on both sides under a hot grill.
2 In a non-stick frying pan, dry-fry the mushroom over a low heat for 5–6 minutes, adding the soy sauce for moisture and seasoning.
3 Combine the salad dressing and the mustard and spread on both pieces of bread.
4 Place the lettuce leaves on one piece and top with the cooked mushroom.
5 Squeeze a little fresh lemon juice on top of the mushroom, top with the remaining piece of bread and serve.

Courgette and semi-dried tomatoes toasted sandwich

Semi-dried tomatoes are sold loose at most delicatessen counters. Check if they are stored in oil. If so, make sure you rinse them well with boiling water before using them.

1 Lightly toast each slice of bread on one side under a medium grill.
2 Preheat a non-stick frying pan, add the courgette and dry-fry for 2–3 minutes until soft.
3 Rinse the tomatoes under boiling water.
4 Finely shred the basil leaves and mix with the salad dressing. Spread on the toasted side of each slice of bread. Place the courgette strips, tomatoes and chillies on one slice, and top with the second slice. Press the sandwich together and place on a grill pan.
5 Toast on both sides until golden brown.
6 Slice in half and serve with corn on the cob or a mixed salad.

SERVES 1
PER SERVING:
192 KCAL/2.3G FAT
PREPARATION TIME:
10 MINUTES
COOKING TIME:
10 MINUTES

2 slices medium-sliced white or
 brown bread
1 courgette, thinly sliced
5–6 semi-dried tomatoes
3–4 fresh basil leaves
1 tablespoon low-fat salad
 dressing
1–2 sweet marinated chillies

Cottage cheese and pepper toasted sandwich

SERVES 1
PER SERVING:
245 KCAL/3G FAT
PREPARATION TIME:
10–15 MINUTES
COOKING TIME:
10 MINUTES

2 slices medium-sliced white or
  brown bread
1 tablespoon low-fat salad
  dressing
1 tablespoon chopped fresh
  chives
2 tablespoons low-fat cottage
  cheese
$\frac{1}{2}$ red pepper, seeded and finely
  chopped
4–5 slices peeled cucumber

A great way to use up the last of the cottage cheese. If you have time, to improve the taste, you can grill the red pepper as large pieces first, before chopping it finely and adding to the sandwich and toasting.

1 Lightly toast each slice of bread on one side under a medium grill.
2 Spread the toasted side of each slice with salad dressing and sprinkle with the chives.
3 Using a fork, spread the cottage cheese on one slice. Cover with the red pepper and the cucumber slices. Top with the second slice of bread, press the sandwich together and place on a grill tray.
4 Toast on both sides until golden brown.
5 Serve hot with a simple tomato salad and fresh salad leaves.

Chilli ham
toasted sandwich

Caperberries are like large capers complete with stalks. As they are virtually fat free, they are a good substitute for olives. Depending on the type of vinegar they are stored in, they are generally not as sharp as capers.

1 Lightly toast each slice of bread on one side under a medium grill.
2 In a small bowl, mix together the salad dressing and chilli sauce and spread on the toasted side of each slice of bread.
3 Add a slice of ham on one slice, spread the ham with mustard, and add the caperberries (if using). Top with the second slice of bread, press the sandwich together and place on a grill tray.
4 Toast the sandwich on both sides until golden brown.
5 Slice in half and serve accompanied with a mixed salad.

SERVES 1
PER SERVING:
216 KCAL/3.9G FAT
PREPARATION TIME:
10 MINUTES
COOKING TIME:
10 MINUTES

2 slices medium-sliced white or brown bread
1 tablespoon low-fat salad dressing
1–2 teaspoons chilli sauce
2 thin slices very lean ham
1 teaspoon coarse grain mustard
2–3 caperberries (optional)

Fresh fruit smoothy

SERVES 1
PER SERVING:
342 KCAL/1.9G FAT
PREPARATION TIME:
5 MINUTES

1 large ripe banana

175g (6oz) fresh strawberries, hulled

150ml ($\frac{1}{4}$ pint) ice cold skimmed milk

150ml ($\frac{1}{4}$ pint) low-fat natural yogurt

1–2 teaspoons runny honey to taste

A liquid lunch! High in nutrients and taste, this is ideal for packing in a vacuum flask to drink at work when you have no time to eat.

1 Peel the banana and slice into a food processor or liquidiser.
2 Slice the strawberries and place in the food processor or liquidiser.
3 Pour the milk and yogurt over the top and process for a few seconds or until all ingredients are fully combined.
4 Pour into a tall glass and serve.

Microwave meals

Although microwave ovens have been around for many years now, they are still a very much underused piece of kitchen equipment. Yet cooking low-fat dishes in a microwave could not be simpler, as vegetables and meats cook perfectly well without the aid of fats and oils.

The crucial element of microwave cooking is in the timing. Like conventional ovens, microwave ovens all vary in temperature and time settings, so check the instruction manual applicable to your model.

Always allow standing time. This is additional time after the allocated cooking time, as the food continues cooking for a short while after it is removed from the oven.

Most foods require to be covered with microwave film or food wrap during cooking. Always pierce the film several times with a sharp knife to allow excess steam to escape during cooking. Always remove the film by peeling back from the far edge of the cooking container to allow any build-up of steam to escape away from your face.

Scrambled eggs with sun-dried tomatoes and smoked salmon

SERVES 2
PER SERVING:
280 KCAL/15G FAT
PREPARATION TIME:
10 MINUTES
COOKING TIME:
15 MINUTES

6 pieces sun-dried tomatoes
(non-oil variety)
4 eggs
2 tablespoons skimmed milk
115g (4oz) smoked salmon,
sliced into thin strips
salt and freshly ground black
pepper

This is a luxurious and delicious lunch or breakfast.

1 Slice the sun-dried tomatoes into thin strips and place in a microwave bowl with enough water to barely cover.
2 Cook, uncovered, on full power for 4 minutes, drain and return to the bowl.
3 Break the eggs into the bowl and beat with a fork. Gradually add the milk, beating until the mixture is fully combined. Season with black pepper and cook, uncovered, on full power for 40-second intervals, stirring between cooking, until the egg mixture is just set.
4 Stir in the smoked salmon strips and add salt and black pepper to taste. Serve immediately.

Quick microwave porridge with dried cherries

1 Place all the ingredients except the sugar in a large non-metallic bowl and stir well. Cover with microwave film and pierce the film several times with the point of a sharp knife.
2 Place the bowl in the oven and microwave on full power for 3 minutes, adjusting the time according to the wattage of your oven.
3 Remove the film carefully and stir well.
4 Cover again and cook for a further 3–4 minutes or until thick and creamy.
5 Add sugar to taste and serve.

SERVES 2
PER SERVING:
330 KCAL/4.7G FAT
PREPARATION TIME:
5 MINUTES
COOKING TIME:
10 MINUTES

115g (4oz) whole rolled porridge oats
600ml (1 pint) skimmed milk
pinch of salt
25g (1oz) dried cherries or other dried fruit
sugar to taste

Smoked haddock with spiced greens

SERVES 1
PER SERVING:
229 KCAL/2.9G FAT
PREPARATION TIME:
10 MINUTES
COOKING TIME:
10 MINUTES

225g (8oz) young spinach
   leaves
pinch of ground cinnamon
1 fresh smoked haddock fillet
   (approximately 120g/4¼oz)
150ml (¼ pint) skimmed milk
2 slices fresh lemon
freshly ground black pepper

As smoked haddock contains some salt, you will probably find you don't need to use any additional salt in this meal.

1 Using a sharp knife, finely shred the spinach and place in a heap in the centre of a microwave dish. Season with black pepper.
2 Lightly dust with cinnamon, then place the haddock fillet on top. Pour the milk over and place the lemon slices on the top of the fish.
3 Cover with microwave food wrap and pierce several times with the point of a sharp knife.
4 Cook in the microwave on full power for 4–7 minutes, according to the wattage of your oven. Check after 4 minutes and return to cook further if required.
5 Allow the fish to stand for 1 minute before removing the food wrap.
6 Transfer to a serving plate and serve with microwaved instant rice.

Marinated gammon with apple and cinnamon sauce

Marinating the gammon helps to draw out some of the salt as well as tenderising the meat. You can substitute the apple juice with orange or even pineapple juice if you prefer.

1 Place the gammon steaks in a shallow dish. In a bowl, mix together the apple juice, sugar and herbs and pour over the gammon.
2 Add the cinnamon stick and orange peel and turn the steaks over to coat all sides. Cover and allow to marinate for 20–30 minutes in the refrigerator.
3 Preheat a microwave-proof browning dish in the microwave for 5 minutes (or according to the manufacturer's instructions). Remove the gammon steaks from the marinade and place in the dish, turning them over to colour on both sides.
4 Cook on full power for 10 minutes. Turn them over and cook for a further 4–5 minutes. Remove from the microwave and cover with foil to keep warm.
5 Pour the marinade, including the cinnamon and orange, into a small microwave bowl, and cook on full power for 4–5 minutes.
6 Slake the cornflour with a little cold water and add to the sauce. Return the sauce to the oven and cook for 1-minute intervals, stirring in between, until the sauce thickens. Allow to cool slightly, then stir in the fromage frais.
7 Place the gammon on a serving dish and pour the sauce over.
8 Serve with potatoes and a selection of fresh seasonal vegetables.

SERVES 2
PER SERVING:
321 KCAL/9.9G FAT
PREPARATION TIME:
10 MINUTES
MARINATING TIME:
20–30 MINUTES
COOKING TIME:
35 MINUTES

2 gammon steaks, with all
   visible fat removed
300ml ($\frac{1}{2}$ pint) fresh apple juice
2 teaspoons soft brown sugar
1 tablespoon chopped fresh
   mixed herbs
1 cinnamon stick
2 pieces orange peel
1 tablespoon cornflour
2 tablespoons virtually fat free
   fromage frais

Dry spiced salmon

Leaving the fish to stand coated with the spices for at least 30 minutes before cooking will add more flavour to the finished dish.

1 Season the salmon fillets with salt and black pepper and place in a shallow microwave dish. Sprinkle the spring onions and the spices over the salmon and place a sprig of dill on top of each fillet.
2 Pour the wine around the fish, cover with microwave food wrap and pierce several times with the point of a sharp knife.
3 Cook in the microwave on full power for 7–8 minutes according to the wattage of your oven. Allow to stand for 3–4 minutes.
4 Serve hot with potatoes and a selection of seasonal vegetables.

SERVES 2
PER SERVING:
367 KCAL/22G FAT
PREPARATION TIME:
15 MINUTES
COOKING TIME:
15 MINUTES

2 × 175g (2 × 6oz) salmon
    fillets
2 spring onions, finely chopped
$1/2$ teaspoon ground cumin
$1/2$ teaspoon ground coriander
grated fresh nutmeg to taste
2 sprigs fresh dill
$1/2$ glass white wine
salt and freshly ground black
    pepper

Sage stuffed chicken

SERVES 2
PER SERVING:
236 KCAL/5.4G FAT
PREPARATION TIME:
20 MINUTES
COOKING TIME:
20 MINUTES

2 skinless boned chicken breasts
   (approximately 130g/4$\frac{1}{2}$oz
   each)
2 slices lean Parma ham
4 large sage leaves
300ml ($\frac{1}{2}$) pint tomato passata
1 teaspoon vegetable bouillon
   stock powder
salt and freshly ground black
   pepper

Chicken breasts tend to microwave better than chicken joints. If you prefer to use skinless chicken thighs, cut out the bone with a sharp knife.

1 Place the chicken breasts on a chopping board and season on both sides with salt and black pepper.
2 Make an incision to form a pocket in the side of each breast. Fold each Parma ham slice into a small oblong and place one inside each breast along with 2 sage leaves.
3 Place the chicken in a microwave dish, with the thickest part of the chicken to the outside of the dish. Cover with greaseproof paper and cook on full power for 7–10 minutes.
4 Mix the stock powder with the passata and pour over the chicken. Cover with microwave film and pierce the film several times with the point of a sharp knife. Return the chicken to the oven for 4–5 minutes. Allow to stand for 4–5 minutes.
5 Cut the breasts in half to check that they are cooked right through to the centre.
6 Serve with potatoes and seasonal vegetables.

Mixed vegetable pilaff

This recipe is very adaptable. You can vary the flavours of stock or use a herb stock cube instead. If you wish, you can substitute the fresh vegetables with leftover cooked ones or a frozen selection; simply add the rice and stock and continue cooking as instructed.

1 Place the onion, celery, red pepper, mushrooms and garlic in a deep microwave casserole dish and cook, uncovered, on full power for 6–8 minutes, stirring occasionally.

2 Add the rice, vegetable stock and the thyme. Cover with microwave film, pierce several times with the point of a sharp knife and cook for 10 minutes.

3 Stir well, then return to the oven for a further 5 minutes. After cooking, allow to stand for 5 minutes until all the stock has been absorbed.

4 Season to taste with salt and black pepper and serve immediately as a vegetable accompaniment or a light lunch.

SERVES 4
PER SERVING:
117 KCAL/1.3G FAT
PREPARATION TIME:
20 MINUTES
COOKING TIME:
30 MINUTES

1 small red onion, finely chopped
1 celery stick, finely sliced
1 small red pepper, seeded and finely diced
115g (4oz) mushrooms, sliced
1 garlic clove, crushed
115g (4oz) easy cook long grain rice
600ml (1 pint) vegetable stock
1 teaspoon chopped fresh thyme
salt and freshly ground black pepper

Pasta vegetable stew

SERVES 2
PER SERVING:
284 KCAL/4.4G FAT
PREPARATION TIME:
5 MINUTES
COOKING TIME:
40 MINUTES

115g (4oz) pasta shapes
1 vegetable stock cube
1 small red onion, finely
chopped
1 garlic clove, crushed
115g (4oz) chestnut or button
mushrooms, sliced
150ml ($\frac{1}{4}$ pint) tomato passata
$\frac{1}{2}$ teaspoon ground cumin
1 mixed herb or basil stock cube
1 × 400g (14oz) can chopped
tomatoes
salt and freshly ground black
pepper

Herb stock cubes are a great standby when you require a little added flavour in soups and sauces. Cooking times for the pasta will depend on the shape and size of the pasta.

1 Place the pasta in a large microwave bowl with the vegetable stock cube and cover with boiling water. Cover the bowl with microwave film, pierce the film several times with the point of a sharp knife, and cook the pasta on full power for 12–14 minutes, stirring occasionally. Allow to stand for 10 minutes.
2 Place the onion, garlic and mushrooms in a separate microwave bowl. Cook on full power for 5–6 minutes until soft.
3 Add the tomato passata and cumin, return to the oven and cook on full power for 2 minutes.
4 Add the herb stock cube, mixing until dissolved, then add the chopped tomatoes.
5 Add the cooked pasta and coat with the sauce, season with salt and black pepper and cook on full power for 5–6 minutes.
6 Allow to stand for 1 minute and serve with a mixed salad.

Soups

Homemade soups can range from simple quick broths, requiring very little preparation, to more complicated bisque-style soups that benefit from long, slow cooking. You can improve the flavour of some soups by making them a day in advance. Try always to use fresh, good-quality ingredients in order to achieve the best possible flavour.

Soups are ideal for home freezing, so you can multiply the quantities of ingredients in a recipe, if you wish, and freeze in small batches. This gives you quick access to a convenient light lunch or a simple starter for unexpected guests.

Presentation is always important and, with a little imaginative flair, a simple-looking soup can be transformed into a stunning and stylish appetiser.

Allow 200ml ($^1/_3$ pint) per serving.

Spring vegetable and fresh tuna broth

SERVES 6
PER SERVING:
89 KCAL / 2.4G FAT
PREPARATION TIME:
20 MINUTES
COOKING TIME:
20 MINUTES

2 carrots, finely diced
2 leeks, finely diced
2 celery sticks, finely diced
2 small courgettes, finely diced
8 spring onions, finely chopped
25g (1oz) risotto rice
1.2 litres (2 pints) vegetable
    bouillon stock
1 teaspoon finely chopped
    lemongrass
175g (6oz) fresh tuna (free from
    skin and bones)
115g (4oz) mange tout, finely
    diced
1 tablespoon finely chopped
    fresh chives
salt and freshly ground black
    pepper
25g (1oz) young rocket leaves,
    finely shredded

Fish soup can sometimes be heavy and strong flavoured. This light and fresh-tasting recipe provides the perfect start to any meal. The fresh tuna adds sufficient flavour without overpowering the vegetables. The basic soup can be prepared in advance and stored in the refrigerator, leaving the last few ingredients to be added just before serving.

1 In a non–stick saucepan dry-fry the carrots, leeks, celery, courgettes and spring onions for 2–3 minutes until they start to soften.
2 Add the rice, stock and lemongrass and bring to the boil. Reduce the heat and simmer for 15–20 minutes. Remove from the heat.
3 Cut the tuna into bite-size pieces. Season well with salt and black pepper.
4 Five minutes before serving, reheat the soup back up to a gentle simmer. Add the tuna, mange tout and chives.
5 Ladle the soup into warm soup bowls and sprinkle with finely shredded rocket leaves.

Crab and tomato chowder

This is a substantial soup, so it is ideally suited as a lunch.

1 In a large non-stick saucepan, dry-fry the onions until soft, add the garlic and 3 tablespoons of the stock.
2 Sprinkle the flour over and beat well with a wooden spoon. Cook for 1 minute in order to cook out the flour, then gradually stir in the remaining stock.
3 Add the chopped tomatoes, chilli, passata and potatoes and simmer gently for 10–15 minutes until the potatoes are just cooked.
4 Stir in the crab meat and herbs and remove the pan from the heat. Add the fromage frais and season to taste with salt and black pepper.
5 Ladle into bowls and garnish with the diced tomato.

SERVES 4
PER SERVING:
309 KCAL/7.7G FAT
PREPARATION TIME:
40 MINUTES
COOKING TIME:
35 MINUTES

2 onions, finely chopped
2 garlic cloves, crushed
600ml (1 pint) vegetable stock
2 tablespoons plain flour
1 × 400g (14oz) can chopped
    tomatoes
1 small red chilli, seeded and
    finely chopped
300ml (½ pint) tomato passata
225g (8oz) small potatoes, cut
    into 1cm (½in) dice
3 dressed crabs, meat removed
1 tablespoon chopped fresh
    parsley
1 tablespoon chopped fresh
    chives
2 tablespoons virtually fat free
    fromage frais
salt and freshly ground black
    pepper
4 ripe tomatoes, skinned, seeded
    and diced

Caramelised onion and lemon soup with chive and parsley cream

This onion soup, with a hint of lemon and a finishing touch of fresh herb cream, really gets the tastebuds tingling. It can be made in advance and is suitable for home freezing, although it may lose some of its delicate lemon flavour.

1 In a large non-stick saucepan, dry-fry the onions with the caster sugar for 4–5 minutes until they start to caramelise and turn brown.
2 Add the garlic, thyme and the lemon zest and juice, then sprinkle the flour over and mix in well with a wooden spoon. Cook over a low heat, stirring well, for 1 minute in order to cook out the flour.
3 Gradually add the vegetable stock, stirring well to prevent any lumps from forming. Bring to the boil, then reduce the heat and simmer for 20 minutes.
4 Taste and season with salt and black pepper. Just before serving, combine the chives and parsley with the yogurt.
5 Serve the soup hot in warmed bowls and garnish each with a slice of lemon and a swirl of chive and parsley cream.

SERVES 8
PER SERVING:
76 KCAL/0.8G FAT
PREPARATION TIME:
20 MINUTES
COOKING TIME:
25 MINUTES

1kg (2$\frac{1}{4}$lb) cooking onions, thinly sliced
1 teaspoon caster sugar
4 garlic cloves, crushed
1 tablespoon chopped fresh thyme
zest and juice of 1 lemon
2 tablespoons plain flour
1.2 litres (2 pints) vegetable stock
1 tablespoon chopped fresh chives
1 tablespoon chopped fresh flat leaf parsley
150ml ($\frac{1}{4}$ pint) low-fat natural yogurt
1 lemon, cut into 8 slices
salt and freshly ground black pepper

Artichoke and leek soup

SERVES 6
PER SERVING:
90 KCAL / 1.2G FAT
PREPARATION TIME:
25 MINUTES
COOKING TIME:
35 MINUTES

6 baby leeks, washed and sliced

2 garlic cloves, crushed

2 teaspoons finely chopped
    fresh thyme

2 vegetable stock cubes,
    dissolved in 300ml (½ pint)
    boiling water

2 tablespoons plain flour

600ml (1 pint) skimmed milk

175g (6oz) Jerusalem
    artichokes, peeled and sliced

salt and freshly ground black
    pepper

1 lemon, thinly sliced

When choosing artichokes, make sure they are dry, firm and unwrinkled in appearance. Freshly harvested, they have a wonderful fragrant flavour, but as they deteriorate it is soon lost.

1 In a large non-stick saucepan, sweat the leeks, garlic and thyme for 2–3 minutes until soft.

2 Add 2–3 tablespoons of the stock and sprinkle the flour over. Cook over a low heat for 1 minute, mixing well with a wooden spoon, in order to cook out the flour.

3 Gradually stir in the remaining stock and the milk.

4 Add the artichokes and bring to the boil. Reduce the heat and simmer for 20–25 minutes until the artichokes are soft.

5 Season to taste with salt and black pepper. Pour into a serving bowl and garnish with the lemon slices.

Double carrot soup

A highly nutritious yet fun party soup. Use only young carrots, as older ones taste less sweet and can be bitter in flavour.

1 Wash the carrots well. Remove the tops with a sharp knife and reserve. Slice the carrots and place in a non-stick saucepan. Add the celery, onions and garlic and dry-fry over a low heat for 2–3 minutes.
2 Add the thyme, stock and bay leaves and simmer gently until the vegetables are soft.
3 Remove the bay leaves, pour the mixture into a liquidiser and liquidise until smooth. Adjust the consistency with a little extra stock if required and season with salt and black pepper. Pour into a serving dish.
4 Rinse out the liquidiser, add the carrot tops and fromage frais, and purée until smooth. Season with salt and black pepper.
5 Serve the soup hot or cold, garnished with the carrot top cream.

SERVES 4
PER SERVING:
120 KCAL / 1.9G FAT
PREPARATION TIME:
20 MINUTES
COOKING TIME:
30 MINUTES

900g (2lb) fresh young carrots, complete with tops
3 celery sticks, sliced
2 medium onions, chopped
1 garlic clove, crushed
$\frac{1}{2}$ teaspoon chopped fresh thyme
1.2 litres (2 pints) vegetable stock
2 bay leaves
salt and freshly ground black pepper
2 tablespoons virtually fat free fromage frais

Spiced noodle soup

SERVES 4
PER SERVING:
160 KCAL/4.7G FAT
PREPARATION TIME:
20 MINUTES
COOKING TIME:
20 MINUTES

6 small shallots, finely sliced

2 teaspoons coriander seeds

1 smoked garlic clove, crushed

2 teaspoons lemongrass, finely chopped

1 × 5cm (2in) piece fresh ginger, peeled and finely chopped

1 small red chilli, seeded and finely chopped

1/2 teaspoon ground turmeric

1 tablespoon desiccated coconut

1.2 litres (2 pints) vegetable stock

115g (4oz) fine egg noodles

115g (4oz) beansprouts

2 tablespoons virtually fat free Normandy fromage frais

mint leaves to garnish

Coconut is extremely high in fat – desiccated coconut has 62% fat, and the fat content of coconut milk or creamed coconut is even higher. This recipe uses a small quantity of desiccated coconut combined with low-fat fromage frais to reduce the overall fat content considerably while still achieving a creamy tropical flavour. You may find this soup easier to serve if you cut the cooked noodles with kitchen scissors.

1 In a large non-stick pan, dry-fry the shallots until soft.

2 Crush the coriander seeds on a chopping board, using the broad side of a chopping knife, and add to the pan, along with the garlic. Cook for 2–3 minutes and then add the lemongrass, ginger, chilli, turmeric and coconut, stirring well to combine the spices.

3 Add the vegetable stock and bring to the boil. Reduce the heat to a gentle simmer and add the noodles. Cook for 5–6 minutes until the noodles become soft, then remove from the heat and stir in the beansprouts and fromage frais.

4 Just before serving, garnish with mint leaves.

Curried butternut squash soup

Butternut squash are readily available most of the year. They have a pale orange flesh, are quite sweet in flavour and make the most delicious soup.

1 Cut the squash in half lengthways. Remove the seeds with a spoon and discard. Using a sharp vegetable knife, peel away the thick skin, and cut the flesh into chunks.
2 Place the squash and the other vegetables in a large non-stick saucepan and dry-fry for 4–5 minutes until they soften and start to colour.
3 Add the curry powder and cook out for 1 minute, keeping the mixture moving to prevent it catching on the bottom of the pan. Gradually add the vegetable stock and the bay leaves, stirring continuously, and bring to the boil.
4 Reduce the heat and simmer until the vegetables are tender.
5 Allow the soup to cool slightly, then place in a food processor or liquidiser and liquidise until smooth. Return the soup to the pan and adjust the consistency with a little extra stock. Season to taste with salt and black pepper and serve.

SERVES 4
PER SERVING:
67 KCAL/1.2G FAT
PREPARATION TIME:
20 MINUTES
COOKING TIME:
30–35 MINUTES

1 small butternut squash
115g (4oz) fresh young carrots, washed and sliced
2 medium onions, chopped
2 garlic cloves, crushed
2 celery sticks, chopped
1–2 tablespoon medium curry powder (e.g. tandoori mix)
1.2 litres (2 pints) vegetable stock
2 bay leaves
salt and freshly ground black pepper

Yellow pea and ham soup

SERVES 6
PER SERVING:
150 KCAL/2G FAT
PREPARATION TIME:
20 MINUTES
COOKING TIME:
30–35 MINUTES

175g (6oz) yellow split peas,
    soaked overnight
2 medium onions, finely
    chopped
2 garlic cloves, crushed
$\frac{1}{4}$ teaspoon turmeric
1.2 litres (2 pints) vegetable
    stock
1 tablespoon chopped fresh
    marjoram
2 bay leaves
115g (4oz) lean smoked ham
salt and freshly ground black
    pepper
4 tomatoes, peeled, seeded and
    finely chopped

Golden, thick and wholesome, this is the type of soup that can simmer away gently unattended. Vegetarians can simply omit the ham and add a few sun-dried tomatoes or dried peppers.

1 Rinse the peas well in plenty of cold running water and place in a large saucepan with the onion, garlic, turmeric and vegetable stock.
2 Bring to the boil, then reduce the heat to a gentle simmer and add the marjoram, bay leaves and smoked ham. Simmer gently for 20–25 minutes until the peas have broken down into a thick pulp and are soft.
3 Season to taste with salt and pepper and adjust the consistency, adding more stock if required.
4 Ladle into warmed serving bowls and garnish with the chopped tomatoes.

Watercress and ginger soup

This light and refreshing soup is very easy and quick to make. Choose really fresh watercress that is vibrant in colour, perky and with open leaves, as watercress becomes bitter when it starts to wither.

1 In a non-stick pan, dry-fry the baby leeks and the carrots for 2–3 minutes over a moderate heat until softened but not coloured.
2 Stir in the bamboo shoots and fresh ginger, then gradually add the stock.
3 Slake the cornflour with a little water and stir into the soup. Add the soy sauce and bring the soup up to the boil. Reduce the heat and simmer gently for 10–15 minutes.
4 Remove the tops from the watercress. Just before serving, season the soup to taste with salt and black pepper. Pour into a warmed serving tureen and garnish with the watercress tops.

SERVES 4
PER SERVING:
55 KCAL/1.5G FAT
PREPARATION TIME:
10 MINUTES
COOKING TIME:
20 MINUTES

4 baby leeks, finely sliced
2 small carrots, cut into thin strips
225g (8oz) canned bamboo shoots
1 tablespoon finely chopped fresh ginger
1.2 litres (2 pints) vegetable stock bouillon
2 teaspoons cornflour
2 tablespoons light soy sauce
1 bunch watercress
salt and freshly ground black pepper

Easy sweet and sour corn soup

The base of this soup can be made using frozen diced vegetables if you wish, and then all you have to do is add the flavourings. Real fast food!

1 Place all the ingredients except the coriander in a large saucepan and simmer for 15–20 minutes until the vegetables have softened.
2 Add salt and black pepper to taste, although you may find the soy and chillies add sufficient flavour.
3 Just before serving, garnish with the chopped fresh coriander.
4 Serve the soup as it is or you can add a few cooked noodles in the base of each bowl.

SERVES 4
PER SERVING:
58 KCAL / 1.2G FAT
PREPARATION TIME:
10 MINUTES
COOKING TIME:
20 MINUTES

225g (8oz) frozen sweetcorn
2 celery sticks, finely sliced
2 fresh red chillies, seeded and finely chopped
1 red pepper, seeded and finely chopped
6 spring onions, finely sliced
1.2 litres (2 pints) vegetable stock
2 tablespoons light soy sauce
1 tablespoon clear honey
1 tablespoon rice wine vinegar
salt and freshly ground black pepper
2–3 tablespoons chopped fresh coriander to garnish

Grilled fresh tomato and rocket soup

SERVES 4
PER SERVING:
84 KCAL/0.8G FAT
PREPARATION TIME:
10 MINUTES
COOKING TIME:
25–30 MINUTES

1kg (2¼lb) fresh ripe tomatoes
1 teaspoon sea salt
1 teaspoon caster sugar
2 medium onions, finely
    chopped
2 garlic cloves, crushed
3 tablespoons tomato purée
2 sage leaves
225g (8oz) fresh rocket leaves,
    washed
300ml (½ pint) vegetable stock
salt and freshly ground black
    pepper

Rocket is a peppery salad leaf often eaten raw, but it can also be used to flavour cooked dishes. For an elegant-looking soup, liquidise the two vegetables separately and serve the rocket drizzled across the tomato soup.

1 Preheat the grill on a medium setting.
2 Cut the tomatoes in half and place, cut side up, on a baking tray. Sprinkle with the sea salt and the sugar and place under the grill for 8–10 minutes until the tomatoes start to colour.
3 In a non-stick saucepan, dry-fry the onions and garlic until soft. Add the tomatoes, complete with their juices, followed by the tomato purée and the sage leaves and cook gently for 10 minutes until the tomatoes have reduced down to a pulp.
4 Allow the mixture to cool, then pour into a liquidiser. Add the rocket leaves and blend until smooth.
5 Strain the mixture through a metal sieve into a saucepan to remove the tomato seeds and the skins. Add enough stock to achieve a good consistency and reheat the soup. Season to taste with salt and black pepper and serve hot.

Cream of wild mushroom soup

When buying dried mushrooms, choose good-sized pieces, and avoid broken or shrivelled dark flakes, as these can be hard and chewy when reconstituted. Fenugreek is a light Indian spice with a slightly nutty flavour and is used to flavour curry dishes.

1 Place the mushrooms, garlic, thyme and stock in a small saucepan and gently simmer for 10 minutes in order to soften the mushrooms.

2 In a separate non-stick pan, dry-fry the onions until soft. Add the fenugreek and 2 tablespoons of the mushrooms and stock. Sprinkle the flour over and cook out for 1 minute, stirring well with a wooden spoon.

3 Gradually add the mushrooms and stock and the skimmed milk. Add the bay leaves and simmer gently for 20–25 minutes until the mushrooms are soft and the soup has slightly thickened.

4 Just before serving, stir in the chopped parsley and season to taste with salt and black pepper.

SERVES 4
PER SERVING:
88 KCAL/0.7G FAT
PREPARATION TIME:
10 MINUTES
COOKING TIME:
35–40 MINUTES

40g (1 $\frac{1}{2}$oz) good quality dried
    wild mushrooms
2 garlic cloves, crushed
1 teaspoon chopped fresh
    thyme
450ml ($\frac{3}{4}$ pint) vegetable stock
2 medium onions, finely
    chopped
$\frac{1}{4}$ teaspoon ground fenugreek
1 tablespoon plain flour
450ml ($\frac{3}{4}$ pint) skimmed milk
2 bay leaves
1 tablespoon chopped fresh
    parsley
salt and freshly ground black
    pepper

Broccoli soup with roquefort cheese

Roquefort is a strong French blue veined cheese with a crumbly texture and a slightly salty flavour. Although it is high in fat (with 30g of fat per 100 grams), it has such a strong flavour that only a small quantity is required.

1 Trim off the broccoli florets with a sharp knife and reserve.
2 Chop the broccoli stalk into pieces and place in a non-stick saucepan. Add the onions, fennel and oregano and cook over a medium heat for 8–10 minutes until the broccoli has softened.
3 Add 2 tablespoons of the vegetable stock, sprinkle the flour over and mix well. Cook for 1 minute to cook out the flour, then gradually add the remaining stock and the milk, stirring continuously to prevent any lumps from forming. Simmer gently for 15–20 minutes.
4 Allow the mixture to cool slightly, then place in a food processor or liquidiser and liquidise until smooth.
5 Return the soup to the pan, add the reserved broccoli florets and the cheese, and simmer for 4–5 minutes until the florets are cooked.
6 Season to taste with salt and black pepper. Pour into a serving bowl and garnish with a little low-fat fromage frais.

SERVES 4
PER SERVING:
166 KCAL/5.5G FAT
PREPARATION TIME:
15 MINUTES
COOKING TIME:
40 MINUTES

3 large heads broccoli
2 medium onions, chopped
1 small head fennel, shredded
2 teaspoons chopped fresh
    oregano
450ml ($^3/_4$) pint vegetable stock
1 tablespoon plain flour
450ml ($^3/_4$ pint) skimmed milk
50g (2oz) Roquefort cheese,
    crumbled
salt and freshly ground black
    pepper
low-fat fromage frais to garnish

Chinese mushroom green soup

SERVES 4
PER SERVING:
86 KCAL/2.4G FAT
PREPARATION TIME:
15 MINUTES
COOKING TIME:
30 MINUTES

3–4 dried Chinese mushrooms

1.2 litres (2 pints) vegetable
  stock

50g (2oz) vermicelli noodles

1 tablespoon dark soy sauce

1 tablespoon cider vinegar

1 tablespoon finely chopped
  fresh ginger

4 spring onions, finely sliced

1 small cucumber, peeled and
  thinly sliced

115g (4oz) spinach leaves, finely
  shredded

2 tablespoons chopped fresh
  coriander

Chinese dried mushrooms have a very strong intense flavour. If you prefer, use fresh chestnut mushrooms or button mushrooms for a lighter flavoured soup.

1 Place the mushrooms in a large saucepan. Add half the vegetable stock and bring to the boil. Reduce the heat and simmer gently for 20 minutes until the mushrooms are soft.

2 In a separate saucepan, cook the noodles in boiling salted water. Drain and set aside.

3 Using a slotted spoon, lift the mushrooms out of the stock, slice into strips and return to the pan. Add the remaining stock and bring back to the boil. Add the remaining ingredients except the coriander and simmer for 3–4 minutes to allow the flavours to combine.

4 To serve, place a few noodles in the bottom of each serving bowl, pour the soup over the noodles and sprinkle with coriander.

Cauliflower and basil soup

A winning combination of fresh seasonal flavours. Do not re-boil the soup after it has been liquidised, as this may impair the flavour.

1 Remove and discard the outer leaves from the cauliflower. Coarsely chop the cauliflower, including the stalk.
2 Place the chopped cauliflower in a large saucepan. Add the onions, garlic, vegetable stock, mustard powder and bay leaves. Bring to the boil, then reduce the heat and simmer gently for 15–20 minutes until the vegetables are soft.
3 Allow to cool slightly, remove the bay leaves, then place the soup in batches in a food processor or liquidiser and liquidise, adding a little of the milk and a few basil leaves to each batch (reserve a few small basil leaves for the garnish), until smooth and lump free.
4 Return the soup to the pan and season to taste with salt and black pepper. Adjust the consistency with a little extra milk if required.
5 Garnish with the reserved basil leaves and serve immediately.

SERVES 4
PER SERVING:
86 KCAL/1.5G FAT
PREPARATION TIME:
10 MINUTES
COOKING TIME:
30 MINUTES

1 large cauliflower
2 medium onions, chopped
1 garlic clove, crushed
600ml (1 pint) vegetable stock
$1/2$ teaspoon English mustard powder
2 bay leaves
300ml ($1/2$ pint) skimmed milk
20 fresh basil leaves
salt and freshly ground black pepper

Fun food for kids

More and more children are becoming interested in cooking thanks to the wide selection of cookery books and television programmes available to them.

Children love being involved, especially when something sticky or messy is on the menu. Forget about too many cooks spoiling the broth and encourage your children to help prepare their own delicious creations from scratch, but always make sure that an adult is there to supervise them. The end result is a satisfying healthy low-fat dish that is free from the food additives found in many prepacked and convenience foods.

Some of these recipes have been developed by young would-be chefs with flavour and simplicity in mind, proving that food for kids can be both fun and interesting.

Zesty turkey kebabs

SERVES 4
PER SERVING:
322 KCAL/4.5G FAT
PREPARATION TIME:
15 MINUTES
MARINATING TIME:
1 HOUR
COOKING TIME:
15 MINUTES

4 × 175g (4 × 6oz) boneless
   turkey breasts, cut into 2.5cm
   (1in) chunks

1 medium onion, cut into chunks

1 large red pepper, seeded and
   cut into chunks

1 large yellow pepper, seeded
   and cut into chunks

for the marinade

3 tablespoons lemon juice

2 garlic cloves, crushed

1 teaspoon salt

1 tablespoon soy sauce

$1/2$ teaspoon herbes de Provence

$1/2$ teaspoon paprika

1 Combine the marinade ingredients in a bowl. Add the turkey chunks and stir until well coated. Cover and chill for 1 hour, stirring twice.
2 Using a slotted spoon, transfer the turkey to a plate.
3 Place the onion and red and yellow peppers in the marinade and mix well.
4 Thread the turkey and the vegetables alternately onto 4 metal skewers. Reserve the marinade.
5 Preheat the grill to high and grill the kebabs for 7 minutes.
6 Turn the kebabs over, brush with marinade and grill for a further 8 minutes or until the turkey is well cooked all the way through.
7 Serve with boiled rice.

Hot chicken stir-fry

1 Place the chicken in a large bowl. Add the lemon juice, ginger, garlic, crushed chilli, salt, sugar and honey. Stir thoroughly and leave to marinate for 45 minutes.
2 When marinated, heat a wok or non-stick frying pan. Add the chicken and dry-fry for 10–12 minutes.
3 Add the green chilli and the coriander and cook for a further 5 minutes.
4 Pour the remaining marinade over the chicken and cook for a further 10 minutes or until the chicken is tender.
5 Serve hot with boiled rice.

SERVES 1
PER SERVING:
270 KCAL / 3.8GFAT
PREPARATION TIME:
15 MINUTES
MARINATING TIME:
45 MINUTES
COOKING TIME:
30 MINUTES

115g (4oz) diced lean chicken, all skin removed
6 tablespoons lemon juice
1 teaspoon ginger pulp
1 teaspoon garlic purée
$\frac{1}{2}$ teaspoon crushed red chillies
pinch of salt
1 tablespoon brown sugar
1 tablespoon clear honey
1 green chilli, finely chopped
1 tablespoon chopped fresh coriander

Mini pork and mango rissoles

MAKES 16
PER RISSOLE:
51 KCAL/2.7G FAT
PREPARATION TIME:
15 MINUTES
COOKING TIME:
20–25 MINUTES

450g (1lb) lean minced pork
1 small onion, finely chopped
1 garlic clove, crushed
2 teaspoons ground coriander
2 teaspoons ground cumin
1 tablespoon mango chutney
2 tablespoons chopped fresh
   parsley
1 teaspoon salt
1 tablespoon tomato purée

These meaty nibbles make ideal party food and are great for children. You can substitute minced turkey or chicken for the pork.

1 Preheat the oven to 190C, 375F, Gas Mark 5.
2 Place all the ingredients in a large bowl and mix well.
3 Mould the mixture into 16 small balls, each about the size of a golf ball, and place on a non-stick baking tray.
4 Bake in the oven for 20–25 minutes. Serve hot or cold.

Toasted cheese bagels

1 Preheat a hot grill, slice the bagels in half horizontally and toast lightly on both sides.

2 In a small bowl combine together the cheeses, spring onions and Worcestershire sauce, and season well with salt and black pepper.

3 Spread the mixture onto the pieces of bagel and arrange the tomato slices on top. Return to the grill until golden brown.

SERVES 4
PER SERVING:
289 KCAL/3.3G FAT
PREPARATION TIME:
10 MINUTES
COOKING TIME:
10 MINUTES

4 virtually fat free bagels
2 tablespoons Quark low-fat soft cheese
2 tablespoons low-fat Cheddar cheese
2 spring onions, finely chopped
1 tablespoon Worcestershire sauce
2 large ripe tomatoes, sliced
salt and freshly ground black pepper

Potato hash browns

SERVES 4
PER SERVING:
132 KCAL/2G FAT
PREPARATION TIME:
20 MINUTES
COOKING TIME:
25 MINUTES

450g (1lb) firm waxy potatoes
1 medium onion, finely chopped
or grated
2 rashers smoked bacon, finely
chopped with all visible fat
removed
salt and freshly ground black
pepper

1 Peel and coarsely grate the potatoes into a mixing bowl. Place the grated potato in the centre of a clean dry tea towel, draw together the corners and squeeze tightly, removing as much liquid as possible.
2 Return the potato to the bowl, add the onion and bacon, and season well with salt and black pepper.
3 Preheat a non-stick frying pan, add the potato mixture to the pan pressing down well with a wooden spatula to a depth of approximately 2.5cm (1in) thick.
4 Place a lid on the pan and cook over a low heat for 15 minutes. Remove the lid, raise the heat and cook until the mixture forms a crisp base. Flip the potato over and brown on the other side.
5 Slide onto a serving plate and serve immediately with a mixed salad.

Sweetcorn stuffed tomatoes

This vegetable dish is easy to prepare and also makes an ideal light lunch – just grate 50g (2oz) low-fat Cheddar cheese on top before baking.

1 Preheat the oven to 200C, 400F, Gas Mark 6.
2 Slice the tomatoes in half and remove the inner pulp and seeds, taking care not to split the outer skin. Season the insides of the tomato halves with salt and black pepper and place on a non-stick baking tray.
3 Combine the remaining ingredients in a small bowl and spoon into the centre of each tomato half.
4 Bake in the oven for 10–15 minutes until golden brown.
5 Serve with a mixed salad.

SERVES 4
PER SERVING:
92 KCAL/1.04G FAT
(WITHOUT CHEESE)
125 KCAL/2.9G FAT
(WITH CHEESE)
PREPARATION TIME:
10 MINUTES
COOKING TIME:
10–15 MINUTES

4 large tomatoes
1 × 180g (6½oz) can sweetcorn with no added sugar, drained
4 spring onions, finely chopped
1 garlic clove, crushed
50g (2oz) Quark low-fat soft cheese
1 tablespoon finely chopped fresh parsley
salt and freshly ground black pepper

Fruity carrot and raisin salad

Simple yet very tasty, this combination of carrot and orange is a delicious accompaniment to the children's lunch box. It will keep for 3-4 days in an airtight container in the refrigerator, and the flavour improves with age. Californian raisins are plumper and slightly larger than ordinary raisins and have succulent juicy skins, so it's worth seeking them out.

1 Grate the carrots on the coarse side of a grater into a large mixing bowl. Add the spring onions and raisins, and mix well.
2 Using a sharp knife, cut the peel from the oranges, then cut out the individual segments between the thin membrane and add to the bowl.
3 In a separate small bowl, combine the orange juice, wine vinegar and coriander and season with plenty of salt and black pepper. Pour the dressing over the carrots and raisins.
4 Spoon into a serving dish or container and sprinkle with pumpkin seeds.

SERVES 6
PER SERVING:
159 KCAL/0.8G FAT
PREPARATION TIME:
15 MINUTES
COOKING TIME:
10 MINUTES

675g (1½lb) carrots, washed
4 spring onions, finely sliced
175g (6oz) Californian raisins
3 oranges
150ml (¼ pint) fresh orange juice
1 tablespoon white wine vinegar
1 tablespoon chopped fresh coriander
salt and freshly ground black pepper
pinch of pumpkin seeds to garnish

Low-fat waffles

SERVES 4
PER SERVING:
284 KCAL/2.9G FAT
PREPARATION TIME:
5 MINUTES
COOKING TIME:
20 MINUTES

225g (8oz) plain flour
2 tablespoons caster sugar
1 teaspoon baking powder
$\frac{1}{2}$ teaspoon bicarbonate soda
1 egg
1 teaspoon vanilla extract
300ml ($\frac{1}{2}$ pint) skimmed milk
a little vegetable oil

1 Combine the flour, sugar, baking powder and bicarbonate of soda in a mixing bowl. Add the egg and vanilla extract.

2 Using a whisk, gradually stir in the milk, beating the mixture to a smooth, lump-free batter.

3 Preheat a waffle iron or a non-stick frying pan with a 12cm cutter. Lightly oil the waffle plate or cutter, then remove the oil with kitchen paper, taking care not to burn your hands.

4 Spoon 3–4 tablespoons of the mixture into the waffle iron or frying pan and cook for 2 minutes. Flip over and cook the other side for a further 2 minutes. Repeat with the remaining mixture.

5 Serve hot with jam or marmalade.

Grilled honey bananas

A delicious hot dessert for all the family. When grilling the bananas, be very careful as the sugar caramelises at a very high temperature and if spilt can cause serious burns.

1 Preheat the grill to high.
2 Peel the bananas, slice in half lengthways and place on a non-stick baking tray.
3 Using a zester, zest the orange peel into a small bowl. Cut the orange in half and squeeze out the juice.
4 Drain the syrup from the ginger into the bowl. Finely chop the ginger and add to the bowl, along with the honey.
5 Mix together well, then spoon onto the bananas. Sprinkle with demerara sugar and place immediately under the hot grill for 3–4 minutes until the sugar has caramelised and the bananas are soft.
6 Serve piping hot with virtually fat free fromage frais or Wall's 'Too Good to be True' iced dessert.

SERVES 4
PER SERVING:
204 KCAL/0.3G FAT
PREPARATION TIME:
10 MINUTES
COOKING TIME:
5 MINUTES

4 medium ripe bananas
1 large orange
1 tablespoon stem ginger in syrup
3 tablespoons runny honey
3 tablespoons demerara sugar

Family meals

This chapter offers a variety of delicious dishes that reflect a diversity of tastes and cuisines. You will find that they will easily slot into your regular repertoire of weekly recipes and become firm family favourites. As with all the other recipes in this book, the cooking methods have been adjusted to reduce unnecessary fat while retaining maximum flavour.

Many of the recipes can be adapted to suit individual tastes by substituting different meats or vegetables to give even more variety. So, ring the changes by adding spice to your pasta dishes or making your stir-fries fruity and wait for the compliments from all the family.

Ratatouille beef

SERVES 4
PER SERVING:
236 KCAL/7.4G FAT
PREPARATION TIME:
20 MINUTES
COOKING TIME:
20 MINUTES

4 × 175g (4 × 6oz) pieces lean
    rump or sirloin steak
2 red onions, finely sliced
2 garlic cloves, crushed
1 red pepper, seeded and finely
    sliced
2 courgettes, sliced
1 aubergine, diced
1 tablespoon chopped fresh
    herbs (thyme, oregano, basil)
1 × 400g (14oz) can chopped
    tomatoes
salt and freshly ground black
    pepper

Good quality beef needs very little cooking and is ideal for this particular recipe. Other meats will require longer cooking, which will in effect spoil the crispness of the vegetables.

1 Trim the steak of any fat and slice the steak into strips. Season well with salt and black pepper and set aside.
2 Preheat a non-stick frying pan. Add the meat to the hot pan and seal very quickly, moving the meat around with a wooden spoon. Once sealed, remove the beef from the pan, place in an ovenproof dish and cover to keep warm.
3 Return the pan to the stove and dry-fry the onion and garlic for 2–3 minutes until they start to colour. Remove from the pan, transfer to the ovenproof dish, and cover to keep warm.
4 Return the pan to the heat. Add the red pepper and courgettes, season with salt and pepper and dry-fry for 2–3 minutes until the vegetables start to colour. Transfer to the ovenproof dish.
5 Return the pan to the heat, add the aubergine, season, and cook briskly for 5–6 minutes moving the aubergine around the pan with the wooden spoon. Add the herbs and tomatoes and stir well.
6 Return the beef and cooked vegetables to the pan and gently simmer until the beef is heated through.
7 Serve with new potatoes or on a bed of steamed rice.

Minced beef and potato pie

To make a richer sauce, you could substitute some of the beef stock with stout or real ale, but this will increase the calories!

1 Preheat the oven to 190C, 375F, Gas Mark 5.
2 Preheat a non-stick frying pan. Add the beef and dry-fry until it changes colour. Drain through a metal sieve to remove as much fat as possible, then wipe out the pan with kitchen paper.
3 Add the onions and garlic to the pan and dry-fry for 2–3 minutes until soft. Add the thyme and return the beef to the pan. Add 2 tablespoons of stock and sprinkle the flour on top.
4 Mix well, cooking over a low heat for 1 minute, then gradually add the remaining stock. Simmer gently for 10 minutes to allow the mixture to thicken, stirring occasionally. Add a little gravy browning for colour if desired and transfer to an ovenproof dish.
5 Cover with slices of potato and brush with the soy sauce. Season well with black pepper and place in the oven for 30–35 minutes until the potatoes are cooked and golden brown.
6 Sprinkle with chopped parsley and serve with a selection of fresh vegetables.

SERVES 4
PER SERVING:
409 KCAL/11.8G FAT
PREPARATION TIME:
15 MINUTES
COOKING TIME:
60 MINUTES

450g (1lb) lean mince beef
2 onions, finely chopped
1 garlic clove, crushed
2 teaspoons chopped fresh thyme
600ml (1 pint) beef stock
2 tablespoons plain flour
a little gravy browning (optional)
4 large potatoes, thinly sliced
1 tablespoon light soy sauce
freshly ground black pepper
1 tablespoon chopped fresh parsley

Beef and mushroom cannelloni

1　Preheat the oven to 200C, 400F, Gas Mark 6.
2　Dry-fry the onions in a non-stick pan until soft. Add the beef and garlic and cook over a high heat for 5–6 minutes.
3　Add the mushrooms and soy sauce, then sprinkle the stock cubes over. Add the chopped tomatoes, purée and herbs, and simmer for 15–20 minutes.
4　Meanwhile, cook the lasagne sheets in plenty of salted water until just cooked. Drain and cover with cold water to prevent further cooking. Drain the lasagne again and lay the sheets out flat. Season well with salt and pepper.
5　Place 1 sheet in an ovenproof dish and cover the centre (about a third) with the beef mixture. Roll up the sheet into a cylindrical shape and place at one end of the dish. Continue with the remaining sheets and pour any remaining mixture over the top.
6　Combine all the topping ingredients, season to taste and pour over the lasagne. Bake in the oven for 25–30 minutes.
7　Serve with salad.

SERVES 4
PER SERVING:
439 KCAL/12.5G FAT
PREPARATION TIME:
20 MINUTES
COOKING TIME: 75 MINUTES

1 large onion, finely diced
450g (1lb) lean minced beef
2 garlic cloves, crushed
225g (8oz) chestnut
　mushrooms, finely sliced
1 tablespoon mushroom soy or
　dark soy sauce
2 beef stock cubes
1 × 400g (14oz) can chopped
　tomatoes
2 tablespoons tomato purée
2 tablespoons chopped fresh
　oregano or marjoram
8 lasagne sheets
salt and freshly ground black
　pepper

for the topping
600ml (1 pint) virtually fat free
　Normandy fromage frais
115g (4oz) chestnut mushrooms,
　very finely chopped
1 teaspoon English mustard
　powder
1 tablespoon white wine
salt and freshly ground black
　pepper

Gingered mango pork

SERVES 4
PER SERVING:
319 KCAL/8.5G FAT
PREPARATION TIME:
10 MINUTES
COOKING TIME:
20 MINUTES

juice of 1 orange
2 tablespoons runny honey
2 teaspoons finely chopped
  fresh ginger
2 teaspoons light soy sauce
2 tablespoons mango chutney
4 lean pork steaks
salt and freshly ground black
  pepper
pineapple slices to garnish

1 In a small bowl, mix together the orange juice, honey, ginger, soy sauce and mango chutney to form a glaze. Season to taste with salt and black pepper.

2 Trim any fat from the pork steaks and place the steaks in a shallow dish. Brush the glaze over the steaks, then turn the steaks over and brush the other side.

3 Cook the steaks on a hot barbecue or under a preheated hot grill for 8–10 minutes each side.

4 Garnish with pineapple slices and serve with boiled rice, a salad made with red onions, red peppers and chicory, and additional mango chutney.

Chilli stuffed peppers

What a feast! A colourful combination that can be made in advance and reheated in a hot oven. If you prefer, you could use white cannelloni beans instead of red kidney beans.

1 Preheat the oven to 200C, 400F, Gas Mark 6.
2 Using a sharp knife, split the peppers lengthways and cut out the central core, including the seeds, and discard, leaving the stalk for easier handling.
3 Place the peppers on a non-stick baking tray and season well with salt and black pepper. Roast in the oven for 15–20 minutes until soft.
4 Preheat a non-stick frying pan, add the mince and dry-fry over a high heat until the meat changes colour. Drain through a metal sieve to remove as much fat as possible, then wipe out the pan with kitchen paper.
5 Add the onion and garlic to the pan and dry-fry for 2–3 minutes until soft. Return the beef to the pan and add the remaining ingredients except the cheese. Bring to the boil, reduce the heat and simmer gently for 20–25 minutes until the meat is tender and the sauce has reduced.
6 Spoon the beef mixture into the roasted pepper shells and top with the grated cheese. Return them to the oven for 10 minutes in order to heat through and melt the cheese.
7 Serve hot with Mock guacamole (see recipe, page 295) and a crisp green salad.

SERVES 4
PER SERVING:
219 KCAL/4.8G FAT
PREPARATION TIME:
15 MINUTES
COOKING TIME:
70 MINUTES

2 red peppers
2 yellow peppers
75g (3oz) lean minced beef
1 red onion, finely chopped
2 garlic cloves, crushed
1 beef stock cube, dissolved in
    150ml ($\frac{1}{4}$ pint) boiling water
1 × 400g (14oz) can chopped
    tomatoes
2 red chillies, seeded and finely
    chopped
1 tablespoon chopped fresh
    mixed herbs
1 × 400g (14oz) can red kidney
    beans, rinsed
50g (2oz) low-fat Cheddar
    cheese
salt and freshly ground black
    pepper

Stir-fried pork in plum and orange sauce

Pork spare ribs are typical of Chinese cuisine, but unfortunately they contain a high percentage of fat. Pork fillet, however, is one of the leanest meats available and can be used either whole as a piece for roasting or sliced for quick stir-fries. Plum sauce, a combination of dried plums, apricots, sweet vinegar and spices, can be found in most food stores.

1 Prepare the pork by removing all traces of fat, then cut it into long thin strips and place in a shallow dish.
2 Combine the sherry, the orange zest and juice, the honey and the plum sauce. Mix well and add the chilli, garlic, tomato purée and spice powder. Pour the mixture over the pork, cover and refrigerate for 1 hour to marinate.
3 Wash the pak choi well and place in a colander to drain.
4 Preheat a non-stick wok or large frying pan, add the pak choi and sesame seeds and cook over a high heat for 3–4 minutes. Season well and place in a serving dish. Keep warm.
5 Return the pan to the heat and add the pork pieces, cooking them quickly over a high heat for 5–6 minutes. Add the remaining marinade and allow to heat through. Spoon onto the pak choi.
6 Garnish with slices of orange and serve with noodles or rice.

SERVES 4
PER SERVING:
394 KCAL/8.4G FAT
PREPARATION TIME:
25 MINUTES
MARINATING TIME:
1 HOUR
COOKING TIME:
20 MINUTES

675g (1½lb) pork fillet
2 tablespoons dry sherry
zest and juice of 2 oranges
2 tablespoons runny honey
2 tablespoons plum sauce
1 small Thai chilli, finely sliced
2 garlic cloves, crushed
1 tablespoon tomato purée
½ teaspoon five spice powder
115g (4oz) pak choi or dark cabbage
2 teaspoons sesame seeds
salt and freshly ground black pepper
orange slices to garnish

Glazed pork steaks with green chilli salsa

SERVES 4
PER SERVING:
224 KCAL/3.8G FAT
PREPARATION TIME:
30 MINUTES
COOKING TIME:
30 MINUTES

4 lean pork steaks
4 tablespoons dry sherry
2 tablespoons runny honey
2 tablespoons Chinese plum
  sauce
1 tablespoon tomato purée
$\frac{1}{2}$ teaspoon caraway seeds
$\frac{1}{2}$ teaspoon five spice powder
2 garlic cloves, finely chopped
zest and juice of 1 lemon

for the salsa
2 limes
2 Granny Smith's eating apples
2 green peppers, seeded and
  diced
$\frac{1}{2}$ cucumber, peeled and diced
1–2 green chillies, seeded and
  finely chopped
good handful of fresh coriander
  leaves, chopped
salt and freshly ground black
  pepper

Delicious sticky pork with a cool salsa that packs a punch! This recipe has a wonderful collection of flavours yet it requires very little preparation. It works equally well with turkey steaks or chicken fillets, but do remember to remove the skin before coating with the sauce.

1 Trim off any fat from the pork steaks with a sharp knife. Place the steaks in a shallow container.

2 Combine the remaining ingredients in a small bowl and mix well. Pour over the pork and turn the steaks over, coating both sides with the glaze.

3 To make the salsa, zest and juice the limes into a bowl. Cut the apples into quarters and remove the core with a small knife. Dice into small pieces and add to the lime, stirring well to coat the apple and prevent it from turning brown.

4 Add the remaining salsa ingredients and mix well, seasoning with salt and black pepper. Spoon into a serving bowl and chill until required.

5 Cook the pork steaks on a hot barbecue or under a preheated hot grill for 8–10 minutes on each side, basting with more glaze if required.

6 Serve the steaks with the salsa, accompanied by Mexican salad (see recipe, page 216) and new potatoes.

Spicy pork and blackeye bean bake

1 Preheat the oven to 200C, 400F, Gas Mark 6.
2 In a preheated wok, dry-fry the onion until soft. Add the garlic and minced pork. Cook over a brisk heat for 5–6 minutes, stirring well.
3 Sprinkle the tandoori mix powder over and cook for 1 minute.
4 Add the herbs, red pepper, beans, stock and tomato purée. Stir well and bring to the boil. Transfer the mixture to a roasting tin or ovenproof dish.
5 Thinly slice the potatoes and place on top of the meat mixture. Season well with salt and black pepper.
6 Place in the oven for 40 minutes or until the potatoes crisp up and turn golden brown.
7 Sprinkle with chopped parsley and serve with plenty of fresh vegetables.

SERVES 4
PER SERVING:
427 KCAL/6.2G FAT
PREPARATION TIME:
20 MINUTES
COOKING TIME:
60 MINUTES

1 medium onion, finely chopped
2 garlic cloves, crushed
450g (1lb) lean minced pork
1 tablespoon tandoori mix powder
2 teaspoons dried herbes de Provence
1 red pepper, seeded and diced
1 × 425g (15oz) can blackeye beans, drained and rinsed
600ml (1 pint) vegetable stock
3 tablespoons tomato purée
675g (1½lb) potatoes, peeled
salt and freshly ground black pepper
1 tablespoon chopped fresh parsley

Lamb burgers
with mint salsa

SERVES 4
PER SERVING:
344 KCAL/3.1G FAT
PREPARATION TIME:
25 MINUTES
COOKING TIME:
35 MINUTES

175g (6oz) bulgar wheat
350g (12oz) lean minced lamb
6 spring onions, finely chopped
1 tablespoon chopped fresh
   herbs
1 teaspoon vegetable stock
   powder
1 teaspoon ground cumin
salt and freshly ground black
   pepper

for the salsa
6 spring onions, finely chopped
1 green pepper, seeded and
   diced
1 small courgette, diced
1 small green chilli, seeded and
   finely chopped
1 tablespoon chopped fresh
   mint
zest and juice of 1 lime
salt and freshly ground black
   pepper

1 Place the bulgar wheat in a mixing bowl and cover with boiling
   water. Allow to stand for 20 minutes until the grains have
   softened and swelled. Drain well and mix with the minced lamb,
   spring onions, herbs, stock powder and cumin. Season well with
   salt and black pepper and mix well until fully combined.

2 Divide the mixture into 4 and form into burger shapes, each
   about 1cm ($\frac{1}{2}$in) thick. Chill for 20 minutes.

3 Cook the burgers under a preheated hot grill or in a ridged
   griddle pan for 5 minutes on each side.

4 Combine the salsa ingredients in a small bowl and season to
   taste.

5 Serve the burgers with the salsa, dry-roast new potatoes and a
   mixed salad.

Grilled lamb steaks with redcurrant and orange

If you are unable to find redcurrants, this recipe works equally well
with cranberries or cranberry sauce.

1 Cut the lamb into steaks and place in a shallow dish. Sprinkle
   the rosemary and garlic on top and season well with salt and
   black pepper. Pour the orange juice over the steaks and leave
   to marinate for 30 minutes.
2 When ready to cook, remove the lamb from the marinade and
   place on a grill tray. Cook under a hot grill for 5–6 minutes each
   side.
3 Pour the marinade into a small saucepan, add the redcurrants
   and redcurrant jelly and heat gently.
4 Slake the cornflour with a little water and add to the sauce,
   stirring continuously, until the sauce starts to thicken.
5 Arrange the lamb steaks on a serving dish and pour the sauce
   over them.
6 Serve with potatoes and vegetables.

SERVES 4
PER SERVING:
290 KCAL/15.7G FAT
PREPARATION TIME:
10 MINUTES
MARINATING TIME:
30 MINUTES
COOKING TIME:
40 MINUTES

450g (1lb) lean lamb fillet
a few sprigs fresh rosemary
2 garlic cloves, crushed
300ml ($\frac{1}{2}$ pint) fresh orange
   juice
salt and freshly ground black
   pepper
50g (2oz) fresh redcurrants
1 tablespoon redcurrant jelly
1 tablespoon cornflour

Irish stew

SERVES 4
PER SERVING:
297 KCAL / 9.3G FAT
PREPARATION TIME:
15 MINUTES
COOKING TIME:
1 HOUR 45 MINUTES

2 medium onions, diced

2 garlic cloves, crushed

450g (1lb) lean diced lamb

1 tablespoon plain flour

1.2 litres (2 pints) meat stock

1 lamb stock cube

bouquet garni

450g (1lb) small charlotte
  potatoes

2 celery sticks, chopped

2 medium leeks, sliced

5–6 outer leaves of Savoy
  cabbage, shredded

salt and freshly ground black
  pepper

2 tablespoons chopped fresh
  parsley

To make a fresh bouquet garni, wrap 2 bay leaves around some fresh thyme, rosemary and marjoram and secure with a piece of string.

1 In a preheated non-stick pan, dry-fry the onions and garlic for 2–3 minutes until soft. Add the lamb, seasoning well with salt and black pepper, and continue to cook over a high heat until well sealed.

2 Sprinkle with the flour and cook for 1 minute to cook out the flour.

3 Mix the meat stock with the stock cube and gradually add to the pan, stirring continuously. Add the bouquet garni, cover and simmer gently for 1 hour or until the meat is tender.

4 Add the potatoes, celery and leeks and cook for a further 25 minutes. Add the cabbage and cook for a further 5 minutes.

5 Just before serving, remove the bouquet garni and sprinkle the parsley over the stew.

Chicken fricassée

1 Preheat a non-stick wok or frying pan. Dry-fry the onion until soft. Add the garlic and chicken. Season well and cook for 2–3 minutes until the chicken is sealed.
2 Sprinkle the flour over the top, stir well and cook for 1 minute to cook out the flour.
3 Gradually stir in the white wine and the stock, a little at a time, and then add the mustard, mushrooms, herbs and milk. Simmer, stirring continuously, until the sauce thickens and the chicken is cooked through.
4 After about 7 minutes, remove the pan from the heat and stir in the fromage frais and parsley. Season with salt and black pepper and serve immediately with boiled rice.

SERVES 4
PER SERVING:
245 KCAL / 3.3G FAT
PREPARATION TIME:
20 MINUTES
COOKING TIME:
20 MINUTES

1 medium onion, finely chopped
2 garlic cloves, crushed
4 skinless chicken breasts, cut into strips
1 tablespoon plain flour
1 wineglass white wine
150ml ($\frac{1}{4}$ pint) chicken stock
2 teaspoons Dijon mustard
225g (8oz) chestnut mushrooms, sliced
1 tablespoon chopped fresh fine herbs (chervil, chives, tarragon)
150ml ($\frac{1}{4}$ pint) skimmed milk
2 tablespoons virtually fat free Normandy fromage frais
1 tablespoon chopped fresh parsley
salt and freshly ground black pepper

Chicken chasseur

SERVES 4
PER SERVING:
278 KCAL/3.9G FAT
PREPARATION TIME:
20 MINUTES
COOKING TIME:
45 MINUTES

1 medium onion, finely chopped
4 large skinless chicken breasts
2 garlic cloves, crushed
150ml (¼ pint) chicken stock
1 tablespoon plain flour
3 tablespoons dry white wine
1 × 400g (14oz) can chopped
   tomatoes
1 tablespoon chopped fresh
   tarragon
115g (4oz) button mushrooms
salt and freshly ground pepper
1 tablespoon chopped fresh
   parsley to garnish

This recipe works equally well with lean pork steaks or even turkey breast fillets. If you wish, you can substitute cider or apple juice for the white wine.

1 Preheat the oven to 200C, 400F, Gas Mark 6.
2 Dry-fry the onion in a non-stick frying pan until soft.
3 Season the chicken on both sides and add to the pan. Lightly brown the chicken breasts on each side. Remove the chicken from the pan and place in an ovenproof dish.
4 Add the garlic and 2 tablespoons of stock to the pan, stir in the flour and cook for 1 minute, stirring continuously, to cook out the flour. Gradually add the remaining stock, the wine and the tomatoes and continue stirring.
5 Add the tarragon and mushrooms and bring to the boil. Pour over the chicken and cover with aluminium foil.
6 Place in the centre of the oven and cook for 30–35 minutes.
7 Just before serving sprinkle with chopped fresh parsley.
8 Serve with potatoes and assorted vegetables.

Sweet and sour chicken

Dry-frying vegetables first before adding to a casserole really adds so much more flavour. This recipe benefits from being made in advance to allow the flavours to develop.

1 Preheat a non-stick frying pan. Add the chicken and season with salt and black pepper. Cook for 8–10 minutes until lightly coloured on all sides.
2 Remove from the pan and place in a large saucepan. Add the pineapple juice, passata, stock cube and vinegar. Simmer gently over a low heat.
3 Place the onion, garlic, carrots and leeks in the frying pan and dry-fry for 5–6 minutes until soft. Add to the saucepan containing the chicken. Stir in the chilli, mushrooms, tomato purée and honey. Simmer for 10 minutes to allow the sauce to thicken.
4 Just before serving add the beansprouts, stir in the mango chutney and season to taste.
5 Serve hot on a bed of boiled rice.

SERVES 4
PER SERVING:
293 KCAL / 4.8G FAT
PREPARATION TIME:
20 MINUTES
COOKING TIME:
30 MINUTES

450g (1 lb) skinless chicken
    breasts, cut into pieces
300ml (½ pint) pineapple juice
300ml (½ pint) tomato passata
1 chicken stock cube
1 tablespoon red wine vinegar
1 red onion, diced
2 garlic cloves, crushed
2 medium carrots, thinly sliced
2 baby leeks, sliced
1 small red chilli, seeded and
    finely chopped
115g (4oz) chestnut mushrooms,
    sliced
2 tablespoons tomato purée
1 tablespoon clear honey
225g (8oz) beansprouts
1 tablespoon mango chutney
salt and freshly ground black
    pepper

Tandoori turkey and mushroom burgers

SERVES 4
PER SERVING:
273 KCAL/8.7G FAT
PREPARATION TIME:
20 MINUTES
COOKING TIME:
20–25 MINUTES

450g (1lb) extra lean minced
   turkey
1 medium red onion, finely
   chopped
2 garlic cloves, crushed
225g (8oz) chestnut
   mushrooms, finely chopped
1 tablespoon tandoori curry
   powder
2 teaspoons vegetable bouillon
   stock powder
1 tablespoon chopped fresh
   mixed herbs (parsley, chives,
   oregano)
50g (2oz) fresh breadcrumbs
freshly ground black pepper

Cooking home-made burgers on a barbecue gives them a delicious smoky roasted flavour. When moulding them together, flatten them with the palm of your hands, as the depth is very important to the cooking time. If the burgers are too thick, they will take much longer to cook through to the centre, causing the outside to overcook or even burn.

1 In a large mixing bowl, combine the turkey, onion, garlic and mushrooms, working the mixture with 2 forks to break up the meat.
2 Sprinkle the tandoori powder and bouillon stock powder over and stir in well to ensure the ingredients are fully combined.
3 Add the herbs and breadcrumbs and season with plenty of black pepper. Mix well, using your hands to bring the mixture together.
4 Take a quarter of the mixture and squeeze it to form a tight ball, then flatten it slightly and set aside. Repeat with the remaining mixture to create 4 burgers.
5 Cook the burgers on a hot barbecue or under a preheated grill for 10 minutes each side.
6 Pull one burger apart to check the centre is fully cooked. If in doubt, return to the barbecue or grill.
7 Serve in burger buns with a mixed salad.

Smoked haddock fish cakes with caper sauce

1 Poach the smoked haddock in a little water until just cooked. Remove from the pan with a slotted spoon and allow to cool.

2 Place the mashed potato in a large bowl. Flake the fish into the bowl, removing any skin and bones.

3 In a non-stick frying pan, dry-fry the leeks until soft. Add to the potato mixture and then add the lemon zest and juice, parsley and mustard. Mix well and season with plenty of salt and black pepper.

4 Shape the mixture into 8 small balls, then gently flatten with a palette knife to form fish cakes. Dry-fry in a non-stick pan on both sides until golden brown, then transfer to the oven to keep warm.

5 Combine all the caper sauce ingredients in a bowl.

6 Serve the fish cakes hot with the caper sauce, boiled potatoes and vegetables.

SERVES 4
PER SERVING:
242 KCAL/1.7G FAT
PREPARATION TIME:
10 MINUTES
COOKING TIME:
35 MINUTES

450g (1lb) fresh smoked
    haddock
450g (1lb) cooked mashed
    potato
2 baby leeks, finely chopped
zest and juice of 1 lemon
2 tablespoons chopped fresh
    parsley
1 teaspoon coarse grain
    mustard
salt and freshly ground black
    pepper

for the caper sauce
175g (6oz) virtually fat free
    fromage frais
1 tablespoon cider vinegar
1 tablespoon lemon juice
$1/4$ teaspoon ground turmeric
2 teaspoons sugar
1 tablespoon chopped fresh
    parsley
1 tablespoon chopped capers
salt and freshly ground black
    pepper

Welsh rarebit

SERVES 4
PER SERVING:
217 KCAL/3.3G FAT
PREPARATION TIME:
10 MINUTES
COOKING TIME:
15 MINUTES

4 slices wholemeal bread
2 medium onions, finely sliced
300ml ($\frac{1}{2}$ pint) skimmed milk
1 bay leaf
4 teaspoons cornflour
50g (2oz) low-fat Cheddar
    cheese
1 teaspoon Dijon mustard
salt and freshly ground black
    pepper

The traditional recipe contains real ale and masses of high-fat cheese. This low-fat version is equally delicious.

1 Toast the bread on both sides.
2 Dry-fry the onions in a non-stick pan until they start to colour, then place in a medium saucepan. Add the milk and the bay leaf. Bring to the boil.
3 Slake the cornflour with a little cold water to form a smooth paste. Gradually add to the milk, stirring until thickened. Simmer for 2 minutes, stirring occasionally, and add the cheese and the mustard.
4 Place the toasted bread on a baking tray and spread the sauce on top. Place under a preheated hot grill for 1–2 minutes, until golden brown.
5 Serve hot with Worcestershire sauce and a selection of salad leaves.

8 topping pizza

Probably the tastiest low-fat pizza yet! The mixture of low-fat salad dressing with cheese melts to form a delicious cheesy coating, rather like the way mozzarella cheese melts on top of a traditional pizza.

1 Place the flour and salt into a large mixing bowl and make a slight well in the centre.
2 Dissolve the yeast in the milk and add to the flour. Using the blade of a round-ended knife, mix the yeast with the milk and flour, adding more liquid if required.
3 Turn out onto a floured surface and knead well to form a soft dough. Cover with a damp cloth for 10 minutes.
4 Preheat the oven to 200C, 400F, Gas Mark 6.
5 Knead the dough again. Roll it out into a large circle and place on a non-stick baking tray.
6 Spoon the passata and garlic over the base, leaving a border around the edge. Arrange the red pepper, onion, ham, mushrooms, tomatoes, herbs and capers or chillies on top. Season with salt and black pepper.
7 Combine the salad dressing and the cheese and blob onto the top.
8 Bake in the oven for 20 minutes.
9 Serve with salad.

SERVES 4
PER SERVING:
276 KCAL/3.5G FAT
PREPARATION TIME:
20 MINUTES
COOKING TIME:
30 MINUTES

225g (8oz) strong white bread flour
1 teaspoon salt
15g (1/2oz) fresh yeast or 2 teaspoons dried yeast
150ml (1/4 pint) warm skimmed milk

for the topping
150ml (1/4 pint) tomato passata
1 garlic clove, crushed
1 red pepper, seeded and sliced
1 small red onion, sliced
2 slices smoked ham, cut into strips
5–6 chestnut mushrooms, sliced
2 tomatoes, sliced
1 tablespoon chopped fresh mixed herbs
a few capers or chopped chillies
2 tablespoons low-fat salad dressing
2 teaspoons Parmesan cheese or 1 tablespoon grated low-fat Cheddar cheese
salt and freshly ground black pepper

Pasta arrabbiata

SERVES 4
PER SERVING:
233 KCAL/1.4G FAT
PREPARATION TIME:
20 MINUTES
COOKING TIME:
30 MINUTES

225g (8oz) rigatoni pasta

1 vegetable stock cube

1 red onion, finely chopped

2 garlic cloves, crushed

1 red pepper, seeded and finely sliced

1 × 400g (14oz) can chopped tomatoes

1 red chilli, seeded and finely chopped

salt and freshly ground black pepper

8–10 basil leaves to garnish

This hot and spicy pasta sauce can be served on many different varieties of pasta. To cool it down slightly, just before serving stir in a little virtually fat free fromage frais. This also creates a creamier sauce.

1 Cook the pasta with the stock cube in boiling water.

2 Meanwhile, in a non-stick pan dry-fry the onion for 2–3 minutes until soft. Add the garlic and red pepper and cook for a further 2–3 minutes. Add the tomatoes and chilli, bringing the sauce to a gentle simmer. Season to taste with salt and black pepper.

3 Drain the pasta and pour into a serving dish. Spoon the sauce over and sprinkle with shredded basil leaves.

Spaghetti carbonara

1 Cook the spaghetti with the stock cube in a large pan of boiling water.
2 In a non-stick pan, dry-fry the onions and garlic until soft. Add 2 tablespoons of vegetable stock and stir in the flour. Cook out the flour for 1 minute, stirring continuously, then gradually stir in the milk.
3 Cut the ham into thin strips and add to the sauce along with the cheese and mustard. Season with salt and black pepper, reduce the heat and simmer for 2–3 minutes until the sauce thickens.
4 Toss the sauce with the spaghetti, mixing well.
5 Garnish with chopped chives and serve with salad.

SERVES 4
PER SERVING:
308 KCAL/4.5G FAT
PREPARATION TIME:
10 MINUTES
COOKING TIME:
30 MINUTES

225g (8oz) spaghetti
1 vegetable stock cube
6 spring onions, finely chopped
1 garlic clove, crushed
150ml ($^1/_4$ pint) vegetable stock
1 tablespoon plain flour
300ml ($^1/_2$ pint) skimmed milk
115g (4oz) smoked ham
50g (2oz) low-fat Cheddar cheese, grated
1 teaspoon Dijon mustard
salt and freshly ground black pepper
a few chopped chives to garnish

Top right: *Tagliatelle with sun-dried tomato and coriander pesto*

Right: *Penne with artichokes, chilli and courgette*

Tagliatelle with sun-dried tomato and coriander pesto

1 Place all the ingredients except the pasta in a food processor and blend until smooth. Season to taste with salt and black pepper.

2 Cook the pasta in plenty of boiling salted water until tender, and drain.

3 Heat the tomato pesto in a saucepan for 2–3 minutes. Add the cooked pasta. Reheat and serve immediately.

See photograph on page 159.

See photograph on page 159.

SERVES 4
PER SERVING:
234 KCAL/3.1G FAT
PREPARATION TIME:
15 MINUTES
COOKING TIME:
30 MINUTES

65g (2½oz) sun-dried tomatoes
  (non-oil variety)
2 garlic cloves, crushed
1 tablespoon ground coriander
2 tablespoons chopped fresh
  coriander
300ml (½ pint) tomato passata
225g (8oz) tagliatelle
salt and freshly ground black
  pepper

Penne with artichokes, chilli and courgette

SERVES 4
PER SERVING:
267 KCAL/3.9G FAT
PREPARATION TIME:
15 MINUTES
COOKING TIME:
25 MINUTES

225g (8oz) penne pasta

1 red onion, finely diced

2 garlic cloves, crushed

2 young courgettes, cut into
  matchsticks

1 × 425g (15oz) can artichoke
  hearts, drained and cut in half

1 small red chilli, finely sliced

300ml ($\frac{1}{2}$ pint) tomato
  salsadina or passata

1 tablespoon chopped fresh
  basil

1 Cook the pasta in plenty of boiling salted water until tender.
2 Meanwhile, make the sauce by dry-frying the onion and garlic
   in a non-stick frying pan until soft. Add the courgette strips,
   artichoke hearts and chilli. Cook for a further 2–3 minutes,
   stirring regularly.
3 Add the salsadina and fresh basil. Simmer until the sauce
   thickens.
4 Drain the pasta and return it to the saucepan. Pour the sauce
   over the pasta.
5 Serve with a crisp salad.

See photograph on page 159.

Fish and shellfish

Fish tends to be an easy option when looking for a low-fat dish, as fish and shellfish are generally very low in fat. Steaming or poaching are the favourable methods of cooking, as well as dry-roasting or grilling. However, finding a suitable low-fat sauce can sometimes be a problem. With this in mind, this chapter contains a selection of fish recipes that use various cooking methods and incorporate a variety of flavourings in the form of spices, marinades and sauces or suggestions for an accompanying side dish.

Although oily fish such as salmon has a high fat content, fish oils are essential to health and are therefore acceptable in moderation on a low-fat eating plan.

Sardine baked peppers

SERVES 4
PER SERVING:
81 KCAL/3.2G FAT
PREPARATION TIME:
10 MINUTES
COOKING TIME:
35 MINUTES

2 medium red peppers
2 medium yellow peppers
8 cherry tomatoes
2 garlic cloves, finely chopped
salt and freshly ground black
    pepper
1 × 115g (4oz) can sardines
juice of 1 lemon
2 tablespoons chopped fresh
    parsley

1 Preheat the oven to 200C, 400F, Gas Mark 6.
2 Slice the peppers in half through the stalk and remove the
   inner core and seeds. Place, cut side up, in an ovenproof dish.
3 Slice the tomatoes in half and arrange 4 halves in each pepper
   half. Sprinkle with the chopped garlic and season well with salt
   and black pepper.
4 Break the sardines into small pieces and distribute between the
   peppers so that they cover the tomatoes. Drizzle with lemon
   juice and place in the top of the oven for 20–25 minutes.
5 Sprinkle with fresh parsley and serve piping hot with boiled
   new potatoes or boiled rice and an accompanying salad.

Crab au gratin

This is an unusual method of serving crab and results in a very different flavour from cold dressed crab. Serve piping hot with a simple tomato salad for a quick and easy lunch.

1 Preheat the oven to 190C, 375F, Gas Mark 5.
2 Check the crab meat for any pieces of shell or tendons and remove. Place the crab meat in a mixing bowl.
3 Cut the bread into small dice and add to the crab meat. Add the mustard, cayenne pepper, chives and fromage frais. Mix well and season with plenty of salt and black pepper.
4 Lightly oil 4 small gratin dishes with a little vegetable oil, then remove the excess oil with kitchen paper.
5 Pile the crab mixture into the gratin dishes and level off the tops. Grate the cheese over the top and place the dishes on a baking tray. Bake in the oven for 15–20 minutes or until golden brown.
6 Serve hot with salad or roasted vegetables.

SERVES 4
PER SERVING:
232 KCAL/7.4G FAT
PREPARATION TIME:
10 MINUTES
COOKING TIME:
15 MINUTES

350g (12oz) fresh crab meat
3 slices white bread, crusts removed
$\frac{1}{4}$ teaspoon English mustard powder
$\frac{1}{4}$ teaspoon cayenne pepper
1 tablespoon chopped fresh chives
300ml ($\frac{1}{2}$ pint) virtually fat free Normandy fromage frais
a little vegetable oil
50g (2oz) low-fat Cheddar cheese
salt and freshly ground black pepper

Steamed red mullet with vegetables

SERVES 4

PER SERVING:

218 KCAL/7G FAT

PREPARATION TIME:

20 MINUTES

COOKING TIME:

25 MINUTES

4 small red mullet, gutted and
    de-scaled

1 lime, sliced

2 baby leeks, finely shredded

1 celery stick, finely sliced

2 carrots, finely sliced

2 courgettes, finely sliced

2 teaspoons rice wine vinegar

salt and freshly ground black
    pepper

a little grated fresh nutmeg

Red mullet are so called because of their attractive rouge colour. They have a light delicate flavour and therefore require only a mild sauce or lightly cooked vegetables as an accompaniment. If red mullet is unavailable, you can substitute small trout or bass.

1 Wash the red mullet well and place in the top of a bamboo or conventional steamer. Season well on both sides with salt and black pepper.

2 Arrange the lime slices on top of the fish and scatter the vegetables over and around. Drizzle the rice wine vinegar and grate a little nutmeg over the top.

3 Cover with a lid and place over a pan of boiling water. Steam for 12–15 minutes until the fish is cooked through.

4 Remove the fish from the steamer and serve with rice and the steamed vegetables.

Steamed sesame prawn balls with lime dip

This unusual dish is ideal as a light lunch or as starter. It can be made in advance and kept in the refrigerator until ready to cook and serve. For a less spicy taste you can substitute ground coriander or a pinch of nutmeg for the garam masala.

1 Place the prawns, spring onions, garam masala and shrimp paste in a food processor and mix until smooth. Scrape the mixture into a bowl and add the ground rice and coriander. Mix well until combined and season with salt and black pepper.

2 Divide the mixture into small balls, then, using wet hands, roll until smooth and dip in the sesame seeds. Place on a plate, cover with food wrap and chill until ready to cook.

3 To make the lime dip, heat the stock with the saffron and allow the saffron to infuse for 2–3 minutes. Combine with the remaining lime dip ingredients and season to taste with salt and black pepper. Cover and chill until ready to serve.

4 Place the prawn balls in a steamer over boiling water and cook, covered, for 3–4 minutes.

5 Serve immediately on a bed of shredded salad leaves with the lime dip.

SERVES 6
PER SERVING:
162 KCAL / 4.8G FAT
PREPARATION TIME:
20 MINUTES
COOKING TIME:
15 MINUTES

450g (1lb) uncooked prawns, shelled and deveined
4 spring onions, finely chopped
$\frac{1}{2}$ teaspoon garam masala
1 teaspoon shrimp paste
115g (4oz) ground rice
2 tablespoons finely chopped fresh coriander
2 tablespoons sesame seeds
salt and freshly ground black pepper
salad leaves to serve

for the lime dip
1 tablespoon fish or vegetable stock
small pinch of saffron
150ml ($\frac{1}{4}$ pint) virtually fat free fromage frais
finely grated zest and juice of 2 limes
salt and freshly ground black pepper

Baked cod with tomatoes and balsamic vinegar

Tomatoes and balsamic vinegar make a delicious topping for this simple and stylish dish. When just cooked, the cod should flake easily when teased with a fork.

1 Preheat the oven to 200C, 400F, Gas Mark 6.
2 Season the fish well on both sides and place, skin side down, in an ovenproof dish.
3 In a non-stick pan, dry-fry the onion until soft. Add the garlic and tomatoes and cook briskly for 4–5 minutes. Add the balsamic vinegar, parsley and lemon juice. Season well with salt and black pepper.
4 Spoon equal amounts onto each cod steak and place, uncovered, in the oven. Bake for 12–15 minutes or until just cooked.
5 Serve with new potatoes and seasonal vegetables.

SERVES 4
PER SERVING:
191 KCAL/1.7G FAT
PREPARATION TIME:
15 MINUTES
COOKING TIME:
25 MINUTES

900g (2lb) thick cod fillet, skinned and cut into 4 steaks
1 large red onion, finely chopped
1 garlic clove, crushed
4 ripe tomatoes, skinned, seeded and diced
2 teaspoons balsamic vinegar
1 tablespoon chopped fresh parsley
juice of $1/2$ lemon
salt and freshly ground black pepper

Seafood kedgeree

SERVES 4
PER SERVING:
339 KCAL/3.1G FAT
PREPARATION TIME:
20 MINUTES
COOKING TIME:
40 MINUTES

1 large onion, finely chopped

225g (8oz) long grain rice

1 teaspoon mild curry powder

450ml (¾ pint) vegetable stock

1 small red chilli, finely sliced

2 bay leaves

450g (1lb) cooked seafood
(mussels, prawns, crab, squid,
smoked fish)

salt and freshly ground black
pepper

This is a simple dish to prepare and offers a complete meal for under 350 calories.

1 In a non-stick saucepan, dry-fry the onion for 2–3 minutes until soft.
2 Add the rice and the curry powder, gradually stir in the stock, then add the chilli and bay leaves. Bring to the boil, reduce the heat and simmer covered for 20 minutes until most of the liquid has been absorbed.
3 Add the seafood, season to taste and heat through for 5 minutes to ensure the seafood is hot, adding a little stock if required.

Marinated griddled squid

Squid is very messy and time-consuming to prepare, so try to get your fishmonger to clean them, or buy them ready prepared. Squid rings are available, but they do not have the full flavour that fresh squid has.

1 If the squid is not already prepared, pull the head and tentacles away from the tail section. Cut the tentacles just above the eyes and discard the rest of the head. Cut away the round cartilage from the base of the tentacles and discard. Remove any reddish brown membrane and rinse the squid well under cold water. Rinse the tail section under cold water, removing the inner semi-transparent 'pen' and any reddish membrane from the outside. Place the squid on a chopping board and slice open from top to bottom, then rinse again to remove any inside membrane.
2 Using a sharp knife, score both sides of the flesh from the squid in a diagonal pattern and place in a shallow dish.
3 Combine all the marinade ingredients in a small bowl and pour over the squid. Leave to marinate for 30 minutes.
4 Preheat a non-stick griddle pan, lightly greasing with a little oil and then removing the excess with kitchen paper, taking care not to burn your fingers.
5 When the pan is very hot, carefully add the squid, cooking it quickly for 1–2 minutes each side. Take care not to overcook, or the texture will become tough and rubbery.
6 Serve hot with salad leaves, rice or noodles.

SERVES 4
PER SERVING:
102 KCAL/2G FAT
PREPARATION TIME:
45 MINUTES
MARINATING TIME:
30 MINUTES
COOKING TIME:
10 MINUTES

4 baby squid

for the marinade
4 tablespoons light soy sauce
zest and juice of 2 limes
1 small red chilli, seeded and
    finely chopped
1 × 2.5cm (1in) piece fresh
    ginger, peeled and finely
    chopped
2 teaspoons oil (to line pan)
salt and freshly ground black
    pepper

Roasted monkfish chermoula

Chermoula is a special mixture of spices used as a marinade to flavour and enhance certain foods. Monkfish is a very dense, coarse fish that requires light cooking, which makes it perfect for grilling or roasting. This recipe works equally well with thick cod or other fish such as sea bass.

1 Prepare the monkfish by removing the thin outer skin and any bones. Rinse well and place the pieces side by side in a large ovenproof dish. Sprinkle the red onion over the top and season well with salt and black pepper.
2 In a small bowl combine the spices with the chilli, lemon zest and juice and the orange juice. Spoon the marinade over the fish, and then turn the fillets to coat all sides with the spices. Cover and place in refrigerator for 30 minutes to allow the spices to penetrate.
3 Preheat the oven to 190C, 375F, Gas Mark 5.
4 When the fish has marinated, transfer to a non-stick roasting tin, pour the marinade over the fish and sprinkle with coriander. Place in the oven for 12–15 minutes until just cooked.
5 Wash the spinach and place in a preheated non-stick wok. Season well with salt and black pepper, add a pinch of cinnamon and cook over a high heat for 1–2 minutes, stirring well.
6 To serve, arrange the monkfish on a bed of spinach and pour the juices over the top.
7 Serve with baby new potatoes.

SERVES 4
PER SERVING:
234 KCAL / 2.8G FAT
MARINATING TIME:
30 MINUTES
COOKING TIME:
45 MINUTES

900g (2lb) monkfish tail fillets, cut into 4 pieces
1 medium red onion, finely diced
1 teaspoon ground cumin
1 teaspoon ground paprika
1 teaspoon ground turmeric
good pinch of saffron
1 small red chilli, seeded and finely chopped
zest and juice of 1 lemon
3 tablespoons fresh orange juice
6 tablespoons chopped fresh coriander
900g (2lb) pousse (baby spinach)
pinch of ground cinnamon
salt and freshly ground black pepper

Prawn curry

SERVES 4
PER SERVING:
129 KCAL/1.2G FAT
PREPARATION TIME:
25 MINUTES
COOKING TIME:
20 MINUTES

1 large red onion, finely
    chopped
2 tablespoons tomato purée
600ml (1 pint) fish or vegetable
    stock
1 tablespoon tamarind paste
4 kaffir lime leaves
450g (1 lb) uncooked peeled
    prawns
2 tablespoons chopped fresh
    coriander

for the paste
3 garlic cloves, peeled
1 tablespoon ground coriander
$1/2$ teaspoon ground turmeric
$1/4$ teaspoon fenugreek seeds
2–3 small whole fresh chillies
4 cardamom pods, crushed and
    seeds removed

As the base to this curry sauce is vegetarian, you could replace the prawns with a selection of diced vegetables to create a vegetarian option.

1 Make the paste by grinding all the paste ingredients in a food processor or liquidiser. Scrape the paste into a bowl, then rinse out the food processor of liquidiser with a little stock and add to the bowl.
2 In a non-stick pan, dry-fry the onion until soft. Add the paste and cook for 2 minutes, stirring continuously.
3 Add the remaining ingredients except the fresh coriander and simmer gently for 15–20 minutes until the sauce thickens and the prawns are cooked through.
4 Just before serving, stir in the fresh coriander.
5 Serve with boiled rice.

Chilli prawn couscous

Prawns take very little cooking. They are perfect when lightly steamed, as in this recipe, since they pick up the flavours from the spiced couscous. Alternatively, you could use white crab meat.

1 In a medium saucepan, bring the vegetable stock to the boil. Add the spices, garlic, chilli and tomatoes.
2 Gradually add the couscous, stirring well. Stir the prawns into the mixture. Cover with a tight-fitting lid and remove from the heat for 1 minute.
3 Fluff up the couscous with 2 forks. Add the coriander, garnish with the lemon wedges and serve immediately.

SERVES 4
PER SERVING:
313 KCAL / 1.8G FAT
PREPARATION TIME:
10 MINUTES
COOKING TIME:
5 MINUTES

450ml ($^3/_4$ pint) vegetable stock
$^1/_4$ teaspoon fennel seeds
$^1/_4$ teaspoon ground cumin
$^1/_4$ teaspoon ground coriander
2 garlic cloves, crushed
1 small red chilli, seeded and finely chopped
1 × 225g (8oz) can chopped tomatoes
450g (1lb) couscous
225g (8oz) uncooked peeled prawns
1 tablespoon chopped fresh coriander
lemon wedges to garnish

Vegetarian

Vegetarianism is becoming an increasingly popular option and a vegetarian diet can be just as healthy as one that includes meat, providing it incorporates foods from each of the four main food groups – proteins, milk and dairy products, cereals and grains, fruit and vegetables.

Today, as well as beans and pulses, there are many new sources of plant-based protein, including foods such as TVP, tofu and Quorn, which can be used as meat substitutes in many recipe dishes. Nuts are also a good source of protein, but they tend to be very high in fat, so use sparingly in dishes.

Dairy products are especially important in the diet to provide calcium. Many vegetarians do eat dairy products based on cow's milk, but others prefer to choose soya milk and other vegetarian alternatives.

Foods such as bread, breakfast cereals, potatoes, pasta, rice and other grains are full of starchy carbohydrates which should provide the bulk of food at every meal. Try to ensure, though, that you do not prepare or serve these foods with added fat. For instance, try preparing pasta with tomato-based, rather than creamy sauces and serve yogurt or cottage cheese as a topping for potatoes instead of butter or hard, full-fat cheese.

When cooking and preparing meals, you can reduce the fat content by replacing oily marinades with fruit juices and low-fat sauces such as soy or stock. Dry-frying or dry-roasting is a very successful way of cooking vegetables, particularly the absorbent types such as aubergine or mushrooms which usually soak up the oil or butter they are cooked in. It is also important to allow plenty of moisture as a fat replacement, particularly when cooking with dry spices, so use flavoursome herb stocks and tomato products such as passata or chopped tomatoes to give volume as well as added flavour.

However, to ensure you don't miss out on essential fatty acids found mainly in oily fish, you may add a drop of oil rich in essential fatty acids, such as soya or rapeseed oil, in your cooking or use the more exotic walnut oil in salad dressings. Remember, though, that pure oils are very concentrated and high in calories – so just a drop!

Onion, potato and fennel bake

Potatoes and fennel make a great combination. Use a piping bag to spread the potato into the dish and create a lattice top for decoration.

1 Preheat the oven to 200C, 400F, Gas Mark 6.
2 Boil the potatoes in salted water until cooked. Drain well and mash with a potato masher, adding the skimmed milk until the mixture is lump free.
3 Dry-fry the fennel in a preheated non-stick pan until it starts to colour. Remove from the pan and set aside. Add the onions, leeks and garlic to the pan and cook over a high heat until they start to colour.
4 Heat the milk and stock powder in a saucepan until boiling. Slake the cornflour with a little water and add to the milk, stirring continuously to prevent any lumps from forming. Mix in the cheese and chives and season with salt and black pepper.
5 In an ovenproof dish, place alternate layers of potato, sauce and onion mixture, finishing with a layer of potato.
6 Bake in the oven for 20–25 minutes until brown and crispy.
7 Serve with vegetables or salad.

SERVES 4
PER SERVING:
299 KCAL / 3.1G FAT
PREPARATION TIME:
30 MINUTES
COOKING TIME:
55 MINUTES

675g (1 1/2lb) potatoes, peeled and chopped
2 tablespoons skimmed milk
1 large bulb fennel, thinly sliced
2 medium onions, finely sliced
4 leeks, washed and sliced
2 garlic cloves, crushed
600ml (1 pint) skimmed milk
2 teaspoons vegetable bouillon powder
2 tablespoons cornflour
50g (2oz) low-fat Cheddar cheese
2 tablespoons chopped fresh chives
salt and freshly ground black pepper

Baked ginger stuffed tomatoes

Tomatoes are available all year round, with many different varieties available. Served with a side salad, these ginger-spiked tomatoes make a tasty lunch. They are also suitable as a vegetable dish alongside grilled meat or fish, or you could serve them cold to dress up a simple salad.

1 Preheat the oven to 190C, 375F, Gas Mark 5.
2 Slice off the tops of the tomatoes and reserve. Using a dessertspoon, remove the inner core and seeds from the tomatoes and discard. Place the tomato shells in an ovenproof dish.
3 Preheat a non-stick frying pan and dry-fry the onion for 2–3 minutes until soft. Add the diced pepper, garlic and ginger and cook for a further 2–3 minutes. Stir in the tomatoes and chervil and simmer until the sauce thickens, seasoning well with salt and black pepper.
4 Spoon the cooked mixture into the tomato shells and place a tomato top over each one.
5 Bake in the oven for 20 minutes. Serve hot or cold.

SERVES 2
PER SERVING:
129 KCAL / 1.6G FAT
PREPARATION TIME:
20 MINUTES
COOKING TIME:
40 MINUTES

4 large ripe beef tomatoes
1 medium onion, finely diced
1 red pepper, seeded and diced
2 garlic cloves, crushed
1 tablespoon finely chopped fresh ginger
1 × 225g (8oz) can chopped tomatoes
1 tablespoon chopped fresh chervil
salt and freshly ground black pepper

Spinach soufflé

SERVES 4
PER SERVING:
119 KCAL/4.3G FAT
PREPARATION TIME:
15 MINUTES
COOKING TIME:
60 MINUTES

300ml (1/2 pint) skimmed milk
1 tablespoon stock bouillon
    powder or 1 vegetable stock
    cube
4 teaspoons cornflour
1 tablespoon Dijon mustard
225g (8oz) young baby leaf
    spinach or large leaf spinach
2 egg yolks
4 egg whites
grated fresh nutmeg to taste
salt and freshly ground black
    pepper

1 Preheat the oven to 190C, 350F, Gas Mark 5.
2 Prepare 4 × 115g (4 × 4oz) ramekin dishes by lightly greasing the insides with a little vegetable oil and then removing the excess with a piece of kitchen paper.
3 Heat the milk and stock in a saucepan. Slake the cornflour with a little water and stir into the milk, stirring continuously as the sauce thickens. Reduce the heat and simmer for 2–3 minutes. Mix in the mustard and the spinach (if using large leaf spinach, roughly chop first). Allow the mixture to cool.
4 When the mixture is quite cool, beat in the egg yolks and season with salt and black pepper.
5 Whisk the egg whites until they form stiff peaks. Using a large metal spoon, gently fold a third of the whites into the spinach mixture until combined, then fold in the remaining whites. Spoon into the prepared ramekin dishes and sprinkle the nutmeg on top.
6 Bake in the oven for 20–25 minutes until well risen and golden brown.
7 Serve immediately with new potatoes.

Rosemary, fennel and potato gratin

1 Preheat the oven to 200C, 400F, Gas Mark 6.
2 Preheat a non-stick frying pan, add the onion and fennel and dry-fry the onion over a high heat until brown.
3 Meanwhile, cover the bottom of an ovenproof dish with a layer of potatoes. Spread with half the onion and fennel mixture, season with salt and black pepper and sprinkle the rosemary on top.
4 Add another layer of potatoes and then onion and fennel, and cover with a final layer of potatoes.
5 Heat the milk in a saucepan along with the garlic and stock cube until boiling.
6 Mix the egg and cheese together in a bowl, pour the hot milk over, whisking well to combine. Pour the mixture over the potatoes and bake in the oven for 30–35 minutes.
7 Just before serving, sprinkle the parsley on top.

SERVES 4
PER SERVING:
266 KCAL / 4.4G FAT
PREPARATION TIME:
30 MINUTES
COOKING TIME:
45 MINUTES

2 large onions, sliced
1 bulb fennel, sliced
675g (1 1/2lb) potatoes, peeled and thinly sliced
1 tablespoon chopped fresh rosemary
600ml (1 pint) skimmed milk
3 garlic cloves, crushed
1 vegetable stock cube
1 egg, beaten
50g (2oz) low-fat Cheddar cheese
salt and freshly ground black pepper
2 tablespoons chopped fresh parsley to garnish

Baked mushrooms with turmeric rice

SERVES 4
PER SERVING:
298 KCAL / 7.1G FAT
PREPARATION TIME:
10 MINUTES
COOKING TIME:
50 MINUTES

8 medium flat or field
    mushrooms
1 medium onion, finely chopped
2 garlic cloves, crushed
$\frac{1}{2}$ wineglass white wine
$\frac{1}{2}$ teaspoon ground turmeric
225g (8oz) Arborio risotto rice
600ml (1 pint) vegetable stock
2 tablespoons virtually fat free
    fromage frais
salt and freshly ground black
    pepper
chopped fresh chives to garnish

1 Preheat the oven to 180C, 350F, Gas Mark 4.
2 Wipe the mushrooms over with a piece of damp kitchen paper.
   Remove the stalks and reserve. Arrange the mushrooms in a
   roasting tin or ovenproof dish. Season well with salt and black
   pepper. Roughly chop the mushroom stalks.
3 In a non-stick pan, dry-fry the onion and garlic with the
   mushroom stalks for 2–3 minutes until soft. Add the wine,
   turmeric and rice. Gradually stir in the stock a little at a time,
   allowing the rice to absorb it before adding more each time.
   Simmer until all has been absorbed and the rice is just cooked.
4 Stir in the fromage frais and remove from heat. Season with salt
   and black pepper to taste.
5 Spoon the mixture onto each mushroom. Cover with foil and
   bake in the oven for 20–25 minutes.
6 Sprinkle with chopped chives and serve with a selection of fresh
   vegetables.

Vegetable kedgeree

This colourful and simple vegetarian dish is ideal as a lunch or light supper.

1 In a large non-stick pan, dry-fry the onion and garlic until soft. Add the celery, peppers, cauliflower and spices and mix well.

2 Stir in the rice and stock, mixing well to coat the rice. Cover with a lid and simmer gently for 20–25 minutes until all the stock has been absorbed and the rice is cooked (you may need to add a little extra stock to prevent the rice from drying out).

3 Just before serving, cut the eggs into quarters and place on top of the rice to heat through. Season with salt and black pepper.

4 Garnish with the diced tomato and fresh coriander and serve hot.

SERVES 4
PER SERVING:
307 KCAL/5.9G FAT
PREPARATION TIME:
30 MINUTES
COOKING TIME:
45 MINUTES

1 medium onion, finely chopped
2 garlic cloves, crushed
2 celery sticks, sliced
1 red pepper, seeded and diced
1 yellow pepper, seeded and diced
1 small cauliflower, broken into florets
1 red chilli, seeded and finely chopped
$1/2$ teaspoon ground turmeric
$1/4$ teaspoon cayenne pepper
225g (8oz) easy cook long-grain rice
600ml (1 pint) vegetable stock
2 hard-boiled eggs, shelled
salt and freshly ground black pepper
2 tomatoes, skinned, seeded and diced
chopped fresh coriander to garnish

Baby vegetable kebabs with fresh basil pesto

SERVES 4
PER SERVING:
62 KCAL / 1.5G FAT
PREPARATION TIME:
20 MINUTES
COOKING TIME:
10 MINUTES

8 shallots, peeled
4 baby aubergine
4 baby courgettes
8 patty pan squash
8 cherry tomatoes
8 small chestnut mushrooms

for the pesto
1 vegetable stock cube
2 good bunches fresh basil
1 garlic clove, crushed
1 tablespoon finely chopped
    cooked chestnuts
2 teaspoons grated Parmesan
    cheese
salt and freshly ground black
    pepper

Baby vegetables have a sweet young flavour coupled with a crisp skin and texture, making them ideal barbecue food. Make the kebabs in advance, brush with pesto and store, covered, in the refrigerator until ready for cooking. Pep them up with whole jalapeno chillies if you dare!

1 Prepare the vegetables by cutting the shallots into chunky wedges, the aubergine and courgettes into thick slices and the patty pan squash in half. Thread the vegetables onto wooden skewers and place into a large shallow dish. Season well with salt and black pepper.
2 To make the pesto, dissolve the stock cube in 150ml ($\frac{1}{4}$ pint) boiling water. Pluck the basil leaves from the main plant stem and place in a food processor or liquidiser. Add the remaining ingredients and blend until smooth. Season to taste with salt and black pepper and scrape out into a bowl.
3 Using a pastry brush, lightly brush the vegetables with the pesto, coating all sides of the vegetables. Leave to stand until required. Before cooking, brush the vegetables again with the pesto.
4 Cook over a hot barbecue or under a preheated hot grill for 4–5 minutes each side or until lightly charred but still crisp.
5 Brush the vegetables again with the remaining pesto and serve with crusty bread and mixed salad.

Marinated broccoli and pepper stir-fry with noodles

1. Combine all the marinade ingredients in a large bowl.
2. Break the broccoli into bite-size pieces. Remove the seeds from the peppers and slice the peppers into thin strips. Add the broccoli and peppers to the marinade and mix well. Leave for 10 minutes.
3. Meanwhile, place the noodles in a heatproof bowl and cover with boiling water. Allow them to stand for 5 minutes.
4. Preheat a non-stick wok. Remove the vegetables from the marinade, reserving the marinade. Stir-fry the marinated vegetables for 5–6 minutes until they start to soften. Add the beansprouts and cook for a further 2–3 minutes.
5. Drain the noodles and place in a saucepan. Add the reserved marinade and bring to the boil, combining well.
6. Serve the vegetables and noodles immediately with a crisp salad.

SERVES 4
PER SERVING:
298 KCAL/5.4G FAT
PREPARATION TIME:
10 MINUTES
MARINATING TIME:
10 MINUTES
COOKING TIME:
20 MINUTES

225g (8oz) broccoli florets
2 medium red peppers
225g (8oz) Chinese noodles
225g (8oz) beansprouts

for the marinade
1 red onion, finely sliced
2 garlic cloves, crushed
1 × 2.5cm (1in) piece fresh
   ginger, finely chopped
3 tablespoons orange juice
1 tablespoon light soy sauce
1 teaspoon sesame seeds
1 teaspoon finely chopped chilli

Risotto primavera

SERVES 4
PER SERVING:
422 KCAL / 7.6G FAT
PREPARATION TIME:
10 MINUTES
COOKING TIME:
25 MINUTES

1 medium onion, finely chopped
2 garlic cloves, crushed
225g (8oz) Arborio risotto rice
600ml (1 pint) vegetable stock
$\frac{1}{2}$ wineglass white wine
115g (4oz) baby asparagus
115g (4oz) young courgettes,
    cut into batons
115g (4oz) fine green beans
115g (4oz) mange tout
2 tablespoons virtually fat free
    Normandy fromage frais
salt and freshly ground black
    pepper
3 tablespoons Parmesan cheese

1 In a non-stick frying pan, dry-fry the onion and garlic until soft.
2 Add the rice and gradually stir in a little of the stock and the wine at a time, allowing the rice to absorb the liquid before adding more (this will take between 15 and 20 minutes).
3 Once all the liquid has been added, stir in the vegetables and cover to allow the vegetables to steam but not overcook.
4 Just before serving, fold in the fromage frais and remove from the heat. Season with salt and black pepper.
5 Sprinkle with Parmesan cheese and serve hot.

Aubergine tagine with roast garlic

The traditional Moroccan tagine is a slowly cooked stew, bursting with unusual flavour from fruits and spices, in a rich succulent sauce. This vegetarian version is simply delicious.

1 Preheat the oven to 200C, 400F, Gas Mark 6.
2 Take 2 of the aubergines and slice down the centre lengthways with a sharp knife. Using a dessertspoon, scoop out the centres, taking care not to damage the outer skin. Season the shells with salt and black pepper and place, skin-side up, on a baking tray. Bake in the oven for 20–25 minutes until soft. Remove and set aside.
3 While the aubergines are baking, wrap the garlic cloves in a small piece of aluminium foil and place in the oven for 20 minutes.
4 Prepare the fennel and the remaining vegetables by cutting into rough pieces, about 1cm (1/2in) thick.
5 Preheat a large non-stick saucepan, add the vegetables and cook briskly for 8–10 minutes, stirring occasionally, until they start to brown. Add the cumin, cinnamon, coriander and roast garlic and cook for 1 minute before adding the chopped tomatoes and stock.
6 Using a vegetable peeler, remove 3 strips of orange peel from the orange, and then squeeze out the juice from the orange. Add the strips of orange peel and the orange juice to the saucepan.
7 Place the cardamom pods on a chopping board. Using the broad blade of a chopping knife, crush the pods and remove the inner black seeds. Discard the pods and crush the black seeds. Add the seeds, tomato purée and parsley to the saucepan. Reduce the heat and simmer gently for 20 minutes until the sauce thickens.
8 Place the pre-roasted aubergine shells into an ovenproof dish, spoon in the tagine and bake in the oven for 10–15 minutes.
9 Just before serving, garnish with parsley.
10 Serve hot with couscous, rice or potatoes.

SERVES 4
PER SERVING:
103 KCAL/1.5G FAT
PREPARATION TIME:
25 MINUTES
COOKING TIME:
90 MINUTES

3 medium aubergines
4 garlic cloves, peeled
1 small bulb fennel
2 medium red onions
2 red peppers, seeded
1 teaspoon ground cumin
1/2 teaspoon ground cinnamon
1 teaspoon ground coriander
1 × 400g (14oz) can chopped tomatoes
150ml (1/4 pint) vegetable stock
1 orange
6 cardamom pods
2 tablespoons tomato purée
2 tablespoons finely chopped fresh flat leaf parsley
salt and freshly ground black pepper
extra chopped fresh flat leaf parsley to garnish

Roast vegetable lasagne

SERVES 4
PER SERVING:
354 KCAL/5.3G FAT
PREPARATION TIME:
30 MINUTES
COOKING TIME:
80 MINUTES

1 large red onion, cut into wedges
1 small aubergine, diced
2 medium courgettes, thickly sliced
1 red pepper, seeded and cut into
    pieces
1 yellow pepper, seeded and cut into
    pieces
1 bulb fennel, sliced
6 fresh ripe tomatoes, cut into
    quarters
2 garlic cloves, sliced
2 tablespoons light soy sauce
2 tablespoons chopped fresh oregano
1 teaspoon finely chopped
    lemongrass
1 × 400g (14oz) can chopped
    tomatoes
300ml (1/2 pint) tomato passata
225g (8oz) 'no pre-cook' lasagne
    sheets

for the topping
300ml (1/2 pint) low-fat natural yogurt
1 egg, beaten
1 teaspoon English mustard powder
2 teaspoons finely grated Parmesan
    cheese
salt and freshly ground black pepper

You won't believe the flavours that come through in this meat-free lasagne. Substituting vegetables for meat certainly results in a lighter dish, and, without the calories and fat from the meat, it allows you to sprinkle a little Parmesan on top to finish.

1 Preheat the oven to 200C, 400F, Gas Mark 6.
2 Place all the vegetables in a large non-stick roasting tray, season well with black pepper and mix well. Scatter the garlic slices over and drizzle with soy sauce, then mix well again to coat the vegetables with the soy.
3 Place the roasting tray in the top of the oven and roast the vegetables for 35–40 minutes until soft, turning occasionally.
4 Remove the roasting tray from the oven and add the oregano, lemongrass, canned tomatoes and tomato passata, mixing all the ingredients together.
5 Spoon a thin layer of the vegetables into an ovenproof dish. Cover with a layer of lasagne sheets, without overlapping them, as they will expand during cooking. Continue layering the remaining vegetables and lasagne sheets, finishing with a layer of lasagne sheets.
6 Combine all the topping ingredients, spread over the top and sprinkle the Parmesan cheese on top. Bake in the oven for 35–40 minutes until brown.
7 Serve with a mixed leaf salad.

Asparagus and black bean pancakes

Crispy spring rolls are hard to resist, but traditional deep-fried ones contain unspeakable amounts of fat. These low-fat pancakes with a tasty filling are baked in the oven, which produces a delicious crisp casing and a flavoursome result.

1 To make the pancake batter, sift the flour and salt into a mixing bowl and make a well in the centre. Add the egg and a little of the milk and combine, using a whisk to make a thick paste. Gradually add the remaining milk and chervil, beating continuously until smooth and lump free. Allow the batter to stand for 20–30 minutes. The consistency should be similar to a thick cream. If necessary, thin it down with a little cold water.

2 To make the filling, cut off the ends of the asparagus and slice the asparagus diagonally into bite-size pieces. Plunge them into a pan of boiling salted water for 2 minutes, drain and immediately refresh under cold water to stop the asparagus cooking further.

3 Preheat a non-stick wok or frying pan until hot, add the spring onions and soften quickly for 1 minute.

4 Drain the beans and add to the pan, together with the asparagus, beansprouts and water chestnuts.

5 Mix the hoisin sauce with the water and pour over the vegetables and toss thoroughly cooking for a further 2 minutes. Remove from the heat and allow to cool.

6 Preheat the oven to 200C, 400F, Gas Mark 6.

7 Preheat a non-stick frying pan with a little oil, then wipe out the pan with kitchen paper, taking care not to burn your fingers. Whisk the batter well, then add 2 tablespoons to the pan, tilting the pan to allow the batter to coat the base. Cook briskly for 30 seconds, then loosen the edges with a wooden spatula, flip the pancake over and cook the other side for 15 seconds and slide onto a plate. Repeat until all the mixture is

SERVES 4
PER SERVING:
125 KCAL/2.4G FAT
PREPARATION TIME:
50 MINUTES
COOKING TIME:
45 MINUTES

for the pancake batter
50g (2oz) plain flour
pinch of salt
1 egg
150ml (¼ pint) skimmed milk
1 tablespoon finely chopped fresh chervil
a little vegetable oil (to line the pan)

for the filling
225g (8oz) thin asparagus spears
4 spring onions, finely sliced
2 tablespoons salted black beans, soaked overnight in cold water
175g (6oz) fresh beansprouts
1 × 225g (8oz) can water chestnuts, sliced
1 tablespoon hoisin sauce
150ml (¼ pint) hot water

used, adding oil to the pan and wiping out after every 2 pancakes.

8 When the pancakes are cool enough to handle, place 2 tablespoons of filling inside each one. Fold in both sides approximately 4cm (1$\frac{1}{2}$in), then roll into a spring roll shape and arrange in an ovenproof dish. Bake, uncovered, for 15–20 minutes until crisp.

9 Serve hot with noodles or rice.

Vegetables and accompaniments

The finishing touch to a dish of vegetables is generally a large knob of butter or a drizzle of olive oil to add a glaze. This unnecessary fat can mask the true flavour of the vegetables and leave a pool of fat at the bottom of the dish. If you omit the fat, you'll notice the difference at first, but replacing the fat with a combination of other ingredients such as herbs and spices not only adds flavour but also transforms an ordinary side dish into an imaginative part of the meal. As we have access to so many varied ingredients, it's a shame not to put them to use.

Thai lemongrass or fine balsamic vinegar can be incorporated into vegetable dishes to offer an alternative flavour, and a simple sprinkling of fennel seeds or chopped fresh herbs adds a finishing touch.

We so easily fall into the trap of serving the same plain accompaniments time and time again, so ring the changes and spice up your vegetable selection with a little imagination and a host of unusual ingredients.

Carrots and fennel with lemon

SERVES 6
PER SERVING:
24 KCAL/0.6G FAT
PREPARATION TIME:
20 MINUTES
COOKING TIME:
30 MINUTES

450g (1lb) young carrots
1 small bulb fennel
1 vegetable stock cube
1 lemon

Fennel is a much underused vegetable, similar to celery in appearance and with a dill-like fern head. Florence fennel is the finest with young long slender bulbs and fresh green sprouts. Try it shredded in salads or braised in vegetable stock – it's quite delicious.

1 Peel or scrape the carrots and cut into small batons. Slice the fennel bulb lengthways and cut into small dice.
2 Place both vegetables in a saucepan with the stock cube. Using a zester, remove the zest from the lemon and add to the pan. Barely cover the vegetables with water. Bring to the boil and simmer until the vegetables are cooked.
3 Drain the vegetables through a colander and place in a warmed serving dish.
4 Cut the lemon in half and squeeze over the vegetables.

Garlic pineapple beans

This colourful combination contains unusual flavours that work particularly well alongside Chinese dishes. Often, when serving a highly spiced main course, it is best to keep the side dishes reasonably plain to balance the meal.

1 In a saucepan, bring 600ml (1 pint) of water to the boil with the stock powder or cube.
2 Top and tail the beans and add to the stock. Cook, uncovered, for 8–10 minutes or until tender, then drain, reserving the cooking liquor.
3 In a non-stick frying pan, dry-fry the onions and garlic over a low heat, taking care not to burn the garlic. Add the pineapple slices and green beans with a little of the reserved cooking liquor.
4 Slake the cornflour with a little cold water and add to the pan, stirring until the sauce starts to thicken. Simmer for 2 minutes. Season well with black pepper and serve immediately.

SERVES 4
PER SERVING:
60 KCAL/0.8G FAT
PREPARATION TIME:
20 MINUTES
COOKING TIME:
20 MINUTES

225g (8oz) fine green beans
1 tablespoon vegetable stock bouillon powder or 1 stock cube
4 spring onions, finely sliced
3 garlic cloves, crushed
1 small fresh pineapple, sliced with skin removed
2 teaspoons cornflour
freshly ground black pepper

Braised pak choi with garlic

SERVES 4
PER SERVING:
42 KCAL/0.6G FAT
PREPARATION TIME:
5 MINUTES
COOKING TIME:
20 MINUTES

115g (4oz) young pak choi
3 garlic cloves, finely chopped
1 cinnamon stick
600ml (1 pint) vegetable stock
2 teaspoons cornflour
2 teaspoons light soy sauce

If you enjoy the flavour of spinach, then try this oriental alternative. Pak choi, with its sweet white stems and lush green leaves, is also the perfect vegetable for stir-fries.

1 Preheat the oven to 200C, 400F, Gas Mark 6.
2 Slice the pak choi in half and arrange in the bottom of an ovenproof dish.
3 In a non-stick wok, lightly dry-fry the garlic over a low heat until soft, taking care not to burn it. Add the cinnamon stick and vegetable stock and bring to the boil.
4 Slake the cornflour with a little cold water and add to the stock, stirring well. Pour the sauce over the pak choi and cover with aluminium foil. Place in the oven for 10 minutes.
5 When cooked, remove the foil. Drizzle the pak choi with soy sauce and serve hot.

Easy ratatouille

Ratatouille is one of my favourite combinations of vegetables. This is a cook-in-one-pot recipe, but to add extra flavour, you could dry-fry the vegetables first in a non-stick pan. If you find green pepper a little bitter, try substituting it with red or yellow pepper, which are sweeter varieties.

1 Cut the green pepper in half lengthways and remove the core and seeds. Cut the pepper into fine strips.
2 Place the chopped tomato in a large saucepan and add the green pepper and the remaining ingredients, except the basil. Bring to the boil and skim off any sediment.
3 Cover and simmer for about 20 minutes or until all the vegetables are tender and most of the liquid has evaporated. If there is too much liquid, reduce this by boiling briskly for a few minutes with the lid removed.
4 Remove the bay leaves, sprinkle the basil over the ratatouille and serve hot.

SERVES 2
PER SERVING:
129 KCAL / 1.4G FAT
PREPARATION TIME:
25 MINUTES
COOKING TIME:
40 MINUTES

1 large green pepper
1 × 400g (14oz) can chopped tomatoes
225g (8oz) courgettes, sliced
2 small aubergines, sliced
2 medium onions, sliced
2 garlic cloves, chopped
2 bay leaves
salt and freshly ground black pepper
a little chopped fresh basil to garnish

Wine glazed beetroot

SERVES 4
PER SERVING:
124 KCAL/0.2G FAT
PREPARATION TIME:
10 MINUTES
COOKING TIME:
50 MINUTES

675g (1 1/2 lb) fresh beetroot
20 baby shallots, peeled
2 teaspoons demerara sugar
150ml (1/4 pint) red wine
salt and freshly ground black
    pepper
1 tablespoon chopped fresh
    chervil

Cooking beetroot can be a messy job, so the tip is to rub away the skins under a running tap, wearing rubber gloves to prevent your hands staining from the strong blood red juices.

1 Wash the beetroot well and place in large saucepan. Cover with water and bring to the boil. Simmer for 30–40 minutes until tender when tested with the point of a knife.
2 Drain the beetroot and rinse with cold water, rubbing the skins away. Trim off the top and bottom and cut into small wedges.
3 In a non-stick frying pan, dry-fry the shallots with the sugar until they start to caramelise.
4 Add the beetroot and wine and simmer gently until most of the liquid has reduced. Season with salt and black pepper and spoon into a serving dish. Sprinkle with chopped fresh chervil.

Ribbon vegetables with ginger and lemongrass

This is a light and delicate way of serving a vegetable selection, and it looks sensational. Prepare the vegetables in advance to allow the ginger and lemongrass flavours to develop.

1 Slice thin strips from the length of the carrots and courgettes with a vegetable peeler, using as much of the vegetables as possible, and place into a large bowl.
2 Add the onion, red peppers, ginger, lemongrass and sesame seeds and mix well. Season with plenty of salt and black pepper.
3 Preheat a non-stick wok and quickly stir-fry the vegetables in batches for 2–3 minutes. Transfer each batch to an ovenproof dish and keep warm in a low oven.
4 Just before serving, drizzle with lemon juice.

SERVES 6
PER SERVING:
49 KCAL/1.1G FAT
PREPARATION TIME:
20 MINUTES
COOKING TIME:
15 MINUTES

3 carrots, peeled
3 courgettes
1 red onion, finely sliced
2 red peppers, seeded and finely sliced
1 × 2.5cm (1in) piece fresh ginger, peeled and finely chopped
1 teaspoon chopped fresh lemongrass
2 teaspoons sesame seeds
salt and freshly ground black pepper
juice of 1 lemon

Broccoli and chickpeas glazed with honey

SERVES 4
PER SERVING:
189 KCAL/4.4G FAT
PREPARATION TIME:
10 MINUTES
COOKING TIME:
20 MINUTES

1 medium onion, finely diced
4 celery sticks, finely chopped
$^1/_2$ teaspoon cumin seeds
150ml ($^1/_4$ pint) vegetable stock
450g (1lb) broccoli florets
1 × 400g (14oz) can chickpeas, drained
1 tablespoon clear runny honey

This unusual combination gives a new dimension to broccoli, resulting in a crisp texture with an almost smoky sweet sauce. As a variation, try using young courgettes or finely shredded cabbage instead of broccoli.

1 In a preheated non-stick wok, dry-fry the onion for 2–3 minutes until soft. Add the celery and the cumin seeds. Cook for a further 1–2 minutes to allow the seeds to lightly toast.
2 Pour the vegetable stock into the wok and add the broccoli florets. Cover and simmer for 6–8 minutes until the broccoli is just cooked.
3 Add the chickpeas and honey and mix well to heat through. Pile into a warm serving dish.

Honey roast parsnips

Using diluted soy sauce on dry-roasted vegetables prevents them from drying out as well as giving a rich golden colour. Many kinds of different honeys are now available, from lavender to sunflower, so do experiment and find your personal favourite.

1 Preheat the oven to 200C, 400F, Gas Mark 6.
2 Peel the parsnips and remove the tops, using a sharp knife.
3 Place the parsnips in a saucepan with the bouillon powder or stock cube and just cover with water. Bring the water to the boil, and then drain the parsnips through a colander, saving the water for gravy or to use as stock in soups. Place the parsnips in a roasting tray.
4 Dilute the soy sauce with 2 tablespoons of water and paint on the parsnips, using a pastry brush. Place the parsnips in the oven and cook for 20–25 minutes until crisp and golden in colour.
5 Five minutes before serving, drizzle the honey over the parsnips and return to the oven to caramelise.
6 Garnish with parsley and serve.

SERVES 4
PER SERVING:
187 KCAL/2.8G FAT
PREPARATION TIME:
15 MINUTES
COOKING TIME:
30 MINUTES

900g (2lb) baby parsnips
1 tablespoon vegetable bouillon powder or 1 vegetable stock cube
1 tablespoon dark soy sauce
1 tablespoon runny honey
chopped fresh parsley to garnish

Leek and sun-dried tomato risotto cakes

SERVES 4
PER SERVING:
262 KCAL/3.6G FAT
PREPARATION TIME:
10 MINUTES
COOKING TIME:
30 MINUTES

1 large onion, finely chopped

2 garlic cloves, crushed

225g (8oz) risotto rice

600ml (1 pint) vegetable stock

2 leeks, finely chopped

4 sun-dried tomatoes, finely
    chopped

1 tablespoon chopped fresh
    chervil

2 tablespoons plain flour

salt and freshly ground black
    pepper

1 In a non-stick pan dry-fry the onion and garlic until soft.
2 Add the rice, and gradually stir in the stock, a little at a time,
   until most of the stock has been absorbed and the rice is
   cooked.
3 Stir in the chopped leeks, tomatoes, chervil and remaining
   stock. Season with salt and black pepper and allow to cool.
4 Mould the risotto mixture into fish cake shapes, allowing 1
   large or 2 small cakes per person. Use the flour to prevent them
   from sticking to your hands. Shape with a palette knife.
5 Preheat a non-stick frying pan. Dry-fry the risotto cakes for 2–3
   minutes on each side until lightly golden. Serve hot.

Honey and lemon roast vegetables

Oven roasting is one of the healthiest ways of cooking vegetables, as it allows them to retain their full vitamin content which is sometimes lost when boiling. Roasted vegetables can be cooked in advance and reheated as required.

1 Prepare the vegetables by slicing into wedges about 1cm (¹/₂in) thick. Place in a roasting tin and season well with salt and black pepper.
2 Combine the lemon juice, honey, soy sauce and marjoram in a small bowl. Pour over the vegetables and allow the vegetables to marinate for at least 30 minutes, turning occasionally.
3 Preheat the oven to 200C, 400F, Gas Mark 6.
4 Give the vegetables a final mix. Sprinkle with the sesame seeds and place in the oven. Roast for 35–40 minutes until the vegetables are soft and tender with slight charring around the edges.
5 Just before serving, sprinkle with chopped fresh parsley.

SERVES 6
PER SERVING:
92 KCAL/2G FAT
PREPARATION TIME:
15 MINUTES
MARINATING TIME:
30 MINUTES
COOKING TIME:
40 MINUTES

2 medium red onions, peeled
3 medium courgettes
1 aubergine
2 bulbs fennel
3 large carrots, peeled
3 young turnips, peeled
juice of 2 lemons
1 tablespoon clear honey
2 tablespoons light soy sauce
2 tablespoons chopped fresh
    marjoram
1 tablespoon sesame seeds
salt and freshly ground black
    pepper
chopped fresh parsley to garnish

Baked chicory with balsamic vinegar

SERVES 4
PER SERVING:
43 KCAL/0.6G FAT
PREPARATION TIME:
10 MINUTES
COOKING TIME:
25 MINUTES

8 chicory heads
1 long shallot, finely chopped
2 tablespoons balsamic vinegar
1 tablespoon demerara sugar
salt and freshly ground black
    pepper
4 ripe tomatoes, skinned, seeded
    and diced

Chicory is one of those very underestimated vegetables that tends to be grouped with salad ingredients. As well as being shredded in salads it can be cooked as a vegetable. As it is naturally bitter in flavour, it requires sweetening with either a sweet vinegar or honey.

1 Preheat the oven to 200C, 400F, Gas Mark 6.
2 Split the chicory in half lengthways with a sharp knife and arrange in a shallow roasting tray.
3 Cover with the shallot and spoon the vinegar and demerara sugar over. Season well with salt and black pepper and cook in the oven for 15–20 minutes until soft.
4 Remove from the oven and add the diced tomato. Bake again for a further 5 minutes.
5 Serve hot straight from the oven.

Leek, mustard and chive mash

Transform mashed potato with lightly cooked leeks and a bite of coarse grain mustard. These potatoes go well with grilled gammon or fish.

1 Cook the potatoes in plenty of boiling salted water for 20–25 minutes.
2 In a non-stick frying pan, dry-fry the leeks until soft.
3 Drain the potatoes well and mash until smooth. Beat in the fromage frais along with the leeks, mustard and chives.
4 Season well with salt and black pepper and spoon into a warmed serving dish.

SERVES 6
PER SERVING:
258 KCAL/1.6G FAT
PREPARATION TIME:
20 MINUTES
COOKING TIME:
20 MINUTES

900g (2lb) potatoes, peeled
225g (8oz) baby leeks, finely chopped
3 tablespoons low-fat fromage frais
1 tablespoon coarse grain mustard
2 tablespoons finely chopped fresh chives
salt and freshly ground black pepper

Wild rice pilaff

SERVES 6
PER SERVING:
186 KCAL/2.2G FAT
PREPARATION TIME:
10 MINUTES
COOKING TIME:
1 HOUR

1 tablespoon vegetable stock
   powder or 1 vegetable stock
   cube
50g (2oz) wild rice
1 large onion, finely chopped
225g (8oz) long-grain rice
450ml (¾ pint) vegetable stock
6 cardamom pods, crushed and
   seeds removed
2 bay leaves
1 small red chilli, seeded and
   finely chopped
1 clove
1 tablespoon chopped fresh
   chervil

Wild rice is totally different from other rice grains. It has a long, dark, tough husk surrounding the kernel that bursts open when cooked. It can be boiled or steamed and, when cooked, has a chewy texture. It becomes much more palatable when mixed with other grains. This dish can be served as an accompaniment to Indian curries or as a lunch with roasted vegetables.

1 Place the vegetable stock powder or vegetable stock cube in a large saucepan with 900ml (1½ pints) of water and bring to the boil. Add the wild rice and boil for 40 minutes or until tender. Drain and set aside.
2 In a non-stick frying pan, dry-fry the onion until soft. Add the long grain rice, stir in the stock and add the cardamom seeds, bay leaves and chilli. Place the clove on top so that it is easy to retrieve later. Cover and simmer for about 20 minutes until all the stock is absorbed and the rice is cooked.
3 Remove the clove, add the drained wild rice to the pan and mix well.
4 Just before serving, stir in the chervil.
5 Serve on a warmed serving plate or, alternatively, press the rice into small moulds or empty yogurt pots and turn out onto individual plates.

Delmonico potatoes

Potatoes cooked in milk are a great accompaniment to grilled or roasted foods that require a sauce or a little extra moisture. You can use sweet potatoes as an alternative or even cook Jerusalem artichokes in the same way.

1 Preheat the oven to 200C, 400F, Gas Mark 6.
2 Wash, peel and then rewash the potatoes and cut into 5mm (¼in) dice. Place in the bottom of an earthenware dish. Add the onion and season well with sea salt and black pepper.
3 Place the milk into a saucepan and add the bay leaf and garlic. Heat until the milk is boiling, then pour onto the potatoes.
4 Bake the potatoes in the oven for 30–40 minutes. Remove from the oven and sprinkle with the breadcrumbs and parsley, then return to the oven for a further 10–15 minutes until golden brown.

SERVES 4
PER SERVING:
185 KCAL/0.8G FAT
PREPARATION TIME:
20 MINUTES
COOKING TIME:
55 MINUTES

450g (1lb) potatoes
1 medium onion, finely diced
600ml (1 pint) skimmed milk
1 bay leaf
1 garlic clove, crushed
50g (2oz) fresh breadcrumbs
1 tablespoon chopped fresh
    parsley
sea salt and freshly ground black
    pepper

Minted saffron couscous

SERVES 4
PER SERVING:
118 KCAL/1G FAT
PREPARATION TIME:
10 MINUTES
COOKING TIME:
10 MINUTES

400ml (14fl oz) vegetable stock
$\frac{1}{4}$ teaspoon ground cumin
$\frac{1}{4}$ teaspoon paprika
$\frac{1}{4}$ teaspoon ground coriander
good pinch of saffron
175g (6oz) couscous
4 tomatoes
salt and freshly ground black
 pepper
juice of $\frac{1}{2}$ a lemon
a few mint leaves to garnish

Couscous is fine grains of semolina rolled in flour. Most couscous in the supermarkets has been precooked and just requires soaking in order to reconstitute it. Saffron adds a luxury touch to this dish, making it a wonderful accompaniment to any main course in place of potatoes. You can make the couscous in advance and then reheat it by either steaming over boiling water for 2 minutes or microwaving on full power for 1 minute.

1 In a saucepan, bring the stock to the boil. Add the cumin, paprika, coriander and saffron and then the couscous, stir well, and cover with a lid for 1 minute.
2 Blanch the tomatoes in boiling water for just 10 seconds and then immediately submerge in cold water and remove the skins.
3 Remove the lid from the couscous and fluff up the couscous, using a fork to separate the grains, and then cover again.
4 Cut the tomatoes in half. Place them in the cold water and remove the seeds, then rinse the tomatoes. Chop into small dice and add to the couscous.
5 Season with salt and black pepper and spoon into a warmed serving dish. Drizzle with lemon juice and garnish with fresh mint.

Salads

The secret behind a delicious salad is the care and attention given to the preparation. The choice of salad leaves is endless, with many prepared combinations available in food shops, including oriental leaves and fresh young herbs blended together.

Fresh crisp vegetables make an ideal base for salads, adding colour and bulk, but they do require a complementary dressing – oil free of course. A more recent trend is to serve a hot salad of noodles or pasta dressed with vegetables or fish and meat.

With all these factors in mind, this chapter brings together a range of unusual and different salads that combine many new and traditional flavours.

Beetroot and orange salad

SERVES 4
PER SERVING:
50 KCAL/0.1G FAT

1 little gem lettuce, separated
    into leaves
2 oranges
2 large cooked beetroot, diced
1 tablespoon orange juice
1 teaspoon balsamic vinegar
salt and freshly ground black
    pepper
snipped chives to garnish

1 Arrange the lettuce leaves on 4 small plates.
2 Remove the pith and rind from the oranges and cut the orange
   into segments.
3 Pile the beetroot in the centre of the lettuce and arrange the
   orange segments around it.
4 Place the orange juice in a small bowl, add the vinegar and
   season to taste with salt and black pepper. Spoon over the
   beetroot and garnish with the chives.

Tomato, chicory and orange salad with fresh raspberry dressing

The sweet and sour flavours in this salad make it an ideal accompaniment to barbecued meats or fish. You can make the salad in advance and chill until required.

1 Cut the tomatoes into dice and place in a mixing bowl. Finely shred the chicory and add to the bowl.

2 Cut the segments from the oranges and then cut each segment into 3 pieces. Add to the bowl, then add the spring onions and mix well.

3 Make the dressing by mashing the raspberries in a small bowl with a fork. Add the remaining ingredients, then pass through a sieve to remove the raspberry seeds. Pour over the salad and toss through.

SERVES 6
PER SERVING:
59 KCAL/0.4G FAT
PREPARATION TIME:
5 MINUTES
COOKING TIME:
15 MINUTES

450g (1lb) firm ripe tomatoes
2 heads chicory
4 oranges
4 spring onions, finely chopped

for the dressing
50g (2oz) fresh raspberries
4 tablespoons orange juice
1 tablespoon balsamic vinegar
a few pink peppercorns, crushed
sea salt to taste

Tarragon and mustard potato salad

SERVES 8
PER SERVING:
77 KCAL/0.4G FAT
PREPARATION TIME:
20 MINUTES
COOKING TIME:
20 MINUTES

675g (1½lb) new potatoes,
     washed and scraped
175g (6oz) virtually fat free
     Normandy fromage frais
2 tablespoons tarragon vinegar
1 small red onion, finely
     chopped
¼ teaspoon ground turmeric
1 tablespoon coarse grain
     mustard
pinch of sea salt
freshly ground black pepper
2–3 sprigs tarragon to garnish

The classic potato salad, made with real mayonnaise, is high in fat. This lighter yet flavoursome alternative uses simple ingredients that are free from the additives often found in readymade products.

1 Cook the potatoes in plenty of salted boiling water until just cooked. Drain through a colander.
2 In a large bowl, whisk together the fromage frais, vinegar, onion, turmeric and mustard and season to taste with salt and black pepper.
3 Add the potatoes and mix until well coated with the dressing.
4 Pull the tarragon leaves from the stem and scatter over the potatoes. Transfer to a serving dish. Serve hot or cold.

Mixed beans with balsamic vinegar and lime

This simple salad is low in fat and calories yet full of flavour.
Making it a day in advance allows the dressing to coat the beans
and results in a much stronger, flavoursome salad.

1 Rinse the canned beans and drain well. Mix with the cooked
   beans.
2 Combine all the dressing ingredients and mix with the beans.
3 Line a serving dish with crisp green lettuce leaves and spoon
   the salad on top.

SERVES 6
PER SERVING:
214 KCAL/1.7G FAT
PREPARATION TIME:
20 MINUTES
COOKING TIME:
10 MINUTES

1 × 450g (14oz) can pinto
   beans
1 × 450g (14oz) can cannellini
   beans
225g (8oz) fine green beans,
   cooked
225g (8oz) baby broad beans,
   cooked
green lettuce leaves to serve

for the dressing
1 red onion, finely chopped
2 tablespoons balsamic vinegar
zest and juice of 1 fresh lime
1 teaspoon coarse grain
   mustard
1 tablespoon chopped fresh
   chives

Warm scallop salad

SERVES 4
PER SERVING:
135 KCAL / 2.9G FAT
PREPARATION TIME:
25 MINUTES
COOKING TIME:
20 MINUTES

2 rashers lean back bacon
$\frac{1}{2}$ slice white bread
2 tomatoes, diced
1 × 5cm (2in) piece cucumber,
    diced
salad leaves
16 fresh scallops
6 spring onions
salt and freshly ground black
    pepper

for the dressing
1 teaspoon French mustard
3 tablespoons lemon juice
1 tablespoon orange juice
1 tablespoon wine vinegar
salt and freshly ground black
    pepper

Scallops are a member of the mollusc family and eaten very much as a delicacy. The attractive fan-shaped shell can be used as a serving dish to present many seafood dishes. The shell contains a small nugget of white meat with an orange coral attached at the side. The scallop is removed from the shell and washed thoroughly. Scallops need very little cooking, as overcooking can cause them to become tough and rubbery in texture.

1 Trim any fat from the bacon. Grill the bacon well and chop into small pieces.
2 Toast the bread on both sides and cut into small squares.
3 Mix the tomato and cucumber with the salad leaves and arrange on a serving plate.
4 Rinse the scallops well under a cold water tap and dry on a piece of kitchen paper.
5 Preheat a non-stick frying pan. Add the scallops and spring onions and dry-fry, seasoning well with salt and black pepper. Cook for 2–3 minutes until they start to firm up but are still lightly cooked in the centre. Take care not to overcook them.
6 Arrange the scallops, bacon pieces and toasted bread on top of the salad.
7 Place all the dressing ingredients into a jam jar with a tight-fitting lid and shake vigorously until well combined. Pour over the salad and serve immediately.

Chicken caesar salad

Traditionally, caesar salad is served with an exceptionally high fat dressing and deep-fried croutons. In this low-fat version, the chicken brings taste and texture and the low-fat dressing tastes delicious. Vegetarians can substitute dry-fried courgettes for the chicken.

1 Preheat a non-stick frying pan. Slice the chicken into strips and season well. Place in the pan and cook briskly, turning regularly, for 8–10 minutes.
2 Shred the lettuce and place in a large bowl. Add the spring onions and cucumber, mix well and arrange on a serving dish.
3 Combine the dressing ingredients in a small bowl. Place the cooked chicken on the salad and drizzle the dressing over.

SERVES 4
PER SERVING:
138 KCAL/5.8G FAT
PREPARATION TIME:
10 MINUTES
COOKING TIME:
15 MINUTES

4 boneless chicken breasts
1 romaine or iceberg lettuce
8 spring onions, sliced
$\frac{1}{2}$ cucumber, cut into batons

for the dressing
4 tablespoons low-fat salad dressing
1 tablespoon virtually fat free fromage frais
1 garlic clove, crushed
fresh lemon juice to taste
salt and freshly ground black pepper

Mexican salad

This colourful crunchy salad can be made in advance and chilled until required. Use fruit vinegar to give a sweet and sour contrast to the peppers, and pep up with as much chilli as you wish!

1 Drain and rinse the kidney beans and sweetcorn and place in a large mixing bowl. Add the remaining ingredients and mix well to combine the flavours.
2 In a small bowl, whisk together the dressing ingredients and season to taste. Pour over the salad and toss through.
3 Spoon into a serving dish and chill until required.

SERVES 8
PER SERVING:
76 KCAL/0.7G FAT
PREPARATION TIME:
30 MINUTES
COOKING TIME:
10 MINUTES

1 × 400g (14oz) can red kidney beans
225g (8oz) can sweetcorn
1 red onion, finely chopped
1 red pepper, seeded and diced
1 yellow pepper, seeded and diced
1 green pepper, seeded and diced
1 small red chilli, seeded and finely chopped
4 ripe tomatoes, skinned, seeded and diced

for the dressing
2 tablespoons Womersley fruit vinegar (raspberry or bilberry)
2 tablespoons lemon juice
2 tablespoons tomato juice
salt and freshly ground black pepper

Tofu, lemon and chive salad

SERVES 2
PER SERVING:
197 KCAL/5G FAT
PREPARATION TIME:
5 MINUTES
COOKING TIME:
10 MINUTES

4 tablespoons low-fat dressing

1 teaspoon wholegrain mustard

juice of 2 lemons

$\frac{1}{2}$ fresh lettuce

1 tablespoon vegetable oil

1 packet (280g) Cauldron Foods Original Tofu cut into 2.5cm (1in) dice

2 tablespoons chopped fresh chives

salt and freshly ground black pepper

Tofu is a high-protein food derived from the white soybean. The soybeans are fermented and the soaked beans are then puréed and strained to extract the white milk-like liquid. This is then mixed with a setting agent to produce a curd-like texture. On its own, tofu is very bland but soon picks up other flavours, making it ideal for use in salads and stir-fries.

1 Mix the low-fat dressing with the mustard, lemon juice, and season with salt and pepper.
2 Arrange the lettuce on 2 plates.
3 Heat the oil in a non-stick pan, add the tofu and cook until golden. Remove with a slotted spoon and drain on kitchen paper.
4 Add the tofu and chives to the dressing, mix and leave to absorb the flavours for a couple of minutes.
5 Spoon the tofu and dressing over the lettuce and serve while still warm.

Smoked mackerel
salad niçoise

The classic French niçoise salad contains olives and anchovies in an oil-rich dressing. This low-fat alternative, while quite different, offers an interesting combination with good strong flavours.

1 Cook the beans in salted boiling water until tender. Drain and refresh under cold running water.
2 Slice the beans in half lengthways and place in a large bowl with the new potatoes.
3 Slice the tomatoes in half and add to the bowl.
4 Remove the skin from the mackerel and flake the mackerel into bite-size pieces, checking for any bones. Add to the salad along with the red onion and grapes.
5 Combine the dressing ingredients in a bowl. Pour over the salad.
6 Arrange a few salad leaves on a serving plate and spoon the salad over. Serve with crusty bread.

SERVES 4
PER SERVING:
426 KCAL/ 27G FAT
PREPARATION TIME:
20 MINUTES
COOKING TIME:
20 MINUTES

115g (4oz) fine green beans
450g (1lb) new potatoes, cooked and sliced
20 cherry tomatoes
350g (12oz) smoked mackerel fillets
1 red onion, finely chopped
20 small black seedless grapes
salad leaves to garnish

for the dressing
2 tablespoons lemon juice
1 tablespoon balsamic vinegar
1 tablespoon chopped fresh chives
1 teaspoon Dijon mustard
salt and freshly ground black pepper

Herby pasta salad with barbecued peppers

Transform a plain herb pasta salad with the addition of barbecued sweet peppers. The salad can be made in advance, leaving you to add the peppers as the final touch.

1 Boil the pasta in a large pan of water together with the stock cubes for added flavour.
2 Place the peppers directly on the barbecue rack or under a preheated hot grill and cook for 5–6 minutes, until they start to blister and change colour.
3 When the pasta is cooked, drain through a colander and transfer to a large mixing bowl. Add the cooked peppers to the pasta.
4 In a separate bowl mix together the remaining ingredients except the paprika, season with salt and black pepper and add to the pasta. Stir well to combine all the ingredients, pour into a serving dish and sprinkle with smoked paprika.
5 Serve the salad hot or cold.

SERVES 6
PER SERVING:
250 KCAL/2.2G FAT
PREPARATION TIME:
15 MINUTES
COOKING TIME:
35 MINUTES

350g (12oz) pasta, e.g. penne or farfalle
2 vegetable stock cubes
2 red peppers, seeded and cut into large pieces
2 yellow peppers, seeded and cut into large pieces
150g (5oz) virtually fat free Normandy fromage frais
2 teaspoons coarse grain mustard
1 tablespoon chopped fresh chives
1 tablespoon chopped fresh chervil
salt and freshly ground black pepper
good pinch of ground smoked paprika

Couscous Salad

SERVES 4
PER SERVING:
114 KCAL/1.3G FAT

400ml (14fl oz) vegetable stock
1/4 teaspoon ground cumin
1/4 teaspoon paprika
1/4 teaspoon ground coriander
175g (6oz) couscous
2 salad tomatoes, diced
1 × 7.5cm (3in) piece cucumber,
    peeled and diced
1 red pepper, finely diced
2 spring onions, finely chopped
2 tablespoons chopped fresh
    mint
2 tablespoons chopped fresh
    parsley
juice of 1/2 lemon
salt and freshly ground black
    pepper

Couscous has become very popular as a base for a salad, and this recipe is ideal as a packed lunch or to accompany a summer barbecue.

1 In a saucepan, bring the stock to the boil, add the spices and couscous and stir well. Remove from the heat and cover with a lid for 1 minute.
2 Fluff the couscous with a fork and pour into a large bowl. Mix in the vegetables and herbs and season to taste.
3 Just before serving drizzle with lemon juice. Serve hot or cold.

Hot salad noodles

Noodles have been part of the Chinese staple diet for more than 2000 years – the ultimate oriental fast food! Soba noodles are made using a blend of wheat flour and buckwheat flour and natural ingredients free from colourings and artificial flavourings. They have a distinctive nutty flavour, rather like that of wholemeal pasta.

1 Place the vegetables and chopped coriander in a large non-metallic mixing bowl.
2 Cook the noodles with the stock cube in plenty of boiling water, drain and add to the vegetables. Add the soy sauce and lemon juice and toss well.
3 Reheat either in a microwave on full power for 2 minutes or in a steamer over boiling water for 2 minutes.
4 Garnish with fresh coriander and serve hot.

SERVES 4
PER SERVING:
270 KCAL/4.4G FAT
PREPARATION TIME:
20 MINUTES
COOKING TIME:
10 MINUTES

1 small red onion, finely sliced
1 red pepper, seeded and finely sliced
1 fresh red chilli, seeded and finely chopped
½ cucumber, peeled and cut into matchsticks
4 ripe tomatoes, skinned, seeded and diced
115g (4oz) mange tout, cut into thin strips
2 tablespoons chopped fresh coriander
225g (8oz) soba noodles
1 vegetable stock cube
2 tablespoons light soy sauce
juice of 1 lemon
chopped fresh coriander to garnish

Puddings

In this chapter, you'll find a tempting selection of hot puddings and mouthwatering creamy desserts suitable for all the family.

Many traditional desserts are high in sugar and fat and, subsequently, high in calories. A low-fat dessert needs to feel luxurious on the tongue as well as flavoursome, which means you may need to adjust your menu planning by serving a lower calorie main meal to compensate for the indulgence later.

Portion control is essential, so use shallow dishes for hot puddings and, when possible, serve cold desserts in individual glasses.

Fruity desserts are always welcome to complete a meal. Make good use of seasonal fresh fruits, and keep some frozen berries reserved in the freezer, ready to create quick forest fruit soufflés – this recipe is a real winner, so do give it a try.

Queen of puddings

SERVES 4
PER SERVING:
289 KCAL/3G FAT
PREPARATION TIME:
10 MINUTES
COOKING TIME:
30 MINUTES

300ml (1/2 pint) skimmed milk

1 teaspoon vanilla extract

2 egg yolks

115g (4oz) caster sugar

75g (3oz) fresh white
  breadcrumbs

4 tablespoons dark plum jam

3 egg whites

There are many variations of this traditional pudding, some using cake crumbs in the base and a thick layer of marmalade in the centre. Here, the vanilla adds richness to the base, which, together with the dark plum jam, makes it a dessert to remember.

1 Preheat the oven to 180C, 350F, Gas Mark 4.
2 Heat the milk and vanilla extract in a small saucepan until boiling.
3 Beat the egg yolks with half the caster sugar, then pour the milk over, whisking to combine.
4 Divide the breadcrumbs between 4 individual ramekin dishes and pour the custard mixture over the breadcrumbs. Transfer to the oven and bake for 20 minutes or until set.
5 Remove from the oven and spread with the jam.
6 Whisk the egg whites to stiff peaks, then continue whisking as you add the remaining sugar very slowly, a teaspoon at a time. Place the mixture in a piping bag with a star nozzle and pipe the mixture over the jam to form a pyramid shape.
7 Return the puddings to the oven for 10 minutes to allow the meringue to crisp.
8 Serve hot or cold with virtually fat free Normandy fromage frais.

Apple and cinnamon charlotte

Traditionally, apple charlotte is made using bread thickly buttered and then baked until crisp. The sponge fingers in this recipe result in a softer texture, fewer calories and much less fat. If you wish, you can add a few redcurrants to the apple mixture for added flavour and colour.

1 In a large saucepan dissolve the sugar and cinnamon in the apple juice over a low heat. Add the apples and simmer gently for 4–5 minutes until tender.
2 Remove the apples, using a slotted spoon, and reserve. Boil the apple liquid until it has reduced by half.
3 Line a 1 litre (2 pint) pudding basin with clear food wrap, leaving an overhang around the basin.
4 Soak the sponge fingers in the reduced syrup to soften them. Line the base and sides of the basin with the sponge fingers. Spoon in the cooked apples and press down. Cover with the remaining sponge fingers and drizzle the syrup over.
5 Fold the overhanging food wrap over and place a small tea plate on the top. Place a weight on top and refrigerate for 2 hours.
6 To serve, place an upturned serving plate over the top of the basin and turn the pudding out. Carefully remove the food wrap.
7 Serve with the redcurrants and virtually fat-free fromage frais.

SERVES 8
PER SERVING:
122 KCAL/0.2G FAT
PREPARATION TIME:
25 MINUTES
COOKING TIME:
15 MINUTES
COOLING TIME:
2 HOURS

115g (4oz) soft light brown sugar
1 teaspoon ground cinnamon
300ml ($\frac{1}{2}$ pint) fresh apple juice
1.5kg (3lb) cooking apples, peeled, cored and thinly sliced
24 sponge fingers
115g (4oz) redcurrants

Barbecued fresh fruit with cinnamon and marsala wine syrup

When barbecuing fruit, choose firm fruits that will hold together after being exposed to high temperatures. Dusting the fruits with icing sugar while they are cooking adds a caramelised flavour. Top up the bowl with soft fruit to add colour and contrasting flavours.

1 Place all the syrup ingredients in a small saucepan and bring to the boil. Pour into a large bowl.
2 To prepare the fruit, cut the pineapple into thick pieces. Slice the bananas lengthways. Cut the peaches and pears in half and remove the stones and cores. Hull the strawberries.
3 Place the fruit on a hot barbecue or under a hot grill and turn regularly until slightly softened.
4 Dust the fruit with icing sugar and place in the bowl containing the cinnamon syrup.
5 Serve hot with low-fat fromage frais.

SERVES 6
PER SERVING:
230 KCAL/0.4G FAT
PREPARATION TIME:
20 MINUTES
COOKING TIME:
10 MINUTES

1 medium pineapple
3 bananas
3 firm peaches
3 firm pears
12 large strawberries
icing sugar to dust

for the syrup
150ml ($\frac{1}{4}$ pint) dry Marsala wine
115g (4oz) sugar
150ml ($\frac{1}{4}$ pint) water
1 stick cinnamon

Rhubarb and ginger marble pudding

SERVES 6
PER SERVING:
201 KCAL/1.4G FAT
PREPARATION TIME:
20 MINUTES
COOKING TIME:
25 MINUTES

225g (8oz) young rhubarb
3 tablespoons ginger preserve
115g (4oz) Quark low-fat soft
   cheese
115g (4oz) caster sugar
1 egg, separated
150g (5oz) plain flour
2 teaspoons baking powder
3 tablespoons skimmed milk
2 teaspoons ground ginger

Young rhubarb is much more tender and less fibrous than the thicker pieces. The redness of the fruit determines the sweetness. The greener it is, the more sour the flavour. Since rhubarb withers and becomes rubbery, use only very fresh rhubarb.

1 Preheat the oven to 180C, 350F, Gas Mark 4.
2 Wash the rhubarb well and cut into small pieces. Place in a saucepan and add the ginger preserve. Cook for 5–6 minutes over a low heat until the rhubarb starts to soften. Remove and allow to cool.
3 Beat together the Quark, sugar and egg yolk until smooth.
4 Sift the flour and baking powder and gradually stir into the Quark mixture alternately with the milk. Add the ground ginger and beat well.
5 Whisk the egg white until stiff and fold into the mixture.
6 Pour the mixture into a lightly greased ovenproof dish. Dot the rhubarb mixture over the top and swirl into the sponge.
7 Place in the oven for 20–25 minutes until golden brown.
8 Serve with low-fat custard or fromage frais.

Peaches poached in cardamom syrup

White flesh peaches are often not quite so easy to come by, although many supermarkets do have them. They have a much sweeter fruity flavour than regular peaches and hold their shape much better when cooked. However, regular peaches or nectarines can be used as a substitute.

1 Preheat the oven to 190C, 375F, Gas Mark 5.
2 Combine the wine, lime zest, sugar, ginger and cardamom in a saucepan and bring to the boil.
3 Cut each peach in half and remove the stones. Place, face down, in an ovenproof dish and pour the hot syrup over the top. Cover with foil and bake in the oven for 30–35 minutes until soft.
4 Allow to cool in the refrigerator until required.
5 Dust with cinnamon and serve chilled with 0% fat Greek yogurt.

SERVES 4
PER SERVING:
84 KCAL/0.2G FAT
PREPARATION TIME:
5 MINUTES
COOKING TIME:
30 MINUTES

300ml ($^{1}/_{2}$ pint) sweet white wine
zest of 1 lime
2 teaspoons caster sugar
$^{1}/_{2}$ teaspoon finely chopped ginger
8 cardamom pods, crushed and seeds removed
4 large white flesh peaches
cinnamon to dust

Exotic fresh fruit salad with ginger and lime

SERVES 4
PER SERVING:
92 KCAL/0.4G FAT
PREPARATION TIME:
10 MINUTES
COOKING TIME:
30 MINUTES

1 medium pineapple
1 papaya
2 passion fruit
2 oranges
zest and juice of 2 limes
1 × 2.5cm (1in) piece fresh
  ginger, peeled and finely
  chopped
sugar to taste

Fruit salad with a difference! Make in advance to allow the flavours to develop and become more concentrated. This dessert will keep overnight.

1 Remove the outer skin from the pineapple with a sharp knife, cut the flesh into small pieces and place in a large bowl.
2 Cut the papaya in half and scoop out the seeds. Peel away the outer skin with a knife, cut the flesh into pieces and add to the bowl.
3 Cut the passion fruit in half, scoop out the seeds with a teaspoon and add to the bowl. Discard the outer skins.
4 Peel the oranges, removing all the pith. Cut the orange into segments and add to the bowl. Add the lime juice, zest and the ginger. Stir well and season to taste with sugar. Chill until ready to serve.

Mulled fruit compote

Mulled wine is achieved by warming wine slowly with a selection of aromatic spices. The same principle can be applied to fruit, resulting in a soft, rich, fruity dessert.

1 Prepare the fruits by removing the peel and core from the apples and the centre stones from the plums. Top and tail the gooseberries. Chop the larger fruits into bite-size pieces.
2 Place the fruits in a medium saucepan and add the remaining ingredients. Cook gently over a low heat, stirring well, for 5 minutes until the fruits start to soften.
3 Cover with a tight-fitting lid and remove from the heat. Allow to stand for 5 minutes.
4 Remove the cinnamon stick and clove before serving.
5 Serve warm with 0% fat Greek yogurt.

SERVES 4
PER SERVING:
103 KCAL/0.3G FAT
PREPARATION TIME:
20 MINUTES
COOKING TIME:
10 MINUTES

450g (1lb) assorted fruits
    (cooking apples, plums,
    rhubarb, gooseberries)
2 tablespoons raisins
zest and juice of 2 oranges
1 cinnamon stick
1 whole clove
1 tablespoon soft brown sugar

Cranberry, passion fruit and raspberry towers

SERVES 4
PER SERVING:
72 KCAL/0.2G FAT
PREPARATION TIME:
10 MINUTES
COOKING TIME:
20 MINUTES

600ml (1 pint) pure cranberry juice
2 large passion fruit, pulp only removed
50g (2oz) caster sugar
1 sachet vegi-gel
225g (8oz) raspberries
extra raspberries to decorate
icing sugar to dust

This easy to prepare dessert can be dressed up with fresh fruit or served on its own. As an alternative, try substituting the orange with kiwi fruit or crushed pineapple.

1 In a saucepan, heat the cranberry juice, passion fruit, sugar and vegi-gel until the mixture starts to thicken, then remove from heat.

2 Spoon a small amount into 4 individual pudding moulds or tea cups. Cover with a few raspberries then add another layer of cranberry mixture. Repeat until the moulds are full, cover with clear food wrap and refrigerate until set.

3 When the mixture is set, dip the moulds briefly in boiling water then turn out onto a serving plate.

4 Decorate with raspberries and dust with a little icing sugar.

Quick forest fruit soufflés

A simple but spectacular hot dessert with a very light texture and a definite favourite of mine. If you have extra fruit, combine it with a little sweet sherry and sugar to make a fruit compote to serve alongside the soufflés.

1 Preheat the oven to 200C, 400F, Gas Mark 6.
2 Lightly grease 4 × 50g (4 × 2oz) ramekins with a little margarine, then dust lightly with caster sugar and set aside.
3 Place the fruit and the caster sugar in a small saucepan and simmer gently for 10–15 minutes until the fruit has reduced to a thick paste. Pour into a bowl and allow to cool.
4 In a clean bowl, whisk the egg whites on full speed, adding only a pinch of caster sugar initially. Once the whites start to peak, gradually add the remaining sugar, 1 dessertspoon at a time, allowing 10 seconds between each addition. Continue whisking until all the sugar is added.
5 Place a dessertspoon of fruit into the bottom of each ramekin.
6 Gently fold the egg whites into the remaining fruit purée. Pile into the ramekins, smoothing the top and sides with a palette knife. The mixture should stand above the dishes.
7 Place the ramekins in the oven and bake for 5–6 minutes.
8 Once cooked, serve the soufflés immediately, as they will start to collapse as soon as they come out of the oven.

SERVES 4
PER SERVING:
187 KCAL/0.1G FAT
PREPARATION TIME:
20 MINUTES
COOKING TIME:
10 MINUTES

225g (8oz) frozen forest fruits
    (blackberries, raspberries,
    etc.)
25g (1oz) caster sugar

for the meringue
3 egg whites
150g (5oz) caster sugar
fresh fruit to decorate

Orange and grand marnier tiramisu

This is a delicious alternative to the traditional Italian coffee and chocolate dessert. It looks stunning layered in individual glasses or just as impressive in a glass dish as a centrepiece. Although this is a very quick and easy dessert to prepare, you can prepare the oranges in advance if you wish and place in the refrigerator until required.

1 Prepare the oranges by slicing off the top and bottom of each one. Remove the peel and pith with a sharp knife, cutting around the oranges like a barrel (reserve the 4 pieces of peel). Using a sharp knife, segment the oranges into a bowl, cutting in between the thin membrane to give perfect orange segments. Squeeze any juice from the centre core into a separate bowl. Add the fresh orange juice and the Grand Marnier or orange liqueur to the bowl.
2 Start to layer the dessert into 4 individual glasses by soaking each sponge finger in the orange liquid briefly and then placing in the glasses, adding a spoonful of yogurt and a few orange segments between each layer, and finishing with a layer of yogurt. Refrigerate until ready to serve.
3 Place the reserved orange peel, orange side down, on a chopping board. Shave away the pith with a sharp knife. Cut each piece of peel into very thin strips, blanch in boiling water for 5 minutes, drain and allow to cool.
4 Just before serving, dust each tiramisu with cocoa powder and decorate with a pinch of orange zest.

SERVES 4
PER SERVING:
203 KCAL / 1.1G FAT
PREPARATION TIME:
15 MINUTES
COOKING TIME:
10 MINUTES

4 large oranges
300ml (½ pint) fresh orange juice
2 tablespoons Grand Marnier or orange liqueur
16 sponge finger biscuits
600ml (1 pint) Total 0% Greek yogurt
1 teaspoon cocoa powder to dust

Lemon syllabub

SERVES 4
PER SERVING:
105 KCAL/0.8G FAT
PREPARATION TIME:
20 MINUTES
COOKING TIME:
15 MINUTES

2 lemons

1 tablespoon caster sugar

1 tablespoon custard powder

250ml (8fl oz) skimmed milk

300g (11oz) low-fat Greek
yogurt

2 egg whites

chopped fresh mint and 4 lemon
slices to decorate

In the old English version of this dessert, thick double cream would be churned together with sour wine or fruit juice. This low-fat version is simply delicious and a perfect way to use up leftover low-fat custard.

1 Zest the lemons on a fine grater into a small bowl. Squeeze the juice from the lemons into the bowl and mix with the sugar and custard powder to form a smooth paste.

2 Heat the milk in a saucepan until boiling, pour onto the custard powder and whisk well. Return to the pan and cook until the mixture starts to thicken. Remove from the heat, cover with food wrap and allow to cool.

3 Once cold, beat the yogurt into the custard mixture and sweeten to taste with a little sugar.

4 Whisk the egg whites to stiff peaks and gently fold into the mixture. Spoon into individual glasses and decorate each with chopped mint and a lemon slice.

Pineapple and papaya salad with lime and ginger yogurt

This makes a refreshing finish to a hot and spicy meal. You can substitute any fresh fruits, but try to get a mixture of flavours and textures. The fruits can be prepared in advance, but the yogurt should be mixed just before serving as it may separate if allowed to stand. Once the seeds have been removed from the vanilla pod, the pod can be stored in a sealed jar of caster sugar, and the sugar will take on the flavour.

1 Prepare the pineapple by slicing off the top and bottom with a sharp knife. Stand the fruit upright and cut away the skin from top to bottom, slicing around it to leave a barrel-like shape. Cut the pineapple in half and then into slices.
2 Using a sharp knife, cut away the skin from the papaya, then slice the papaya in half lengthways. Remove the black seeds from the centre and discard. Cut the fruit into long slices and arrange with the pineapple slices in alternate layers on a serving plate.
3 Place the sesame seeds (if using) in a non-stick frying pan and lightly toast over a low heat until browned, then scatter them over the pineapple and papaya slices.
4 Split the vanilla pod down the centre with a sharp knife. Scrape out the seeds from the inside with the edge of the knife and place in a bowl.
5 Add the yogurt, lime juice, ginger and sugar to taste. Mix well and serve alongside the fruit salad.

SERVES 4
PER SERVING:
115 KCAL/4G FAT
PREPARATION TIME:
20 MINUTES
COOKING TIME:
5 MINUTES

1 large ripe pineapple
2 ripe papaya
2 tablespoons sesame seeds (optional)
1 vanilla pod
300ml (½ pint) low-fat natural yogurt
zest and juice of 1 lime
1 × 2.5cm (1 in) piece fresh ginger, skinned and finely chopped
caster sugar to taste

Elderflower and blueberry sorbet

1 In a saucepan, dissolve the sugar in 300ml (½ pint) water and bring to the boil. Add the blueberries and elderflower cordial. Pour into a food processor and blend until smooth.

2 Pour the mixture into a shallow freezer container and allow to cool, then freeze for about 2 hours or until it is mushy.

3 Whisk the egg white until stiff. Remove the blueberry mixture from the freezer and break up with a fork. Fold the egg white into the mixture and re-freeze for 3 hours until firm.

4 Twenty minutes before serving, transfer the sorbet to the refrigerator to enable it to soften slightly, making it easier to serve. Decorate with extra blueberries.

See photograph on page 242.

SERVES 4
PER SERVING:
133 KCAL/0.1G FAT
PREPARATION TIME:
5 MINUTES
COOKING TIME:10 MINUTES
FREEZING TIME: 5 HOURS

115g (4oz) demerara sugar
350g (12oz) fresh blueberries
150ml (¼ pint) elderflower cordial
1 egg white
extra blueberries to decorate

Damson and apple fool

1 Wash the damsons and remove the stalks. Place the damsons in a saucepan.

2 Peel, core and slice the apples and add to the saucepan.

3 Cook the damsons and apples over a low heat until soft, stirring from time to time to prevent sticking.

4 Pass the fruit through a sieve to remove the stones, then return the fruit to the saucepan. Add sugar or artificial sweetener to taste and place over a low heat to reduce to a thick purée.

5 Add the Calvados and allow to cool.

6 Add the Quark to the fruit purée and beat to a smooth consistency.

7 Whisk the egg whites until they stand in stiff peaks. Gently fold into the fruit purée and sweeten to taste.

8 Spoon into individual glasses and decorate with the fresh mint.

See photograph on page 242.

SERVES 4
PER SERVING:
106 KCAL/0.1G FAT
PREPARATION TIME:
15 MINUTES
COOKING TIME:
20 MINUTES

225g (8oz) damson plums
225g (8oz) eating apples
sugar or artificial sweetener to taste
2 tablespoons Calvados brandy
225g (8oz) Quark low-fat cheese
2 egg whites
fresh mint to decorate

Raspberry tofu ice

SERVES 4
PER SERVING:
158 KCAL/4.9G FAT
PREPARATION TIME:
40 MINUTES
FREEZING TIME:
6–7 HOURS

225g (8oz) tofu
300ml (½ pint) low-fat yogurt
   (suitable for freezing)
50g (2oz) vanilla-flavoured
   caster sugar
115g (4oz) fresh raspberries
1 egg white

1 Prepare a 450g (1 pint) loaf tin by greasing with the smallest amount of vegetable oil, then line with clear food wrap, pushing down into the corners and leaving an excess on top.

2 Drain the tofu in a sieve and then place in a food processor or liquidiser and blend until smooth. Add the yogurt and half of the sugar and blend again. Pour into a bowl and stir in the raspberries. Transfer to the freezer container and freeze for about 1 hour until it starts to set.

3 When the tofu mixture is set, remove from the freezer, place in a large bowl and mash with a fork until lump free.

4 Whisk the egg white with the remaining sugar until stiff. Fold the egg white into the tofu mixture and return to the freezer for approximately 4–5 hours until firm.

5 Half an hour before serving, transfer the tofu ice from the freezer to the refrigerator.

6 Just before serving, slice into portions, using a knife dipped in boiling water.

See photograph on page 242.

Left: *Damson and apple fool*
Below: *Elderflower and blueberry sorbet*
Bottom: *Raspberry tofu ice*

Quick raspberry fool

SERVES 4
PER SERVING:
90 KCAL/0.5G FAT
PREPARATION TIME:
5 MINUTES
COOKING TIME:
20 MINUTES

225g (8oz) fresh raspberries
50g (2oz) caster sugar
2 egg whites
150ml (¼ pint) 0% fat Greek
  yogurt
fresh mint to decorate

You can substitute any fruit for the raspberries. Make sure they are softened sufficiently so that they can be folded into the yogurt and egg white. This dessert can also be served slightly frozen.

1 Gently heat the raspberries with the caster sugar in a saucepan over a low heat until the raspberries start to soften. Remove from the heat and pour into a mixing bowl. Allow to cool.
2 Whisk the egg whites until they form stiff peaks.
3 Gently fold the yogurt into the raspberries and then fold in the egg white.
4 Spoon into individual glasses or dishes and decorate with fresh mint.

Strawberry semi freddo

Semi freddo is a creamy Italian dessert, and its name literally means 'half cold'. Traditionally it is made using large quantities of double cream to prevent hard freezing. Strawberries are not as well suited as other soft fruits to freezing, since once they are defrosted they become soggy and watery. However, frozen strawberries work very well in this delicious dessert.

1 Place the sponge fingers into a food processor and reduce to fine crumbs. Alternatively, place the sponge fingers in a plastic in a plastic food bag and crush with a rolling pin.
2 Gently heat the frozen strawberries in a small saucepan over a low heat for 2–3 minutes until soft.
3 Whisk the egg whites until stiff, then gradually fold in the yogurt and icing sugar.
4 Assemble the dessert in layers in a glass serving dish: first, place half the sponge finger crumbs in the dish, sprinkle with a tablespoon of sherry, top with half the strawberries and, finally, half the yogurt mixture. Repeat the layers, reserving a few sponge finger crumbs for decoration.
5 Dust the top with the remaining crumbs, then place in the freezer for 4 hours.
6 Twenty minutes before serving, transfer the dish to the refrigerator in order to make the serving easier.

SERVES 8
PER SERVING:
134 KCAL/1.9G FAT
PREPARATION TIME:
20 MINUTES
COOKING TIME:
15 MINUTES
FREEZING TIME:
4 HOURS

225g (8oz) low-fat sponge fingers
225g (8oz) frozen strawberries
2 egg whites
300ml (1/2 pint) 0% fat Greek yogurt
2 tablespoons icing sugar
2 tablespoons dry sherry

Mandarin and cointreau mousse

SERVES 4
PER SERVING:
80 KCAL/0.1G FAT
PREPARATION TIME:
10 MINUTES
COOKING TIME:
5 MINUTES

1 × 275g (10oz) can mandarin
   segments
2 tablespoons Cointreau
1 sachet vegi-gel
275g (10oz) virtually fat free
   Normandy fromage frais
caster sugar to taste
2 egg whites
fresh fruit to decorate

In this recipe, choose a good quality low-fat fromage frais or yogurt, as these tend to have a richer texture and a less sharp flavour than some. You can make this mousse in advance and store in the refrigerator until ready to serve.

1 Reserve a few mandarin segments and empty the remainder into a saucepan, add the Cointreau and sprinkle the vegi-gel on top. Heat slowly, stirring until the mixture starts to thicken. Pour into a food processor and blend until smooth.
2 Add the fromage frais and a little caster sugar and blend again until combined.
3 Scrape out the mixture into a bowl. Whisk the egg whites until stiff and fold into the mixture.
4 Spoon into individual dishes and decorate with fresh fruit and the reserved mandarin segments.

Fresh pineapple with strawberry and kirsch cream

1 Prepare the pineapple by cutting off the top and bottom. Stand the fruit upright and remove the outer skin by slicing around the fruit from top to bottom to leave a barrel shape. Cut the pineapple into thin slices. Remove the centre core with a small pastry cutter and arrange the pineapple slices on individual serving plates.

2 Reserve a few strawberries for the decoration and place the remainder in a food processor. Add the Kirsch and chop roughly.

3 Pour the strawberries and Kirsch into a bowl, add the yogurt and and mix well.

4 Spoon the mixture over the pineapple slices and decorate with the reserved strawberries. Dust with icing sugar.

SERVES 4
PER SERVING:
63 KCAL/0.2G FAT
PREPARATION TIME:
10 MINUTES
COOKING TIME:
15 MINUTES

1 large ripe pineapple
450g (1lb) fresh ripe
   strawberries
300ml (½ pint) 0% fat Greek
   yogurt
1 tablespoon Kirsch
icing sugar to dust

Grilled peach melba

SERVES 4
PER SERVING:
144 KCAL/0.9G FAT
PREPARATION TIME:
5 MINUTES
COOKING TIME:
10 MINUTES

4 large ripe peaches

2 teaspoons vanilla sugar

450g (1lb) fresh raspberries

50g (2oz) caster sugar

4 scoops virtually fat free vanilla
  ice cream or iced dessert

fresh mint leaves to decorate

A combination of peaches, raspberries and ice cream is what peach melba is all about. Pouring a hot fruit syrup or sauce over ice cream makes a really refreshing dessert. Here, we go one step further by adding pieces of juicy hot fruit, making it a little more substantial.

1 Cut the peaches in half and remove the stones. Place, cut side up, on a baking tray and sprinkle with vanilla sugar.
2 Place the raspberries and sugar in a small saucepan with 2 tablespoons of water and heat over a low heat for 5 minutes.
3 Preheat the grill to medium and place the peaches near the top for 2–3 minutes or until the sugar starts to caramelise.
4 Arrange the peaches on 4 serving plates with a scoop of ice-cream or iced dessert on each plate.
5 Spoon the hot raspberries over the top and decorate with mint leaves.

Saffron rice pudding

Saffron transforms this basic pudding into a rich and colourful dessert which can be enjoyed hot or cold.

1 Place the rice, milk, sugar and saffron in a saucepan. Bring to the boil then reduce the heat to a gentle simmer. Cover and cook for 35–40 minutes, stirring from time to time. Alternatively, place the ingredients in a large bowl, cover with food wrap and microwave on full power for 10 minutes. Stir well and cook for a further 20 minutes. Adjust the consistency with a little extra milk if required.
2 Just before serving add the lemon juice.
3 Serve with a little virtually fat free fromage frais and decorate with chopped fresh mint.

SERVES 6
PER SERVING:
82 KCAL/0.2G FAT
PREPARATION TIME:
5 MINUTES
COOKING TIME:
40 MINUTES

60g (2¼oz) pudding rice
600ml (1 pint) skimmed milk
1 tablespoon caster sugar
good pinch of saffron
juice of ½ lemon
chopped fresh mint to decorate

Rum and raisin crunch

SERVES 4
PER SERVING:
175 KCAL/1.6G FAT
PREPARATION TIME:
10 MINUTES
COOKING TIME:
5 MINUTES

75g (3oz) Californian raisins

150ml (¼ pint) dark rum

8 sponge finger biscuits

600ml (1 pint) 0% fat Greek
yogurt

1 teaspoon cocoa powder to
dust

If you prefer, you can replace the yogurt with virtually fat free fromage frais and gently mix the ingredients together for a dessert with a marbled effect appearance.

1 Place the raisins and rum in a small saucepan and warm gently over a low heat for 2–3 minutes until the raisins are plump.

2 Take 4 individual glasses and break a sponge biscuit into small pieces into the bottom of each glass. Add a spoonful of raisins and then yogurt. Continue layering the desserts until all the ingredients are used, ending with a topping of yogurt.

3 Dust with cocoa powder and refrigerate until ready to serve.

Banana custard tart

In this recipe, the sponge base can be frozen in advance. The frozen base can then be filled with the hot custard, which helps the custard to cool down much more quickly.

1 Preheat the oven to 180C, 350F, Gas Mark 4.
2 To make the sponge base, whisk together the eggs and sugar for several minutes until pale and thick in consistency.
3 Lightly grease an 20cm (8in) non-stick flan case with a little oil, then dust with caster sugar, discarding the excess.
4 Sift the flour and, using a metal spoon, carefully fold the sifted flour into the egg mixture, followed by the vanilla essence. Pour into the flan case and level off with a knife.
5 Bake in the centre of the oven for 20 minutes until golden brown.
6 Loosen the sponge from the flan case with a blunt knife, then allow the sponge to cool.
7 Using a sharp serrated knife, cut away a 1cm ($\frac{1}{2}$in) layer of sponge from the centre of the flan case to make a deeper 'well', then use a spoon to scrape away any crumbs to leave a smooth surface.
8 To make the filling, mix the custard powder and sugar with a little of the milk to form a paste. Pour the remaining milk into a saucepan.
9 Split the vanilla pod lengthways with a sharp knife, scrape away the inside seeds and add the seeds to the milk in the saucepan. Heat until boiling, pour onto the custard powder and mix well.
10 Pour the mixture back into the saucepan and bring to the boil until the mixture thickens. Pour into the flan case and allow to cool.
11 Peel and slice the bananas into a bowl. Pour the lemon juice over the bananas and arrange the bananas on top of the flan.
12 Heat the apricot jam and brush over the bananas to form a glaze. Serve immediately.

SERVES 8
PER SERVING:
184 KCAL / 1.8G FAT
PREPARATION TIME:
10 MINUTES
COOKING TIME:
60 MINUTES

2 eggs
75g (3oz) caster sugar
75g (3oz) self-raising flour
1 teaspoon vanilla essence

for the filling
1 tablespoon low-fat custard powder
1 tablespoon caster sugar
250ml (8fl oz) skimmed milk
1 vanilla pod
2 large bananas
juice of $\frac{1}{2}$ lemon
2 tablespoons sieved apricot jam

Pineapple bread pudding

Adding the demerara sugar just before baking gives a delicious crunchy topping to this nutritious dish.

1 Preheat the oven to 200C, 400F, Gas Mark 6.
2 Prepare the pineapple by using a sharp knife to slice off the top and bottom. Remove the outer skin by slicing down around the sides of the fruit to leave a barrel shape. Cut the pineapple into thin slices, remove the central core with a small pastry cutter, and set aside.
3 Slice the bread into thin discs and arrange alternately with the pineapple in a shallow ovenproof dish.
4 Sprinkle a light covering of grated fresh nutmeg over the top.
5 Place the milk and vanilla extract in a saucepan and heat to near boiling.
6 Whisk the eggs in a bowl and pour the milk over the eggs. Continue whisking until fully combined.
7 Pour the mixture over the bread and allow to stand for 20 minutes for the bread to soak up the liquid.
8 Sprinkle the pudding with demerara sugar and bake in the oven for 25–30 minutes until golden brown.
9 Serve hot or cold with low-fat custard.

SERVES 4
PER SERVING:
252 KCAL/4.4G FAT
PREPARATION TIME:
20 MINUTES
COOKING TIME:
30 MINUTES

1 small fresh pineapple
115g (4oz) thin French bread
   stick
grated fresh nutmeg
450ml (3/4 pint) skimmed milk
1 teaspoon vanilla extract
2 eggs
2 tablespoons demerara sugar

Steamed lime and ginger pudding

SERVES 6
PER SERVING:
168 KCAL/2.2G FAT
PREPARATION TIME:
20 MINUTES
COOKING TIME:
15 MINUTES

2 limes
50g (2oz) light brown sugar
2 eggs
50g (2oz) lighterbake
75g (3oz) plain flour
25g (1oz) rice flour
2 teaspoons baking powder
2 tablespoons preserved ginger
   in syrup
fresh fruit to decorate

Lime and ginger transform this light and airy sponge cake into an interesting, low-fat pudding. Bamboo steamers are very cheap to buy and are available in many different sizes, so this recipe can be adapted to serve fewer people.

1 Finely zest the limes into a mixing bowl. Add the sugar, eggs and lighterbake and beat well. Sift the flours and the baking powder and fold into the mixture.
2 Line a 20cm (8in) bamboo steamer with parchment baking paper, first around the inside edges, then cut out a circle for the base.
3 Pour the mixture into the steamer and cover with a lid. Place over a pan of boiling water and steam for 15 minutes or until the cake is cooked.
4 Extract the juice from the limes. Slice the preserved ginger and mix with the lime juice and the ginger syrup. Pour over the cake and decorate with fresh fruit.

Mincemeat and cherry plait

This recipe doubles as a hot dessert or tasty pastry fingers, making an alternative to mince pies, with considerably less fat, of course. Once baked, the plait can be frozen, but take great care, as filo pastry is very delicate and can damage easily.

1 To make the mincemeat, place the dried fruit in a saucepan. Add the grated apples, mixed spice and cider. Simmer for 20 minutes or until the mixture has formed a pulp and most of the liquid has evaporated. Stir in the rum. Pack in sterilised jars and store in the refrigerator until required.
2 When ready to make the plait, preheat the oven to 180C, 350F, Gas Mark 4.
3 Beat together the egg and milk. Place a sheet of filo pastry on a large baking tray. Brush lightly with the egg and milk mixture, using a pastry brush. Place another sheet of filo pastry on top and repeat, brushing each layer, until all 8 sheets are used.
4 Using a tablespoon, place a line of mincemeat down the centre of the pastry, leaving a small border at the top and bottom. Dot the cherries on top, along the mincemeat line.
5 Using a pair of scissors, cut strips of pastry (finger thickness) from each side of the mincemeat. Fold each strip of pastry over the mincemeat alternately to form a plait effect.
6 Brush with the beaten egg mixture and place in the oven for 20–25 minutes or until golden brown.
7 Serve hot with low-fat fromage frais, or allow to cool and cut into fingers.

SERVES 10
PER SERVING:
182 KCAL/0.9G FAT
PREPARATION TIME:
15 MINUTES
COOKING TIME:
MINCEMEAT: 30 MINUTES
PLAIT: 35 MINUTES

1 egg
2 tablespoons skimmed milk
8 sheets filo pastry (30 × 20cm/ 12 × 8in)
1 × 425g (15oz) can black cherries, pitted
2 teaspoons caster sugar

for the spicy fat-free mincemeat
225g (8oz) mixed dried fruit
150g (5oz) cooking apples, peeled and grated
$\frac{1}{2}$ teaspoon mixed spice
150ml ($\frac{1}{4}$ pint) sweet cider
2 teaspoons rum

Top right: *Mincemeat and cherry plait*

Right: *Individual valrhona chocolate puddings*

Individual valrhona chocolate puddings

Valrhona cocoa is a high-quality chocolate product from France. It is different from other cocoa powders in that it is higher in cocoa solids and lower in fat. These puddings may overflow when cooked if too much mixture is used – it's a case of trial and error – so always place a piece of kitchen paper under each pudding while cooking in the microwave, just in case. The end result is a light chocolate sponge standing on a chocolate sauce.

1 In a mixing bowl, beat together the sugar, fromage frais and eggs. Sift the flour, baking powder and cocoa powder and gradually mix into the fromage frais and egg mixture.
2 Lightly grease 6 teacups with a little oil, wiping out the excess with kitchen paper.
3 Place sufficient sponge mixture in each cup until each is a third full.
4 Combine the topping ingredients and pour the liquid over the sponge mixture in each cup.
5 Cook each pudding individually in a microwave for 1 minute on full power (stand the cup on a piece of kitchen paper). Allow each pudding to stand for 1 minute before turning out. Keep the puddings warm in the top of a vegetable steamer until all are cooked.
6 Turn out the puddings onto individual plates and sprinkle each pudding with icing sugar.
7 Serve with virtually fat free fromage frais or low-fat ice cream.

See photograph on page 255.

SERVES 6
PER SERVING:
211 KCAL／4.5G FAT
PREPARATION TIME:
10 MINUTES
COOKING TIME:
10 MINUTES

for the sponge
115g (4oz) caster sugar
115g (4oz) virtually fat free
    fromage frais
2 eggs
75g (3oz) plain flour
1 teaspoon baking powder
25g (1oz) valrhona cocoa
    powder

for the topping
12 tablespoons boiling water
6 teaspoons valrhona cocoa
    powder
6 teaspoons soft dark brown
    sugar
icing sugar to dust

Baked pears with chocolate sauce

SERVES 4
PER SERVING:
145 KCAL/2.3G FAT
PREPARATION TIME:
10 MINUTES
COOKING TIME:
30 MINUTES

4 ripe dessert pears
2 tablespoons lemon juice
300ml (1/2 pint) semi-skimmed milk
1 tablespoon valrhona cocoa powder
2 teaspoons cornflour
1 tablespoon caster sugar or to taste

A delicious, simple pudding that can be served hot or cold. To save time, you can cook the pears in a microwave – just cover and cook on full power for 2–3 minutes.

1 Preheat the oven to 180C, 350F, Gas Mark 4.
2 Peel the pears, slice in half and remove the central core with a dessertspoon. Immediately place the pears in a bowl with the lemon juice to prevent them from turning brown. Transfer to an ovenproof dish and cover with foil.
3 Place in the oven and bake for 15–20 minutes or until the pears are soft.
4 Place the milk and cocoa powder in a small saucepan, whisking continuously. Slake the cornflour with a little cold milk and whisk into the milk and cocoa powder. Simmer for 1 minute as the sauce thickens, then add the sugar.
5 Arrange the pears on a serving plate and spoon the sauce over the top.

Entertaining

We are always on the the lookout for that easy recipe that takes very little time to produce yet leaves everyone speechless at the dinner table. These recipes may not be the quickest but they certainly will impress and your guests won't even guess that they're low in fat.

Select from both simple and challenging starters that look great, through to celebratory main courses for all occasions.

You can choose suitable vegetable or salad accompaniments as well as puddings to finish from the relevant chapters in this book.

Starters

If you are watching your waistline, fruit and salad dishes make simple low-fat options for starters. However, if you are looking for something a little more elaborate to grace your dinner table, here is a selection of imaginative starters that will enable you to extend your dinner party repertoire. Remember, though, they are only starters, designed to whet your appetite for the main course, so watch the portion sizes.

Garlic mushroom bruschetta

SERVES 4
PER SERVING:
133 KCAL/2.3G FAT
PREPARATION TIME:
10 MINUTES
COOKING TIME:
10 MINUTES

$^1/_2$ French stick
2 garlic cloves
6 spring onions, finely chopped
225g (8oz) chestnut
    mushrooms, finely chopped
juice of $^1/_2$ lemon
1 tablespoon Normandy
    virtually fat free fromage frais
1 teaspoon chopped fresh dill
salt and freshly ground black
    pepper
salad leaves to garnish

Bruschetta generally consists of fried or grilled pieces of bread spread with garlic butter and topped with a tomato Provençale mix made with a large quantity of olive oil. This low-fat mushroom alternative can be prepared in advance and oven baked or grilled as required.

1 Slice the bread diagonally into 8 thick pieces and toast lightly under a hot grill on both sides. Slice one garlic clove in half and rub both sides of the bread with the cut side. Place the bread on a baking tray.
2 Preheat a non-stick frying pan and dry-fry the spring onions for 2–3 minutes until soft. Crush the second garlic clove and add to the pan along with the mushrooms and lemon juice. Cook until the moisture has evaporated to leave a paste-like consistency.
3 Remove the pan from the heat, stir in the fromage frais and dill and season with salt and black pepper. Spread the mixture onto the toasted bread and place under the grill to brown.
4 Garnish with salad leaves and serve hot.

Potted wild mushrooms

Fresh wild mushrooms are readily available in supermarkets and specialist food shops. Buy a mixture so that you have an assortment of flavours and textures. Always buy them fresh and use quickly, as they soon deteriorate in warm weather.

1 In a non-stick frying pan, dry-fry the mushrooms quickly until they start to soften. Add the garlic and white wine. Cook for 2–3 minutes, seasoning well with salt and black pepper. Add the breadcrumbs and herbs and remove from the heat.

2 Spoon into a food processor and add the remaining ingredients. Using a pulse motion, process for 3–4 seconds until combined but not smooth.

3 Spoon the mixture into individual ramekin dishes and chill until required.

4 Garnish with chervil and serve chilled, accompanied by warm Rosemary and tomato focaccia (see recipe opposite).

SERVES 6
PER SERVING:
58 KCAL/0.6G FAT
PREPARATION TIME:
5 MINUTES
COOKING TIME:
20 MINUTES

450g (1lb) mixed fresh wild
    mushrooms
2 garlic cloves, crushed
$\frac{1}{2}$ wineglass white wine
50g (2oz) fresh brown
    breadcrumbs
1 tablespoon chopped fresh flat
    leaf parsley
1 tablespoon chopped fresh
    chervil
2 tablespoons virtually fat free
    fromage frais
juice of $\frac{1}{2}$ freshly squeezed
    lemon
salt and freshly ground black
    pepper
a few sprigs chervil to garnish

Rosemary and tomato focaccia

SERVES 6
PER SERVING:
142 KCAL/0.6G FAT
PREPARATION TIME:
30 MINUTES
COOKING TIME:
55 MINUTES

225g (8oz) strong white bread
   flour
1 teaspoon salt
1 teaspoon chopped fresh
   rosemary
2 teaspoons dried yeast
150ml (¼ pint) warm water
4 tablespoons tomato salsadina
   or passata
2 garlic cloves, finely chopped
1 teaspoon sea salt
fresh rosemary sprigs to garnish

Focaccia is a rustic Italian bread flavoured with fine olive oil, sea salt and fresh pungent rosemary. It usually contains a large amount of olive oil and is also coated in oil before baking. This version offers all the authentic flavours while excluding the oil.

1 Preheat the oven to 200C, 400F, Gas Mark 6.
2 Sift the flour and salt into a large mixing bowl and add the rosemary. Whisk the yeast into the water until dissolved.
3 Make a well in the centre of the flour and add the liquid, stirring with a knife to bring the dough together. Turn out onto a floured board and knead until smooth. Cover with a damp cloth and leave for 10 minutes.
4 Knead the dough again, roll it out into a large circle and place on a non-stick baking tray. Spoon the salsadina over, leaving a border around the edge. Dot with chopped garlic and sprinkle with sea salt. Press random indentations using your finger and place a sprig of rosemary in each one.
5 Allow to prove for 5 minutes, and then bake in the top of the oven for 15–20 minutes. When cooked, slice and serve warm with Potted wild mushrooms (see recipe opposite).

Garlic king prawns with smoked bacon and horseradish dressing

This impressive starter looks fantastic on the plate, yet it's so easy to prepare. If you are unable to get large king prawns, smaller ones will suffice. Do not overcook them or the prawns will become firm and rubbery. This dish needs to be cooked quickly and carefully – not one to be left unattended.

1 Remove any fat from the smoked bacon. Slice the bacon into strips, place in a non-stick frying pan with the garlic and spring onions and cook over a high heat for 2–3 minutes.
2 Add the prawns and ground cumin and cook quickly for 1 minute on each side. Add the diced tomato and the parsley, and season well with salt and black pepper.
3 Using a whisk, combine the dressing ingredients in a small bowl.
4 Remove the frying pan from the heat and pour the dressing over the bacon and prawn mixture.
5 Serve hot on a bed of baby spinach mixed with rocket leaves.

SERVES 4
PER SERVING:
111 KCAL/3.9G FAT
PREPARATION TIME:
25 MINUTES
COOKING TIME:
35 MINUTES

50g (2oz) lean smoked bacon
2 garlic cloves, crushed
8 spring onions, finely chopped
16 large king prawn tails, peeled
1 teaspoon ground cumin
6 tomatoes, skinned, seeded and diced
1 tablespoon chopped fresh parsley
salt and freshly ground black pepper
150g (5oz) rocket and spinach leaves to serve

for the dressing
2 tablespoons fresh apple juice
1 tablespoon white wine vinegar
1 teaspoon horseradish sauce
salt and freshly ground black pepper

Smoked salmon pâté with spinach overcoats

SERVES 4
PER SERVING:
72 KCAL / 1.8G FAT
PREPARATION TIME:
10 MINUTES
COOKING TIME:
5 MINUTES

150g (5oz) sliced smoked
   salmon
juice of 1 lemon
115g (4oz) virtually fat free
   Normandy fromage frais
6 pink peppercorns
freshly ground black pepper to
   taste
50g (2oz) fresh spinach

1 Place all the ingredients except the spinach in a food processor and blend until smooth to form a pâté.
2 Wash the spinach well and dry in a salad spinner. To wilt the spinach, place in a non-metallic bowl and microwave on full power for 1 minute or, alternatively, pour boiling water over the spinach and drain well.
3 Divide the salmon pâté into equal-sized portions and shape with a palette knife.
4 Carefully wrap the spinach around the outside of the pâté to leave a smooth finish.
5 Serve with melba toasts and salad leaves.

Smoked fish terrine

This starter can be made in advance, as it will keep refrigerated for 3–4 days. If you prefer, you can use fresh salmon and a few prawns or diced vegetables instead of the smoked fish.

1 Wash the spinach well and drain in a colander. Place in a non-metallic bowl. Wilt the spinach either in the microwave for 1 minute on full power, or pour boiling water over it and drain well.
2 Take a 1.2 litre (2 pint) terrine mould and line the inside with clear food wrap, pressing it well into the corners. Cover this with a layer of wilted spinach leaves and place in the refrigerator.
3 Poach the fish separately in water or milk and drain on kitchen paper. Season with salt and black pepper.
4 Soak the gelatine in cold water for 2–3 minutes until soft, then squeeze out the liquid and place in a saucepan with the wine and saffron. Heat gently until the gelatine dissolves, then remove from heat and add the fish stock and chervil.
5 Cut the fish into strips, removing any bones. Arrange the strips in layers in the terrine mould, pouring some of the wine and stock mixture in between each layer. Pour in sufficient liquid to cover the fish, then add a layer of spinach. Cover with food wrap and refrigerate until set (ideally overnight).
6 To serve, slice with a sharp knife and garnish with salad leaves and fresh lemon slices.

SERVES 6
PER SERVING:
122 KCAL/1.4G FAT
PREPARATION TIME:
40 MINUTES
COOKING TIME:
15 MINUTES
SETTING TIME:
OVERNIGHT

225g (8oz) fresh spinach
225g (8oz) naturally smoked cod or haddock, free from skin and bones
225g (8oz) fresh cod or other white fish, free from skin and bones
6 sheets leaf gelatine
300ml ($\frac{1}{2}$ pint) white wine
pinch of saffron
150ml ($\frac{1}{4}$ pint) fish stock
2 teaspoons chopped fresh chervil
salt and freshly ground black pepper
salad leaves and lemon slices to garnish

Grilled grapefruit suzette

SERVES 4
PER SERVING:
140 KCAL/0.3G FAT
PREPARATION TIME:
20 MINUTES
COOKING TIME:
10 MINUTES

2 large pink grapefruit
4 teaspoons demerara sugar
pinch of cinnamon
4 oranges, cut into segments
4 tablespoons brandy

Grapefruit is generally eaten cold for breakfast. However, when cooked it takes on a very different flavour.

1 Cut each grapefruit in half and place on a baking tray. Using a grapefruit knife, cut around the inside edge of the fruit and in between each segment.
2 Sprinkle the demerara sugar and the cinnamon on top of the grapefruit and place under a hot grill for 4–5 minutes until golden brown.
3 Preheat a non-stick frying pan, add the orange segments and heat through. Add the brandy and flame the pan by tilting it slightly, making sure the pan is at arm's length.
4 Remove the pan from the heat, place each grapefruit half on a separate plate and pour the hot oranges over.

Coarse pork and chicken pâté with spiced plums

This dense, meaty pâté uses only lean ingredients to cut down on the fat and leave pure flavours. The syrupy plums form the perfect accompaniment to any cold meats or spicy foods. They will keep in the refrigerator for up to 2 weeks.

1 Preheat the oven to 180C, 350F, Gas Mark 4.
2 Roughly chop the chicken livers and place in a large bowl with the minced pork. Add the garlic, peppercorns, herbs, brandy and stock. Season well with salt and black pepper and mix well until fully combined.
3 Cut the chicken breast into thin strips. Place a thin layer of the chicken livers and pork mixture in a 900g (2lb) non-stick loaf tin, just enough to cover the base. Add a third of the sliced chicken. Continue with additional layers, ending with the chicken livers and pork mixture. Cover with foil.
4 Place the loaf tin inside a roasting tin. Pour sufficient water in the roasting tin to come halfway up the sides of the loaf tin and place in the oven for 1½ hours.
5 When cooked, remove the pâté from the oven. Allow to cool, and then refrigerate overnight.
6 To make the spiced plums, dissolve the sugar in the cider vinegar in a large saucepan over a low heat. Add the spices, lemon juice, zest and salt.
7 Cut the plums in half and remove the centre stones. Add the plums to the pan, cover, and simmer gently for 15 minutes. Remove from the heat and allow to cool, still covered. Pour into a container and refrigerate until ready for use.
8 When read to serve, slice the pâté thinly and garnish with the spiced plums and the salad leaves.
9 Serve with melba toasts.

SERVES 10
PER SERVING:
187 KCAL/5.5G FAT
PREPARATION TIME:
30 MINUTES
COOKING TIME:
1 HOUR 30 MINUTES
SETTING TIME (FOR PÂTÉ):
OVERNIGHT

225g (8oz) chicken livers
450g (1lb) lean minced pork
2 garlic cloves, crushed
8 whole green peppercorns
1 tablespoon chopped fresh flat leaf parsley
2 tablespoons chopped fresh mixed herbs (tarragon, chervil, chives)
2 tablespoons brandy
150ml (¼ pint) vegetable stock, cooled
2 skinless chicken breasts
salt and freshly ground black pepper
salad leaves to garnish

for the spiced plums
115g (4oz) soft dark brown sugar
150ml (¼ pint) cider vinegar
2 teaspoons coriander seeds
½ teaspoon allspice
juice and zest of 1 lemon
pinch of sea salt
450g (1lb) fresh dark Victoria plums

Roast asparagus with low-fat hollandaise sauce

Hollandaise is a rich golden sauce made by pouring hot melted butter onto beaten egg yolks to form a warm mayonnaise that is very high in fat. This recipe offers a lighter, low-fat alternative. The sauce should be of a smooth consistency, not thick.

1 Preheat the oven to 220C, 425F, Gas Mark 7.

2 Prepare the asparagus by trimming off the stem approximately 2.5cm (1in) from the bottom. Plunge into a large pan of boiling water for 2 minutes, drain and place in a large roasting tin. Season to taste with sea salt and black pepper and place in the middle of a hot oven for 5–6 minutes.

3 Make the sauce by heating the milk and the turmeric in a small saucepan. Slake the cornflour with a little water and add to the milk along with the stock powder or cube. Stir continuously with a wooden spoon as the sauce thickens. Reduce the heat and simmer for 2–3 minutes. Just before serving, beat in the egg.

4 Arrange the asparagus on a serving plate and pour the sauce over the asparagus.

SERVES 6
PER SERVING:
82 KCAL / 1.9G FAT
PREPARATION TIME:
10 MINUTES
COOKING TIME:
30 MINUTES
SETTING TIME:
1 HOUR

1kg (2lb) fresh asparagus
pinch of sea salt
freshly ground black pepper
300ml ($\frac{1}{2}$ pint) skimmed milk
$\frac{1}{4}$ teaspoon ground turmeric
1 heaped tablespoon cornflour
1 teaspoon vegetable stock
   powder or $\frac{1}{4}$ vegetable stock
   cube
1 egg yolk

Cucumber and tomato timbales with fresh basil

SERVES 4
PER SERVING:
96 KCAL/3.6G FAT
PREPARATION TIME:
15 MINUTES
COOKING TIME:
30 MINUTES
SETTING TIME:
1 HOUR

350g (12oz) cucumber
225g (8oz) baby leeks
1 tablespoon chopped fresh
    basil
450ml (³/₄ pint) tomato passata
1 tablespoon vodka
1 sachet vegi-gel
1 small radicchio lettuce,
    shredded
salt and freshly ground black
    pepper

for the dressing
2 tomatoes, skinned, seeded and
    diced
1 teaspoon fresh lime juice
1 tablespoon chopped fresh
    chives
1 teaspoon coarse grain
    mustard
1 teaspoon runny honey
salt and freshly ground black
    pepper

A refreshing start to any meal, these vegetable timbales spiked with vodka are bursting with flavour. This dish is made using vegi-gel, a gelatine alternative which is very easy to use and is totally odourless and tasteless, making it ideal for delicately flavoured dishes. The timbales can be made in advance and kept in the refrigerator until ready to serve.

1 Peel and finely dice the cucumber. Wash the leeks thoroughly under cold running water, shake dry and chop very finely.
2 Place the leeks in a preheated non-stick frying pan and dry-fry gently until softened. Add the diced cucumber, remove from the heat and season well with salt and black pepper. Mix in the chopped basil.
3 Place the tomato passata and vodka in a small saucepan. Sprinkle the vegi-gel over them and heat gently to near boiling. As soon as the sauce starts to thicken, remove from the heat and season with salt and black pepper.
4 Take 4 × 300ml (4 × ¹/₂ pint) moulds or glass tumblers. Spoon alternate layers of cucumber and tomato mixture into the moulds, reserving any leftover mixture for the garnish. Place in the refrigerator for 1 hour to allow to set.
5 When ready to serve, dip the chilled moulds, one at a time, into a bowl of boiling water for 2–3 seconds. Place a small serving plate upturned on top of the mould, quickly turn it over and remove the mould. Repeat with the remaining moulds. Place a little shredded radicchio around the timbales.
6 Combine the dressing ingredients and spoon the mixture around the timbales. Garnish the top with any reserved cucumber and leek mixture.

Sweet potato and red pepper terrine

A stunning starter, this vegetarian pâté is also suitable for picnics and lunchboxes. Roasting the peppers is time-consuming, but it does add a much stronger flavour throughout the dish. Once cooled, the terrine will keep in the refrigerator for 4–5 days.

1 Preheat the oven to 180C, 350F, Gas Mark 4.
2 Place the peppers, skin side up, on a baking tray and grill under a high heat until the skins start to blacken and blister. Place the peppers inside a plastic food bag and seal to make airtight. Once cool, remove the peppers, peel away the skin and cut into small dice.
3 Cut the sweet potatoes into large chunks and cook in a pan of boiling salted water until soft. Drain well and mash until smooth, seasoning with grated nutmeg and black pepper.
4 Mix the garlic, herbs and tomato purée with the potatoes, and then beat in the eggs one at a time. Fold in the diced red pepper and spoon into a 600ml (1 pint) terrine mould or baking tin.
5 Place the terrine mould or baking tin in a roasting tin and pour in enough boiling water to come halfway up the side of the terrine mould or baking tin.
6 Bake in the oven for 45 minutes. Allow to cool and refrigerate until ready to serve.
7 To serve, turn out onto a serving plate, cut into slices and serve on a bed of mixed salad leaves.

SERVES 6
PER SERVING:
186 KCAL/2.7G FAT
PREPARATION TIME:
60 MINUTES
COOKING TIME:
90 MINUTES

3 red peppers, cut in half and seeded
900g (2lb) sweet potatoes, peeled
grated fresh nutmeg to taste
2 garlic cloves, crushed
1 tablespoon chopped fresh mixed herbs
2 tablespoons tomato purée
2 eggs
salt and freshly ground black pepper

Chilli corn fritters with red pepper salsa

In this light and tasty combination, both mixtures can be made in advance, leaving the fritters to be cooked quickly at the last minute. You can use fresh corn cobs instead of frozen sweetcorn. Cook them well in boiling salted water, refresh in cold water and then remove the kernels with a sharp knife.

1 In a medium saucepan, combine the milk, chilli, spring onions and sweetcorn and bring to the boil.
2 Slake the cornflour with a little cold water and add to the pan, stirring continuously as the mixture thickens. Reduce the heat and simmer for 3–4 minutes.
3 Pour the mixture into a bowl and allow to cool, then refrigerate for 1 hour.
4 To make the salsa, cut the peppers in half and remove the seeds. Place, skin side up, under a preheated hot grill and leave until black and blistered. Immediately place them into a plastic food bag and tie it to make it airtight.
5 When the peppers are cold, carefully peel away the skin under a cold running tap. Dice the peppers and combine with the remaining salsa ingredients. Season to taste.
6 Preheat a non-stick frying pan. Drop tablespoon-size amounts of the corn fritter mixture into the pan and dry-fry for 2–3 minutes on each side.
7 Serve the fritters (allow 2 fritters per person) with the red pepper salsa and salad leaves.

SERVES 6
PER SERVING:
144 KCAL/1.4G FAT
PREPARATION TIME:
20 MINUTES
COOKING TIME:
20 MINUTES
COOLING TIME:
1 HOUR

150ml (¼ pint) skimmed milk
1 small red chilli, seeded and finely chopped
6 spring onions, finely chopped
450g (1lb) frozen sweetcorn, defrosted and drained
1 tablespoon cornflour
1 tablespoon chopped fresh parsley
salt and freshly ground black pepper

for the salsa
2 red peppers
6 spring onions
3 ripe tomatoes, skinned and seeded
zest and juice of 1 lime
1 tablespoon fresh coriander
salt and freshly ground black pepper

Main courses

Choose from a tempting array of main course dishes that will delight your guests and add a touch of pazazz to any dinner party menu. When selecting vegetable or salad accompaniments, try to aim for a balance of colours, textures and flavours, but keep an eye on the calories!

Tomato braised beef with oyster mushrooms

In this recipe, ripe tomatoes form the base to this rich sauce. For a lighter sauce you can use beef stock instead of wine.

1 Preheat the oven to 180C, 350F, Gas Mark 4.
2 Preheat a non-stick frying pan. Season the meat well with salt and black pepper and dry-fry in the pan until browned on both sides. Transfer to an ovenproof casserole.
3 Add the onions to the pan and soften for 3–4 minutes. Sprinkle the thyme over the onions and add the wine and stock cube. Stir well.
4 Scatter the tomatoes over the beef and then pour the wine mixture over. Cover and cook in the oven for 35 minutes.
5 Remove the beef from the oven and add the mushrooms and the tomato purée. Cover and return to the oven for a further 25 minutes or until the beef is tender.
6 Just before serving, sprinkle with chopped fresh coriander.
7 Serve with potatoes and unlimited vegetables.

SERVES 6
PER SERVING:
264 KCAL/9G FAT
PREPARATION TIME:
20 MINUTES
COOKING TIME:
1 HOUR 10 MINUTES

900g (2lb) lean rump or
   braising steak
2 red onions, finely sliced
2 teaspoons chopped fresh
   thyme
300ml ($\frac{1}{2}$ pint) red wine
$\frac{1}{2}$ beef stock cube
450g (1lb) fresh plum tomatoes,
   skinned and halved
350g (12oz) oyster mushrooms
2 tablespoons tomato purée
salt and freshly ground black
   pepper
chopped fresh coriander to
   garnish

Lemon roast turkey with cornbread stuffing and herb gravy

Cornbread stuffing is an American treat often served with the traditional Thanksgiving dinner. Fine cornmeal and plain flour are used in the stuffing to give it a golden cake-like texture, much lighter than a breadcrumb stuffing. The turkey is cooked inside and out with lemon and fresh thyme to keep it beautifully moist and add a unique flavour to the accompanying gravy.

1 Preheat the oven to 180C, 350F, Gas Mark 4.
2 Wash the turkey in cold water and remove the giblets and any fat. Place the giblets, onion, bay leaves and 2 sprigs of thyme in the centre of a large roasting tin and sit the turkey on top.
3 Cut the lemons in half and squeeze the juice from all three over the turkey. Place the lemon shells and the remaining thyme inside the turkey. Season the turkey with sea salt and lemon pepper. Pour 600ml (1 pint) of water around the outside of the turkey to prevent the base from burning, cover with aluminium foil and place in the oven. Allow 15 minutes per 450g/lb Cooking time plus an extra 20 minutes, turning the roasting tin every hour to ensure even cooking.
4 While the turkey is cooking, lightly grease and line a 20cm (8in) cake tin with baking parchment. Prepare the stuffing by mixing together the dry ingredients and herbs in a large bowl. Beat together the egg and milk and add to the dry ingredients. Mix until smooth, then pour into the prepared cake tin. Place to one side.
6 Once the turkey is cooked, remove from the roasting tin and place on a serving dish. Keep it covered with foil and allow 30 minutes' standing time for easier carving.

SERVES 10
PER SERVING:
302 KCAL/3.5G FAT
PREPARATION TIME:
20 MINUTES
COOKING TIME:
3 HOURS 40 MINUTES

1 × 5.4kg (12lb) fresh turkey
1 large onion, diced
3 bay leaves
4–5 sprigs fresh thyme
3 lemons
pinch of sea salt
1 teaspoon lemon pepper
1 tablespoon arrowroot
a few drops gravy browning
   (optional)

for the cornbread stuffing
175g (6oz) plain flour
175g (6oz) fine cornmeal
1 tablespoon baking powder
1 teaspoon salt
1 tablespoon caster sugar
2 tablespoons chopped fresh
   mixed herbs (oregano, thyme,
   marjoram, parsley)
1 egg, beaten
300ml (½ pint) skimmed milk

7 Meanwhile, increase the oven temperature to 200C, 400F, Gas Mark 6. Place the cornbread stuffing in the oven and bake for 25–35 minutes until golden brown.
8 While the stuffing is cooking, drain the contents of the roasting tin into a saucepan. Remove the giblets and bay leaves and discard. Use a ladle to skim away any fat from the top of the pan. Bring the liquid to the boil, slake the arrowroot with a little water and gradually add to the gravy, stirring well. Add a few drops of gravy browning, if desired, to colour the gravy. Thin down with vegetable stock if required.
9 When ready to serve, carve the turkey, cut the stuffing into pieces and serve hot with the herb gravy.

Individual beef wellingtons with red wine sauce

Beef Wellington is traditionally made with high-fat puff pastry and stuffed with either foie gras or rich pâté. This simplified recipe reduces the fat and calorie content considerably. The individual Wellingtons can be made in advance, covered with a damp cloth and stored in the refrigerator.

1 Preheat the oven to 200C, 400F, Gas Mark 6.
2 Prepare the beef by removing all the fat and trimming the sides with a sharp knife to give 4 equal-sized steaks.
3 Preheat a non-stick pan and seal the steaks on both sides, seasoning well with salt and black pepper. Once browned, remove from the pan and set aside, leaving the pan for later.
4 Place the wild mushrooms in a small saucepan with the stock, garlic and thyme. Cook over a low heat and simmer gently for 15–20 minutes until soft.
5 In a non-stick frying pan, dry-fry the onion until it just starts to colour. Add the mushrooms and stock and the parsley and continue to cook until all the liquid has reduced to a paste. Allow to cool.
6 Take 1 sheet of filo pastry and brush with the beaten egg. Fold the sheet in half, place a teaspoon of the mushroom mixture in the centre, sit a steak on top and spread with another teaspoon of the mushroom mixture. Trim the excess pastry with scissors, then fold the pastry around, enclosing the beef in a tight parcel. Repeat with the remaining 3 steaks.
7 Place the parcels on a non-stick baking tray and brush with beaten egg. Bake in the oven for 12–20 minutes, according to your preference.

SERVES 4
PER SERVING:
348 KCAL/12.7G FAT
PREPARATION TIME:
30 MINUTES
COOKING TIME:
60 MINUTES

$4 \times 175g$ ($4 \times 6oz$) fillet steaks
25g (1oz) dried mixed forest wild mushrooms
150ml ($^1/_4$ pint) beef stock
2 garlic cloves, crushed
1 teaspoon finely chopped fresh thyme
1 medium onion, finely chopped
1 tablespoon chopped fresh parsley
4 sheets filo pastry
1 egg, beaten with 2 tablespoons milk
salt and freshly ground black pepper

for the sauce
2 small shallots, finely chopped
150ml (¹/₄ pint) beef stock
2 teaspoons plain flour
300ml (¹/₂ pint) red wine
gravy browning

8 Meanwhile, make the sauce by dry-frying the shallots in the meat pan until soft. Add 1 tablespoon of stock and sprinkle the flour over. Mix well and cook for 1–2 minutes to cook out the flour, then gradually stir in the remaining stock and the wine. Simmer gently for 10 minutes until thickened adding a drop of gravy browning for colour.

9 Serve the Wellingtons straight from the oven with a selection of vegetables and the accompanying sauce.

Grilled marinated lamb with caramelised shallots

Some cuts of lamb contain high quantities of fat. Lamb fillet is the eye meat in the centre of the loin – similar to fillet beef – and therefore very lean. In this recipe, you can use other lean cuts of lamb, such as neck or lean lamb steaks cut from the leg.

1 Combine all the marinade ingredients in a bowl.
2 Prepare the meat by removing all visible fat with a sharp knife. Place the meat in a shallow dish and pour the marinade over the meat. Turn the meat so that all sides are coated with the marinade. Cover with food wrap and chill for at least 4 hours.
3 Thirty minutes before cooking, remove the lamb from the marinade and place on a grill tray. Pour the marinade into a small saucepan and reduce it over a low heat for 10 minutes.
4 Preheat the grill to the hottest setting. Season the lamb all over with salt and black pepper and place under the hot grill. Cook for 15–20 minutes, turning regularly. Allow to stand for 10 minutes before carving.
5 While the lamb is cooking, preheat a non-stick frying pan. Add the shallots and the sugar and cook over a high heat for 5–6 minutes until golden. Add the mushrooms and season well with salt and black pepper.
6 Just before serving add the tomatoes, balsamic vinegar and parsley. Mix well, then transfer the vegetables to a serving plate.
7 To serve, carve the lamb into small chunky slices. Place on top of the vegetables and drizzle the marinade over.
8 Serve with potatoes and green vegetables.

SERVES 6
PER SERVING:
355 KCAL/21G FAT
PREPARATION TIME:
10 MINUTES
CHILLING TIME:
4 HOURS
COOKING TIME:
50 MINUTES

1 kg (2lb) lamb fillet
24 button shallots, peeled
1 teaspoon sugar
24 button mushrooms
24 pomodorino tomatoes or cherry tomatoes
1 tablespoon balsamic vinegar
1 tablespoon chopped flat leaf parsley
sea salt and freshly ground black pepper

for the marinade
1 tablespoon finely chopped fresh rosemary
1 red onion, finely chopped
2 garlic cloves, chopped
3 tablespoons mint jelly
1 teaspoon coarsely ground black pepper
1 wineglass white wine

Chicken liver stroganoff

SERVES 4
PER SERVING:
175 KCAL/3.6G FAT
PREPARATION TIME:
20 MINUTES
COOKING TIME:
20 MINUTES.

450g (1lb) chicken livers
1 medium onion, finely chopped
2 garlic cloves, crushed
1 tablespoon plain flour
2 tablespoons Madeira wine
150ml ($\frac{1}{4}$ pint) chicken stock
2 teaspoons Dijon mustard
225g (8oz) small chestnut
   mushrooms, sliced
300ml ($\frac{1}{2}$ pint) virtually fat free
   fromage frais
2 tablespoons chopped fresh
   parsley
salt and freshly ground black
   pepper
pinch of paprika
lemon wedges to garnish

Cooked properly, chicken livers are delicate, moist and almost melt in the mouth. However, there is a fine line between just cooked and overcooked when they take on a tough dry texture. Give this recipe a little extra attention and I'm sure you will appreciate the results.

1 Check the chicken livers and remove any sinews or fat. Rinse the chicken livers well in clean water and leave to dry on kitchen paper.
2 Preheat a non-stick frying pan or wok. Add the onion and dry-fry for 2–3 minutes until soft. Add the garlic and cook for a further minute.
3 Toss the chicken livers in the flour, season well with salt and black pepper and add to the pan. Cook quickly over a high heat for 1 minute. Add the Madeira wine and then gradually add the stock, stirring all the time to form a thick sauce.
4 Sprinkle the mushrooms over, stir in the mustard and cook for a further minute. The chicken livers should be firm but not overcooked.
5 Remove the pan from the heat. Stir in the fromage frais and the parsley and season to taste with salt and black pepper.
6 Sprinkle with a dusting of paprika, garnish with lemon wedges and serve with boiled rice.

Smothered chicken with madeira

This chicken dish is served in a delicious low-fat mushroom sauce. For a stronger and more intense flavour, you could substitute dried wild mushrooms for the chestnut mushrooms.

1 Season the chicken breasts on both sides with plenty of salt and black pepper and place in a preheated non-stick pan.
2 Dry-fry the chicken on both sides for 5–6 minutes until lightly browned, then transfer to a plate.
3 Add the onions to the pan and cook gently until lightly coloured. Add the ginger and 2 tablespoons of stock. Sprinkle the flour over and cook for 1 minute to cook out the flour.
4 Gradually add the remaining stock, the mushrooms and wine, stirring continuously. Return the chicken to the pan and add the herbs.
5 Simmer gently for 15–20 minutes until the sauce has reduced and the chicken has cooked through.
6 Serve with baby new potatoes and a selection of steamed vegetables.

SERVES 4
PER SERVING:
287 KCAL / 4G FAT
PREPARATION TIME:
20 MINUTES
COOKING TIME:
40 MINUTES

4 lean skinless chicken breasts (approximately 175g/6oz each)
1 medium red onion, finely chopped
1 × 2.5cm (1 in) piece of fresh ginger, peeled and finely chopped
1 chicken stock cube, dissolved in 300ml (½ pint) water
1 tablespoon plain flour
225g (8oz) chestnut mushrooms, sliced
1 wineglass Madeira wine
2 tablespoons chopped fresh mixed herbs
salt and freshly ground black pepper

Tikka chicken with mango rice

SERVES 4
PER SERVING:
414 KCAL / 2.9G FAT
PREPARATION TIME:
10 MINUTES
COOKING TIME:
25 MINUTES

4 skinless chicken breasts
225g (8oz) basmati rice
1 vegetable stock cube
1 ripe mango, peeled and diced
fine zest and juice of 1 lime
150ml (¼ pint) low-fat yogurt
1 tablespoon ground fresh
    coriander
chopped fresh mint to garnish

for the tikka paste
1 small red onion
4 tablespoons tomato purée
1 teaspoon ground cumin
½ teaspoon ground cinnamon
1 × 2.5cm (1in) piece fresh
    ginger, grated
2 garlic cloves, crushed
1 small red chilli, seeded and
    chopped
juice of 1 lime
salt and freshly ground black
    pepper

1 Cut the chicken into chunks and thread onto 8 skewers.
   Place on a baking tray and season well with salt and black
   pepper.
2 Place the tikka paste ingredients in a food processor and blend
   until smooth. Spread the mixture over the chicken, coating on
   all sides, and leave to marinate for at least 20 minutes, longer if
   possible.
3 Boil the rice, adding a vegetable stock cube to the cooking
   water for extra flavour.
4 Cook the chicken under a preheated hot grill for 20–25
   minutes, turning regularly.
5 Drain the rice, add the mango and the lime zest and juice, and
   mix well. Combine the yogurt with the coriander.
6 Serve the chicken on a bed of rice, spoon the yogurt on top and
   garnish with the mint.

Chicken cooked in a salt crust with a white wine and onion sauce

A truly low-fat way of roasting chicken. Although the salt crust is not edible, it provides a double purpose of seasoning the bird as well as keeping it moist. If you serve the cooked chicken cold, the crust need not be removed until just before serving.

1 Preheat the oven to 180C, 350F, Gas Mark 4.

2 Prepare the chicken by washing well inside and out. Remove as much skin as possible from the surface of the chicken and season the chicken well with freshly ground black pepper. Push the lemon inside the body cavity and place on a non-stick baking tray.

3 In a large mixing bowl, combine the flour, garlic, salt and herbs. Slowly pour the water into the mixture, mixing the ingredients together with a round-ended knife until the mixture comes together as a stiff dough. You may need to add a little extra liquid.

4 Roll out the dough onto a floured surface. Cover the chicken with the dough, pressing the dough together all around the top and sides to ensure the chicken is completely covered.

5 Place in the oven and cook for 1–1½ hours, depending on the size of the chicken (allow 20 minutes per 450g/1lb plus an extra 20 minutes).

6 Meanwhile, make the sauce. Dry-fry the onions in a non-stick pan for 2–3 minutes until soft. Add 2 tablespoons of the stock and stir in the flour. Cook out the flour for 1–2 minutes, then gradually stir in the wine and the remaining stock, beating well to prevent any lumps forming. Stir in the milk and mustard and simmer gently for 3–4 minutes.

7 When ready to serve the chicken, remove the salt crust completely and discard. Carve the chicken in the traditional way.

8 Sprinkle with chives and serve with the sauce, accompanied by vegetables or salad.

SERVES 4
PER SERVING:
341 KCAL/13G FAT
PREPARATION TIME:
30 MINUTES
COOKING TIME:
1–1½ HOURS

1 medium free range or organic chicken (approx. 1.75kg/4lb)
1 lemon
900g (2lb) plain flour
2 garlic cloves, crushed
450g (1lb) sea salt
2 teaspoons chopped fresh thyme
2 teaspoons chopped fresh rosemary
150ml (¼ pint) cold water
freshly ground black pepper

for the sauce
2 medium onions, finely sliced
150ml (¼ pint) chicken stock
1 heaped tablespoon plain flour
½ wineglass white wine
150ml (¼ pint) skimmed milk
2 teaspoons Dijon mustard
1 tablespoon chopped fresh chives

Braised artichokes with peppers

SERVES 6
PER SERVING:
149 KCAL/1.9G FAT
PREPARATION TIME:
20 MINUTES
COOKING TIME:
1 HOUR 20 MINUTES

6 large artichokes

1 lemon

1 medium red onion, finely chopped

2 garlic cloves, finely chopped

2 red peppers, seeded and finely chopped

2 yellow peppers, seeded and finely chopped

1 teaspoon chopped fresh thyme leaves

1 tablespoon chopped fresh parsley

1 wineglass white wine

1 × 225g (8oz) can cannelloni beans

300ml ($\frac{1}{2}$ pint) vegetable stock

50g (2oz) reduced-fat Cheddar cheese, grated

Artichokes have a distinctive flavour that is enhanced when braised with other vegetables.

1 Prepare the artichokes by trimming off the stalks and cutting the tops off. About one third of the way down the vegetable, trim the outer leaves with scissors, removing the ends of the leaves. Rub immediately with lemon to prevent discolouration.

2 Plunge the artichokes into a pan of boiling salted water and simmer for 25 minutes. Drain the artichokes and place upside down on a cake rack to remove the excess water.

3 Grasp the centre leaves of the artichokes with your fingers, twist and pull them out to reveal the central choke. Carefully spoon out the choke with a teaspoon, removing any hair-like fibres.

4 Preheat the oven to 190C, 375F, Gas Mark 5.

5 Preheat a non-stick frying pan. Add the onion, garlic, peppers and herbs and cook briskly for 7–8 minutes until the vegetables start to colour. Pour the wine into the pan and reduce it by half. Stir in the cannelloni beans.

6 Place the artichokes in an ovenproof dish and carefully fill each centre with the vegetables. Pour the stock around and cover with aluminium foil.

7 Bake in the oven for 30 minutes.

8 Remove from the oven, sprinkle the cheese on top and place under a hot grill to brown. Serve immediately.

Polenta and roasted vegetable stacks

This impressive-looking, colourful and tasty vegetarian dish is ideal as a light main course. You can vary the vegetables and accompany with a red pepper sauce (see recipe, page 289) or a low-fat pesto. To make pesto, simply liquidise fresh basil with a little vegetable stock.

1 Weigh the polenta flour into a large jug so that it can be poured easily.
2 In a large saucepan, bring the stock to the boil. Add the mixed herbs, garlic and black pepper.
3 Slowly pour the polenta flour into the pan in a continuous stream, stirring with a whisk to prevent lumps from forming, then beat well with a wooden spoon until smooth. Reduce the heat to a gentle simmer and cook for 40–45 minutes, stirring occasionally. Pour into a shallow dish or baking tray and allow to cool and set.
4 Prepare the vegetables by slicing into wedges about 1cm ($\frac{1}{2}$in) thick. Place in a roasting tin and season well with salt and black pepper.
5 Combine the soy, lemon, garlic and fennel seeds in a small bowl and drizzle over the vegetables. Allow the vegetables to marinate for 30 minutes.
6 Preheat the oven to 200C, 400F, Gas Mark 6.
7 When the vegetables have marinated, mix well and place in the oven to roast for 35–40 minutes until soft with slight charring around the edges.
8 Cut the polenta into portion shapes – square, triangle or round – using a pastry cutter. Preheat a non-stick griddle pan until hot, then sear the polenta pieces for 2–3 minutes on each side.
9 Arrange the polenta pieces on a serving plate with layers of vegetables, then sprinkle with chopped coriander.

SERVES 4
PER SERVING:
269 KCAL / 3.1G FAT
PREPARATION TIME:
20 MINUTES
MARINATING TIME:
30 MINUTES
COOKING TIME:
1 HOUR 20 MINUTES

225g (8oz) Bramata polenta flour
1.2 litres (2 pints) vegetable stock
1 tablespoon chopped fresh mixed herbs
2 garlic cloves, crushed
freshly ground black pepper
2 medium courgettes
1 red pepper, seeded
1 yellow pepper, seeded
1 red onion
2 tablespoons light soy sauce
juice of 1 lemon
1 garlic clove, crushed
$\frac{1}{2}$ teaspoon fennel seeds
salt and freshly ground black pepper
1 tablespoon chopped fresh coriander to garnish

Parsnip and chestnut cutlets with red pepper sauce

Sweet parsnips taste quite different when blended with leeks, cumin and herbs. The chestnuts add an interesting texture as well as a rich nutty flavour. All this is served with a tasty colourful sauce. Both the cutlets and the sauce can be made in advance and frozen until required.

1 Top and tail the parsnips. Cut into small pieces, place in a saucepan, cover with water and add 2 teaspoons of salt. Boil until tender then drain and mash well with a potato masher.
2 In a non-stick saucepan, dry-fry the leeks with the ground cumin until soft.
3 Using a wooden spoon, beat the fromage frais into the parsnip mixture. Add the leeks, chestnuts and herbs and season well with salt and black pepper. Allow to cool.
4 Preheat the oven to 200C, 400F, Gas Mark 6.
5 Divide the parsnip mixture into 8 small pieces. Using a palette knife, form each piece into a teardrop shape. Place the breadcrumbs on a plate and dip each side of the cutlets into the breadcrumbs to coat them all over.
6 Place on a baking tray and bake in the oven for 10–15 minutes or until golden brown.
7 Serve the cutlets (allow 2 cutlets per person) with the red pepper sauce.

SERVES 4
PER SERVING:
(EXCLUDING RED PEPPER SAUCE) 285 KCAL/3.9G FAT
PREPARATION TIME:
25 MINUTES
COOKING TIME:
50 MINUTES

900g (2lb) young parsnips
2 teaspoons salt
350g (12oz) leeks, washed and finely chopped
2 teaspoons ground cumin
50g (2oz) low-fat fromage frais
115g (4oz) peeled chestnuts, finely chopped
1 tablespoon chopped fresh chervil
1 tablespoon chopped fresh parsley
115g (4oz) fresh breadcrumbs
salt and freshly ground black pepper
red pepper sauce (see recipe) to serve

SERVES 4
PER SERVING:
136 KCAL/1.7G FAT
PREPARATION TIME:
10 MINUTES
COOKING TIME:
40 MINUTES

8 medium red peppers, cut in
   half and seeded
1 large onion, diced
1 garlic clove, crushed
150ml ($\frac{1}{4}$ pint) strong
   vegetable stock
salt and freshly ground black
   pepper
2–3 drops Tabasco chilli sauce
   or to taste

Red pepper sauce

1 Preheat the oven to 200C, 400F, Gas Mark 6.
2 Place the peppers in a roasting tray and season well with salt
   and black pepper. Place in the top of the oven and roast for
   20–25 minutes.
3 In a non-stick pan, dry-fry the onion and garlic until soft. Add
   the red peppers and the vegetable stock and bring to the boil.
   Pour into a food processor or liquidiser and liquidise until
   smooth. Push the mixture through a fine sieve to remove the
   pepper skin. Adjust the seasoning to taste.
4 Reheat as required, thinning down with a little extra vegetable
   stock, and add a little Tabasco sauce to taste.

Saffron ravioli of leek and rocket with a light mustard sauce

Making fresh pasta is very simple and you can vary the ravioli fillings and shapes as required. Keep the dough covered at all times, as it easily dries out.

1 To make the pasta, place 150ml ($^1/_4$ pint) of water in a small saucepan, add the saffron, bring to the boil and then allow to cool. Sift the flour and salt into a mixing bowl and make a well in the centre. Add the egg and some water, mix to a stiff dough, turn out onto a floured board, and knead for 10 minutes. Wrap in clear food wrap and refrigerate for 1 hour.

2 Meanwhile, make the filling by dry-frying the leeks until soft. Add the oregano and parsley. Remove from the heat and mix in the rocket and Quark. Season well with salt.

3 To make the ravioli, divide the pasta dough in half. Roll out one half on a floured surface or with a pasta machine until paper-thin. Place on a sheet of floured greaseproof paper.

4 Using a teaspoon, place blobs of filling over the dough at 2.5cm (1in) intervals. Brush between the fillings with beaten egg.

5 Roll out the other half of the dough and use to cover the first, pressing down firmly between the fillings.

6 Using a pastry wheel, cut out the individual ravioli. Dust each piece with flour and set aside, allowing 3–4 per person. Refrigerate for 30 minutes.

7 Meanwhile make the sauce by heating the milk, onion and stock powder in a non-stick saucepan. Slake the cornflour with a little cold water to form a paste and add slowly to the milk, stirring well until the milk comes to the boil. Cook for 2–3 minutes, add the mustard and season to taste with salt and black pepper.

SERVES 6
PER SERVING:
245 KCAL/3.8G FAT
PREPARATION TIME:
55 MINUTES
COOLING TIME:
1 HOUR 30 MINUTES
COOKING TIME:
35 MINUTES

for the pasta
good pinch of saffron
225g (8oz) double zero pasta
    flour
$^1/_2$ teaspoon salt
1 egg, beaten

for the filling
4 baby leeks, finely chopped
1 teaspoon chopped fresh
    oregano
1 tablespoon chopped fresh flat
    leaf parsley
50g (2oz) young rocket leaves,
    shredded
50g (2oz) Quark low-fat soft
    cheese
salt
1 egg, beaten

for the sauce

600ml (1 pint) skimmed milk

1 medium onion, finely chopped

1 tablespoon vegetable stock powder

1 tablespoon cornflour

2 teaspoons coarse grain salt and
   freshly ground black pepper

8 Cook the ravioli in a large pan of boiling salted water for
   2–3 minutes. Drain on kitchen paper. Arrange the ravioli
   on a serving plate and pour the hot sauce around.

9 Serve with vegetables or a mixed leaf salad.

Fillets of sole veronique

This classic combination brings together sweet white grapes with a delicate white fish, all dressed in a delicious creamy wine sauce. The traditional garnish is Muscat grapes, but seedless white grapes will suffice. If you wish, you can use a Muscatel wine for a sweeter sauce.

1 Preheat the oven to 180C, 350F, Gas Mark 4.
2 Dry-fry the leeks in a non-stick pan until soft and place in the bottom of an ovenproof dish.
3 Season the fillets on both sides with salt and black pepper and place, skin side down, on top of the leeks. Pour the wine over the fish and cover with a piece of greaseproof paper.
4 Bake in the oven for 6–8 minutes until firm but not overcooked.
5 Meanwhile, heat the milk and stock powder in a saucepan. Slake the cornflour with a little cold milk and stir into the hot milk, stirring continuously. Reduce the heat and simmer for 2–3 minutes as the sauce thickens.
6 Transfer the fish to a serving dish, add the leeks and cooking liquor to the sauce and pour over the fish.
7 Cut the grapes in half and arrange on top of the fish.
8 Serve with new potatoes and a selection of vegetables.

SERVES 4
PER SERVING:
170 KCAL/1.5G FAT
PREPARATION TIME:
25 MINUTES
COOKING TIME:
35 MINUTES

3 baby leeks, finely chopped
4 × 175g (4 × 6oz) half fillets sole, skinned
150ml (¼ pint) dry white wine
300ml (½ pint) skimmed milk
2 teaspoons vegetable bouillon stock powder
1 tablespoon cornflour
salt and freshly ground black pepper
50g (2oz) seedless white grapes to garnish

Golden trout with béarnaise sauce

SERVES 4

PER SERVING:
280 KCAL/8.5G FAT

PREPARATION TIME:
50 MINUTES

COOKING TIME:
25 MINUTES

COOLING TIME:
6 HOURS

4 fresh golden or rainbow
   trout
2 lemons, sliced
4–5 sprigs fresh rosemary
sea salt
black pepper
2 tablespoons Womersley
   rosemary jelly

for the sauce
2 shallots, finely chopped
1 tablespoon fresh
   tarragon leaves
6 green peppercorns,
   crushed
50ml (2fl oz) white wine
   vinegar
225g (8oz) virtually fat
   free Normandy
   fromage frais
1/4 teaspoon ground
   turmeric
1 teaspoon caster sugar
1 tablespoon lemon juice

Lightly cooked trout retains its moist, delicate flavour, making it an ideal fish for serving hot or cold.

1 Preheat the oven to 180C, 350F, Gas Mark 4.
2 Wash the trout well and, using sharp scissors, trim away the small fins.
3 Cut 4 pieces of greaseproof paper large enough to accommodate each trout in a wrapped parcel.
4 Place 1 trout on a piece of paper, season the inside with salt and black pepper and place 2 slices lemon with a sprig of rosemary inside the trout. Season the top of the trout, fold the edges of the paper over to form a parcel and twist the paper to prevent it from unfolding. Repeat with the 3 remaining trout.
5 Place the trout in an ovenproof dish and bake in the oven for 15–20 minutes.
6 Remove from the oven and allow to cool. Once cooled, transfer to a large plate or tray and refrigerate for at least 6 hours or overnight.
7 To dress the trout, turn the fish over and run a sharp knife along the centre of the backbone and around the head and tail. Carefully lift off the top layer of fish to reveal the bones. Pull the bones away from the head towards the tail in one section and remove any remaining stray bones. Replace the top layer of fish, then carefully peel away the skin. Flip the fish over directly onto a serving dish and peel away the top layer of the skin, cutting around the head and tail for decoration. Brush with warmed rosemary jelly to glaze and prevent them from drying out.
8 To make the sauce, dry-fry the shallots in a non-stick frying pan until soft. Add the tarragon, peppercorns and vinegar and reduce over a low heat until almost dry.
9 Scrape into a small bowl, add the fromage frais, turmeric, caster sugar and lemon. Using a whisk, combine all the ingredients.
10 Season to taste with salt and black pepper and serve the sauce alongside the dressed trout.

Buffet and party food

Nothing looks more impressive than a banquet of food displayed and presented as a complete spread for parties and celebrations. But often this visual splendour turns out to be a sea of hidden calories and fat. The majority of buffet foods tend to be pastry based, often using puff pastry which has a 75 per cent fat content. It is suprising how soon the calories add up, even with small finger-sized bites.

A low-fat buffet can look equally inviting and in this chapter you will find lighter yet substantial flavoursome recipes which don't use high-fat pastry or other high-fat ingredients, leaving room for your guests to enjoy a slice of orange and passion fruit cheesecake or a fresh fruit tartlet.

Mock guacamole

SERVES 4
PER SERVING:
31 KCAL/0.6G FAT
PREPARATION TIME:
20 MINUTES
COOKING TIME:
10–15 MINUTES

225g (8oz) fresh asparagus,
    trimmed
2 garlic cloves, crushed
1 green chilli, seeded and finely
    chopped
juice of 2 limes
4 tomatoes, skinned, seeded and
    diced
salt and freshly ground black
    pepper

Traditional guacamole is made using ripe avocado pears which are very high in fat. This low-fat substitute looks and tastes just like the real thing.

1 Cook the asparagus in boiling salted water, cooking it for slightly longer than you would if serving as a vegetable accompaniment. Drain through a colander and rinse with cold water.
2 Place the asparagus, garlic, chilli and lime juice in a food processor or liquidiser and blend until smooth. Scrape out into a bowl and season well with lots of salt and black pepper.
3 Stir in the diced tomato and serve with crusty bread and salad.

See photograph on page 143.

Courgette and oregano tart

This layered tart works equally well with young trimmed asparagus or a combination of leeks and sun-dried tomatoes.

1 Preheat the oven to 190C, 375F, Gas Mark 5.
2 Wash the courgettes, trim the ends and slice into 3mm ($^1/_8$in) disks. Place in a colander and sprinkle lightly with sea salt. Stand to one side to allow to drain.
3 Lightly grease a 23cm (9in) non-stick pie dish with a little vegetable oil, then remove excess oil with kitchen paper.
4 Brush 1 sheet of filo pastry with beaten egg and place over the pie dish so that the corners hang over the edge of the dish. Repeat with the remaining pastry.
5 In a medium mixing bowl, combine both cheeses and the onion with the beaten egg (reserving a little beaten egg for the glaze), skimmed milk and oregano. Season well with salt, black pepper and nutmeg.
6 Spread half the cheese and onion mixture over the base of the lined pie dish. Cover with the drained courgettes. Spread the remaining mixture over and fold the overhanging pastry into the centre of the dish. Press down well with the back of a spoon, pressing the pastry down into the mixture. Brush the top with beaten egg.
7 Bake in the oven for 35 minutes or until the filling has set and is golden brown. Serve hot or cold.

SERVES 6
PER SERVING:
186 KCAL/4.5G FAT
PREPARATION TIME:
20 MINUTES
COOKING TIME:
35 MINUTES

675g (1$^1/_2$lb) young courgettes
pinch of sea salt
6 sheets filo pastry (20 × 30cm/ 8 × 12in)
2 eggs, beaten
3 tablespoons grated low-fat Cheddar cheese
115g (4oz) Quark low-fat soft cheese
1 medium red onion, finely chopped
150ml ($^1/_4$ pint) skimmed milk
1 tablespoon chopped fresh oregano
salt and freshly ground black pepper
grated fresh nutmeg

Roasted pepper and basil terrine

SERVES 6
PER SERVING:
62 KCAL / 2.9G FAT
PREPARATION TIME:
20 MINUTES
COOKING TIME:
20 MINUTES
CHILLING TIME:
OVERNIGHT

2 red medium peppers
2 yellow medium peppers
1 medium aubergine
115g (4oz) baby ruby chard or
    young spinach
300ml (1/2 pint) tomato passata
1 tablespoon chopped fresh
    basil
1 sachet vegi-gel
salt and freshly ground black
    pepper

In this colourful and delicious terrine, roasting the peppers brings out their full sweetness and rich flavours. This dish benefits from being made 1–2 days in advance to allow the flavours to develop.

1 Preheat the oven to 200C, 400F, Gas Mark 6.
2 Prepare the peppers by slicing in half and removing the centre core and seeds. Place the peppers, skin-side up, in a non-stick roasting tin.
3 Slice the aubergine lengthways into 1cm (1/2in) slices and add to the roasting tin. Season well with salt and black pepper.
4 Place the roasting tin in the oven and roast the vegetables, uncovered, for 15–20 minutes until the pepper skins start to blister and brown.
5 Remove from the oven, move the peppers and aubergine to one end of the tin and add the chard or spinach. Cover the tin completely with clear food wrap to make it airtight. The steam generated will enable the pepper skins to be removed easily as well as wilting the chard. Leave covered for 5 minutes.
6 Meanwhile, place the passata and basil in a small saucepan. Sprinkle the vegi-gel over and heat to near boiling. As soon as the sauce starts to thicken remove from the heat and season with salt and black pepper.
7 Spray the inside of a 450g (1lb) loaf tin or terrine mould with water and line with food wrap, allowing it to overhang.
8 Remove the peppers from the roasting tin and peel away the skins. Slice the peppers into strips.
9 Place alternate layers of vegetables and passata into the loaf tin or terrine mould. Press the terrine down and fold the overhanging food wrap over the top. Refrigerate overnight to set firm.
10 When set, turn out the terrine, slice and serve with salad leaves.

Lamb samosas with dipping sauce

Samosas are deep-fried, highly spiced pasties. In this recipe, the fat is reduced considerably by using filo pastry and then baking rather than frying.

1 Preheat a non-stick frying pan, add the onion and garlic and dry-fry until soft. Add the minced lamb and continue cooking over a high heat to seal the meat.

2 Sprinkle the curry powder over and cook out for 1 minute, stirring well, then add the bouillon powder and passata. Simmer gently for 15–20 minutes until the liquid has reduced to leave a thick paste. Allow to cool.

3 Preheat the oven to 200C, 400F, Gas Mark 6.

4 Beat together the egg and the milk. Take a sheet of filo pastry and brush with the egg mixture. Fold a third of the long side into the centre and again on the other side to leave a long strip of pastry. Brush again with egg, then place a good tablespoon of the lamb mixture at one end of the pastry and fold over diagonally, enclosing the mixture in a triangle. Fold the pastry back over along the length of the pastry, retaining the triangle shape and tucking in any spare ends.

5 Brush with egg, place on a baking tray and dust lightly with paprika. Repeat this process for the remaining 7 parcels.

6 Bake the samosas in the oven for 20–25 minutes until golden brown.

7 Combine all the sauce ingredients, season with salt and black pepper and place in a small bowl.

8 Serve the samosas on a bed of mixed salad leaves with the dipping sauce.

MAKES 8
PER SAMOSA:
174 KCAL / 6.4G FAT
PREPARATION TIME:
20 MINUTES
COOKING TIME:
60 MINUTES

1 medium onion, finely diced
2 garlic cloves, crushed
225g (8oz) lean minced lamb
1 tablespoon curry powder
2 teaspoons vegetable bouillon powder
300ml ($\frac{1}{2}$ pint) tomato passata
1 egg
3 tablespoons skimmed milk
8 sheets filo pastry
1 teaspoon paprika

for the sauce
150ml ($\frac{1}{4}$ pint) tomato passata
1 tablespoon mango chutney
1 small red chilli, seeded and finely chopped
1 tablespoon chopped fresh coriander
salt and freshly ground black pepper

Barbecued stuffed chicken legs with salsa verde

Pancetta is an Italian smoked bacon used to flavour many traditional recipes. It can be quite salty, so this dish may not require any additional salt. The accompanying salsa verde is another simple combination using fresh herbs and robust flavours.

1 Preheat the oven to 200C, 400F, Gas Mark 6.
2 Prepare the chicken legs by scoring a sharp knife along the visible bone on the underside of each joint. Carefully cut away the bone from the flesh, working all the way down the bone towards the drumstick and turning the joint inside out. Remove the knuckle end tip and pull the bone through. Remove the bone and re-form the chicken joint.
3 Make the stuffing by finely chopping all the ingredients or by placing everything into a food processor and processing until combined. Season with black pepper and divide the stuffing between the 6 chicken joints.
4 Carefully press the filling down into each joint and secure each joint with a cocktail stick.
5 Combine the dry coating ingredients in a bowl. Dip each piece of chicken into the beaten egg then coat with the dry mixture.
6 Place the chicken on a non-stick baking tray and cook in the oven for 30–35 minutes.
7 To make the salsa verde, place all the salsa ingredients in a food processor and process until fully combined.
8 Serve the chicken hot with the salsa verde.

SERVES 6
PER SERVING:
353 KCAL/15.2G FAT
PREPARATION TIME:
20 MINUTES
COOKING TIME:
25–35 MINUTES

6 large chicken legs, with skin removed

for the stuffing
50g (2oz) lean pancetta or smoked bacon
1 red onion, finely chopped
150g (5oz) lean chicken breast meat
3 celery sticks
2 garlic cloves, crushed
finely grated zest of 1 lemon
1 tablespoon finely chopped flat leaf parsley
freshly ground black pepper

for the coating
2 tablespoons plain flour
1 tablespoon finely chopped fresh parsley
1 teaspoon ground coriander
salt and freshly ground black pepper
1 egg, beaten

for the salsa
a good handful fresh basil
a good handful flat leaf parsley
1 tablespoon fresh mint leaves
2 garlic cloves, crushed
1 teaspoon Dijon mustard
salt and freshly ground black pepper

Spiced orange glazed gammon

SERVES 16
PER SERVING:
223 KCAL / 6.9G FAT
PREPARATION TIME:
20 MINUTES
COOKING TIME:
1 HOUR 35 MINUTES

1 × 1.75kg (4½lb) piece
    gammon
3 oranges, sliced
2 star anise
6 whole cloves
2 cinnamon sticks
4 bay leaves
2 tablespoons runny honey
1 orange and 12 whole cloves to
    garnish

A truly delicious way to prepare and serve gammon. Star anise (its name derives from its star-like shape) is popular in Asian cookery and adds a sweet aniseed flavour throughout the dish. Use in moderation, as it can be bitter if used in excess.

1 Prepare the gammon by removing all the outer skin and fat with a sharp knife. Place the gammon in a large saucepan and cover with cold water.
2 Add the orange slices, star anise, cloves, cinnamon and bay leaves. Bring the pan to the boil, cover and simmer gently for 1 hour.
3 Preheat the oven to 200C, 400F, Gas Mark 6.
4 Transfer the gammon to an ovenproof dish. Pour some of the stock around to prevent it from sticking to the bottom of the dish. Coat the meat with honey, place in the oven and bake, uncovered, for 30–35 minutes until golden brown.
5 Allow to cool, then garnish with orange slices and whole cloves.
6 Slice before serving and serve cold with fruit chutney.

Lime tuna roll ups

Garlic creamy cheese makes an ideal base for these rolls. Vary the fillings by using cooked ham or roasted vegetables and slice into finger food for parties.

1 In a small bowl, combine the Quark, garlic, chives and lime juice, season well with salt and black pepper and mix together.
2 Place the pitta breads on a chopping board and spread with the Quark mixture.
3 Cover with the tomato slices, tuna and watercress. Roll up tightly and secure with wooden cocktail sticks if necessary.
4 Chill until ready to serve.

SERVES 4
PER SERVING:
194 KCAL/0.9G FAT
PREPARATION TIME:
20 MINUTES
COOKING TIME:
10 MINUTES

225g (8oz) Quark low-fat soft cheese
1 smoked garlic clove, crushed
2 tablespoons chopped fresh chives
juice of 1 lime
4 flat large pitta breads
2 ripe tomatoes, sliced
1 × 200g (7oz) can tuna steak in brine, drained
1 bunch watercress, washed
salt and freshly ground black pepper

Sun-dried tomato and garlic cheese celery sticks

Quark is a good substitute for the usual cream cheese or other high-fat cheeses that are commonly used as fillings in party food. However, it is very bland on its own and needs the flavours of herbs and other highly flavoured ingredients to pep it up.

1 Cut each celery stick into 3 pieces.
2 Combine all the remaining ingredients together to form a smooth paste. Place in a piping bag and pipe into the celery sticks.
3 Dust with additional paprika or chopped chives.

SERVES 4
PER SERVING:
54 KCAL/ 0.3G FAT
PREPARATION TIME:
15 MINUTES
COOKING TIME:
10 MINUTES

4 celery sticks
225g (8oz) Quark low-fat soft
    cheese
1 garlic clove, crushed
1 tablespoon chopped fresh
    parsley
1 tablespoon chopped fresh
    chervil
1 teaspoon sweet paprika
4 pieces sun-dried tomato (non-
    oil type), finely chopped
2 teaspoons lemon juice
salt and freshly ground black
    pepper
a few chopped chives to garnish

Pasta and herb salad with barbecued peppers

Transform a plain herb pasta salad with the addition of barbecued sweet peppers. The salad can be made in advance, leaving you to add the peppers as the final touch.

SERVES 6
PER SERVING:
250 KCAL/2.2G FAT
PREPARATION TIME:
15 MINUTES
COOKING TIME:
35 MINUTES

350g (12oz) penne or farfalle

1 vegetable stock cube

2 red peppers, seeded and cut into large pieces

2 yellow peppers, seeded and cut into large pieces

150g (5oz) virtually fat free Normandy fromage frais

2 teaspoons coarse grain mustard

1 tablespoon chopped fresh chives

1 tablespoon chopped fresh chervil

salt and freshly ground black pepper

good pinch of ground smoked paprika

1 Boil the pasta with the stock cube in a large pan of water.
2 Place the peppers on a grill pan and cook under a preheated hot grill for 5–6 minutes, until they start to blister and change colour.
3 When the pasta is cooked, drain through a colander and transfer to a large mixing bowl.
4 Chop the cooked peppers into smaller pieces and add to the pasta.
5 In a separate bowl, mix together the remaining ingredients except the paprika, season with salt and black pepper and add to the pasta. Stir well to combine all the ingredients, pour into a serving dish and sprinkle with smoked paprika.
6 Serve the salad hot or cold.

Ruby chard roulade with garlic and herb cheese

Ruby chard is very similar to spinach but it has a purple stem and veins and a slight peppery flavour. If you wish, you can substitute spinach in this dish or even use a mixture of both. This roulade freezes very well.

SERVES 8
PER SERVING:
117 KCAL/3.8G FAT
PREPARATION TIME:
20 MINUTES
COOKING TIME:
45 MINUTES

1 Preheat the oven to 200C, 400F, Gas Mark 6.
2 Line a large swiss roll tin with parchment paper.
3 Heat the milk, stock and mustard in a non-stick saucepan. Slake the cornflour with a little cold milk and add to the pan, stirring continuously, and bring to the boil. Reduce the heat and simmer for 4–5 minutes to thicken the sauce.
4 Remove from the heat and beat in the ruby chard. Allow to cool slightly, then beat in the egg yolks, one at a time, and season with cayenne pepper.
5 Whisk the egg whites and salt with an electric whisk until they form stiff peaks, then carefully fold into the sauce, using a metal spoon. Once fully combined, pour into the prepared swiss roll tin and level off with a palette knife.
6 Bake in the middle of the oven for 20 minutes until well risen and brown.
7 Turn out onto aluminium foil, remove the parchment paper and leave to cool.
8 Make the filling by softening the Quark in a bowl with a fork. Add the remaining ingredients and season to taste.
9 Spread the roulade with the cheese mixture. Roll up as tightly as possible and place on a serving plate. Slice off the ends with a sharp knife to reveal the filling.
10 Serve with a selection of side salads.

600ml (1 pint) skimmed milk
1 tablespoon vegetable stock powder
1 tablespoon Dijon mustard
2 tablespoons cornflour
225g (8oz) ruby chard, finely shredded
4 eggs, separated
pinch of salt
1/4 teaspoon cayenne pepper

for the filling
115g (4oz) Quark low-fat soft cheese
1 garlic clove, crushed
1 tablespoon finely chopped fresh chives
1 tablespoon finely chopped fresh chervil
salt and freshly ground black pepper

Roasted vegetable greek salad

Roasting peppers transforms their flavour and texture, making them far more palatable in salads and vegetable dishes. This version can be served hot or cold. If serving cold, allow the peppers to cool in the roasting tray before adding to the lettuce.

1 Preheat the oven to 200C, 400F, Gas Mark 6.
2 Cut the peppers into quarters and place in a roasting tray.
3 Cut the tomatoes in half and place a piece inside each pepper quarter.
4 In a small bowl combine the Quark, garlic and basil and season well with salt and black pepper. Dot small amounts of the mixture inside the peppers, then season the peppers with salt and black pepper
5 Place the peppers in the top of the oven. Roast for 20–25 minutes until the peppers start to soften.
6 Meanwhile wash and the lettuce and arrange on a serving plate.
7 Dice the cucumber and add to the plate along with the onion and grapes. Sit the roasted peppers on top and drizzle over any juices left in the pan. Sprinkle with chopped fresh flat leaf parsley and serve.

SERVES 4
PER SERVING:
56 KCAL/0.4G FAT
PREPARATION TIME:
20 MINUTES
COOKING TIME:
35 MINUTES

2 red peppers, seeded
2 yellow peppers, seeded
8 cherry tomatoes
115g (4oz) Quark low-fat soft cheese
1 garlic clove, crushed
1 tablespoon chopped fresh basil
1 romaine or crisp lettuce
$1/2$ cucumber
1 small red onion, finely sliced
salt and freshly ground black pepper
a few black grapes to garnish
chopped flat leaf parsley

Orange and passion fruit cheesecake

SERVES 6
PER SERVING:
237 KCAL / 2.4G FAT
PREPARATION TIME:
20 MINUTES
COOKING TIME:
30 MINUTES

for the base

2 eggs

75g (3oz) caster sugar

75g (3oz) self-raising flour

1 teaspoon pure vanilla
    extract

for the filling

3 oranges

1 heaped tablespoon
    custard powder

2 tablespoons caster sugar

250ml (9fl oz) skimmed
    milk

1 teaspoon pure vanilla
    extract

225g (8oz) Quark low-fat
    soft cheese

3 tablespoons elderflower
    cordial

4 passion fruit, with seeds
    removed

1 teaspoon arrowroot

This dessert needs to be made in advance. The custard powder gives it body and aids setting without the use of gelatine. It is best left overnight to allow it to set completely. You can adapt the topping according to taste. Mixed soft berries form a sharp contrast to the cheese base.

1 Preheat the oven to 180C, 350F, Gas Mark 4.

2 Grease a 20cm (8in) flan case with a little vegetable oil, and then dust with caster sugar.

3 To make the sponge base, whisk together the eggs and sugar for several minutes until thick and pale in consistency.

4 Using a metal spoon, gently fold the flour into the egg mixture and add the vanilla. Pour quickly into the flan case and level off with a knife. Bake in the oven for 20 minutes until golden brown.

5 Allow the sponge to cool. When cool, use a sharp knife to cut away a 1cm ($\frac{1}{2}$in) layer of sponge from the centre of the flan case, then use a spoon to scrape away any crumbs to leave a smooth surface. Take care not to tear the base. It must stay intact.

6 To make the filling, finely zest the oranges on a fine grater.

7 In a small bowl mix the custard powder and sugar with a little of the milk to form a paste. Place the orange zest, vanilla extract and remaining milk in a saucepan, bring to the boil, then pour onto the paste and mix well. Transfer to the saucepan and bring back to the boil until the mixture thickens. Allow to cool for 5 minutes, and then beat in the Quark with a wooden spoon. Pour into the flan case and allow to cool before chilling in the refrigerator for 2 hours.

8 Prepare the zested oranges by removing the outer skin with a sharp knife and cut the orange into segments, removing all membranes and any pith. Place in a saucepan with the elderflower cordial and passion fruit. Slake the arrowroot with a little water and add to the fruit. Bring to the boil until the sauce thickens. Remove from the heat and allow to cool. When cool, spoon onto the cheesecake and chill until ready to serve.

Roast fresh figs in caramel meringue nests

These caramel meringue nests are very easy to make and will keep for up to a month in an airtight container. They do tend to have a more chewy consistency than regular meringue. The roast figs are quick and easy to prepare, so if you make the meringue nests in advance, you have the flexibility of a hot dessert in minutes.

1 Preheat the oven to 140C, 240F, Gas Mark 1.
2 To make the meringue, whisk the egg whites in a clean dry bowl, using an electric whisk, until they form stiff peaks. Continue whisking and gradually add the brown sugar, one dessertspoon at a time, allowing 20 seconds between each addition.
3 Spoon the mixture into a piping bag that has a large star nozzle. Place a sheet of baking parchment onto a baking tray and pipe 4 small round discs, approximately 6cm (3in) in diameter. Pipe a circular edge around each disc to form a nest shape. Any remaining mix can be piped as small dots and used as decoration.
4 Bake the meringue nests in the oven for 1 hour until completely dried out.
5 When the meringue nests are cooked, remove from the oven and increase the oven temperature to 200C, 400F, Gas Mark 6.
6 Prepare the figs by removing any stalk from the tips of the fruit. Make 2 cuts on the top of each fig to form a cross and gently open the figs out.
7 Place the figs in an ovenproof dish and spoon the rum over the top. Place in the oven for 2–3 minutes until hot.
8 When ready to serve, place a scoop of the iced dessert in each meringue nest, place 2 figs on top, and dust with icing sugar. Serve immediately.

SERVES 4
PER SERVING:
318 KCAL/4.2G FAT
PREPARATION TIME:
30 MINUTES
COOKING TIME:
FIGS: 5 MINUTES
MERINGUE NESTS: 60 MINUTES

for the meringue nests
3 egg whites
175g (6oz) soft brown sugar

for the filling
8 ripe fresh figs
2 tablespoons rum
4 scoops Wall's 'Too Good to be True' Toffee iced dessert
icing sugar to dust

Top right: *Roast fresh figs in caramel meringue nests*

Right: *Fresh fruit tartlets*

Fresh fruit tartlets

In these impressive low-fat tartlets you can vary the fruits to make 6 individual flavours or combine them to create a mixed fruit dessert. The baked cases will keep in an airtight container for 2–3 days. Add the fruit just before serving, as the juice from the fruit may cause the pastry to become soggy.

1 Preheat the oven to 190C, 375F, Gas Mark 5.
2 Stack the filo pastry sheets on top of each other. Using scissors, cut the stack into 6 equal square sections, so that you end up with 36 individual squares. During preparation, keep the remaining filo pastry covered to prevent it drying out.
3 Take 6 non-stick individual tartlet tins 10cm (4in) in diameter. In each tin, place 6 individual pastry squares in layers, placing the squares at slight angles to each other and brushing with beaten egg white in between each layer.
4 Cut 6 greaseproof paper discs slightly larger than the tartlet tins and place a disc inside each tin, adding a few baking beans to weight it down.
5 Bake in the oven for 5 minutes, remove the paper and baking beans and return to the oven for a further 4–5 minutes until crisp and golden. Allow to cool.
6 To make the filling, in a mixing bowl combine the custard powder and sugar with a little cold water, mixing to a smooth paste. Heat the milk with the vanilla pod in a saucepan until boiling. Remove the vanilla pod and pour the milk onto the custard powder, mix well and return to the pan. Bring back to the boil, whisking continuously until it thickens. Pour into the pastry cases and allow to cool.
7 Prepare the fruits and arrange on the top of each tart.
8 Heat the apricot jam either in a microwave or a saucepan and brush over the fruit to form a glaze.

See photograph on page 311.

MAKES 6
PER TARTLET:
123 KCAL/4G FAT
PREPARATION TIME:
40 MINUTES
COOKING TIME:
20 MINUTES

6 sheets filo pastry
    (30cm × 20cm/12 × 8in)
1 egg white, beaten
1 tablespoon custard powder
1 tablespoon caster sugar
300ml (½ pint) skimmed milk
1 vanilla pod
selection of fresh fruits
2 tablespoons sieved apricot
    jam

Cranberry and orange punch

SERVES 6
PER SERVING:
88 KCAL/0G FAT
PREPARATION TIME:
10 MINUTES

10–12 ice cubes
600ml (1 pint) cranberry juice
300ml ($\frac{1}{2}$ pint) freshly
    squeezed orange juice
300ml ($\frac{1}{2}$ pint) Pimms or cider
600ml (1 pint) lemonade
1 lime
a few fresh mint leaves
fresh fruit to decorate

This refreshing fruity cocktail is the party drink. You can make in advance, as it will maintain its fizz for 1–2 hours, and this will allow time for the lime and mint to add flavour.

1 In a food processor or liquidiser, crush the ice using a pulse motion and place in the bottom of a large bowl.
2 Pour in the liquids, mixing well. Cut the lime into thin slices and add to the bowl.
3 Finely chop the fresh mint leaves and stir into the bowl.
4 Decorate the bowl with floating pieces of interestingly shaped fruits, such as star fruit and physalis, or thread alternate pieces of fruit onto short wooden skewers.

Strawberry lambrusco cake

An impressive strawberry gateau with a hint of Italian fizz. Serve with a purée of fresh strawberries or simply on its own – delicious!

1 Preheat the oven to 180C, 350F, Gas Mark 4.
2 Grease a 25cm (10in) high-sided cake tin with a little vegetable oil and then dust with caster sugar.
3 To make the sponge, whisk together the egg yolks and hot water until foamy. Slowly add two-thirds of the sugar and continue whisking on a high speed until thick and creamy. This will take several minutes.
4 In a separate bowl, whisk the egg whites until stiff. Slowly add the remaining sugar, a tablespoon at a time, allowing 20 seconds between each addition.
5 Combine the egg whites with the egg yolk mixture. Sift the flour, cornflour and baking powder over and then, using a large metal spoon carefully fold into the mixture; now spoon the mixture into the prepared tin.
6 Bake immediately in the centre of the oven for 20–25 minutes until firm to the touch. Allow to cool and then turn out onto a wire cooling rack. When the cake is completely cold, use a serrated knife to slice it horizontally into 3 sections.
7 To make the filling place the yogurt in a small bowl. Use a sharp knife to slit the vanilla pod along the centre and then, using the edge of the knife, scrape away the vanilla seeds and add to the bowl. Mix well to combine with the yogurt.
8 Slice two-thirds of the strawberries, saving some regular-sized ones for decoration.

SERVES 8
PER SERVING:
187 KCAL / 2.6G FAT
PREPARATION TIME:
25 MINUTES
COOKING TIME:
25 MINUTES
CHILLING TIME:
1 HOUR

for the sponge cake
3 egg yolks
3 tablespoons hot water
115g (4oz) caster sugar
2 egg whites
50g (2oz) plain flour
50g (2oz) cornflour
1 level teaspoon baking powder
icing sugar to dust

for the filling
450g (16oz) Total 0% Greek
   yogurt
1 vanilla pod
450g (1lb) fresh strawberries
120ml (4fl oz) Lambrusco wine

9 Place the base sponge on a serving plate, drizzle with a third of the Lambrusco wine, spread evenly with half of the vanilla yogurt and add a layer of sliced strawberries. Top with the centre sponge, drizzle with a third of the Lambrusco wine, spread with the remaining yogurt and add a layer of sliced strawberries. Top with the remaining sponge. Drizzle with the remaining wine, dust with icing sugar and decorate with strawberries. Chill for 1 hour before serving.

Index of recipes